QUANTITATIVE STRATEGIES

Hayden Van Der Post

Reactive Publishing

CONTENTS

COPYRIGHT © 2025 REACTIVE PUBLISHING. ALL RIGHTS RESERVED.

Published by Reactive Publishing

Preface

In the ever-evolving landscape of financial markets, the quest for outperformance, or alpha generation, is an enduring ambition for investors. The realm of quantitative finance opens a plethora of opportunities to achieve this goal by leveraging data and advanced mathematical models. "Quantitative Strategies for Alpha Generation: Advanced Models for Outperforming the Market" is designed to serve as a comprehensive guide for those who seek to harness the power of quantitative strategies to gain a competitive edge in the financial markets.

The journey through this book is both a deep dive into the fundamental principles of quantitative finance and an exploration of the frontiers of modern financial technology. Each chapter meticulously builds on the previous one, offering a structured and systematic approach to mastering quantitative strategies. We begin with an introduction to the core concepts and historical context, setting the stage for the in-depth exploration of data acquisition, statistical foundations, and model building that follows.

Quantitative finance is as much an art as it is a science. It requires an amalgamation of various disciplines such as statistics, computer science, economics, and behavioral science. This book endeavors to bridge the gap between theoretical concepts and real-world applications, providing readers with a holistic understanding of how quantitative models can be developed, tested, and deployed to generate alpha.

Our exploration starts with the fundamentals of data acquisition and management, acknowledging that high-quality data is the bedrock of any robust quantitative model. From accessing diverse data sources to preprocessing techniques and ethical considerations, we cover the essential steps required to assemble and maintain a high-integrity data repository.

Statistical foundations are crucial for any quantitative strategy. Basic concepts such as mean, variance, and correlation, along with advanced techniques like ARIMA and GARCH, form the toolkit needed to understand market dynamics and build predictive models. These statistical tools empower traders and researchers to glean actionable insights from vast datasets.

Building alpha models, the heart of our discussion, delves into the intricacies of factor models, risk-adjusted return metrics, and systematic trading strategies. With a focus on practical implementation, we guide readers through the process of designing, backtesting, and continuously refining their models to adapt to market changes and enhance performance.

The advent of advanced machine learning techniques has revolutionized quantitative finance. Ethical considerations in machine learning are also discussed, ensuring that readers remain mindful of the broader implications of their work.

Risk management is an indispensable component of successful quantitative strategies. With chapters dedicated to measuring and mitigating various types of risk, readers will learn how to balance risk-reward trade-offs and implement robust risk management frameworks. Case studies of risk management failures highlight the importance of vigilance and adaptability in navigating financial markets.

Algorithmic trading represents another frontier of quantitative finance, and this book outlines the types and execution strategies of trading algorithms. Emphasizing performance metrics, regulatory considerations, and the role of technology, we offer readers a comprehensive understanding of this high-stakes domain.

Behavioral finance sheds light on the often-irrational behaviors that influence market movements.

Effective portfolio construction and optimization are paramount for achieving consistent returns. The book covers principles of portfolio theory, techniques for optimization, and dynamic adjustment methodologies. We also explore strategies for incorporating alternative assets and balancing multiple quantitative strategies within a portfolio.

Finally, real-world applications and case studies provide concrete examples of successful and failed strategies, offering valuable lessons from industry practitioners. Through interviews and analysis, readers gain insights into the practical deployment of quantitative models and the evolving challenges faced by professionals in the field.

"Quantitative Strategies for Alpha Generation" is not merely a compendium of theories and models; it is a practical guide aimed at equipping readers with the tools and knowledge necessary to innovate and excel in the competitive world of finance. Whether you are a seasoned practitioner or a newcomer to quantitative investing, this book aspires to be your trusted resource on the path to discovering and capturing alpha.

Your journey to mastering quantitative finance starts here. Welcome to a world where data-driven strategies hold the key to outperformance.

CHAPTER 1:
INTRODUCTION

Understanding the multi-faceted nature of quantitative finance is akin to peeling back the layers of the intricate tapestry that makes up today's financial markets. At its essence, quantitative finance marries mathematics, statistics, and data analysis to redefine conventional investment strategies. These strategies depend on sophisticated algorithms and statistical models that sift through immense data sets, revealing patterns and insights that can be translated into actionable investment opportunities.

What Is Quantitative Finance? A Comprehensive Definition

Quantitative finance is best understood as the strategic application of mathematical and statistical methods to demystify and address complex financial challenges. This discipline revolves around the creation and application of models designed to represent financial phenomena quantitatively. Rather than depending on instinct or anecdotal evidence, quantitative finance emphasizes a rigorous, objective approach, often leading to high-speed, high-volume strategies that can swiftly adapt to changing market conditions.

The Broad Spectrum of Quantitative Finance

The realm of quantitative finance extends far beyond simple data mining; it encapsulates a variety of critical areas within the financial sector, including asset pricing, risk management, portfolio optimization, algorithmic trading, and derivative modeling. Practitioners employ quantitative methodologies to dissect market dynamics, enabling them to predict future price movements with greater accuracy. A prime example is the Black-Scholes model, which transformed options pricing by offering a systematic framework for valuing derivatives, significantly impacting trading strategies globally.

Furthermore, as financial data grows ever more complex and granular, quantitative analysts—often referred to as 'quants'—emerge as vital architects of market behavior. Utilizing cutting-edge technology and analytical precision, quants integrate alternative data sources (such as social media sentiment analysis or satellite imagery) and employ machine learning techniques to refine prediction capabilities. Through these innovations, quantitative finance is continually pushing the boundaries of conventional financial analysis.

Vivid Illustrations of Quantitative Applications

To clarify the definition and expansive reach of quantitative finance, let's consider a concrete application: the development of a financial trading algorithm. This process initiates with the detection of a market inefficiency or potential opportunity, which is then modeled mathematically. For example, a quant might devise a momentum-based strategy that meticulously analyzes historical price data to predict upcoming trends. This model undergoes rigorous backtesting to ensure its robustness before being deployed in real-time trading environments.

Moreover, quantitative finance is integral to effective risk management practices. Value-at-risk (VaR) models, for instance, utilize advanced quantitative techniques to quantify the potential losses a portfolio may face under various adverse market scenarios. Through simulation and scenario analysis, these models empower investors with a clearer insight into risk exposure, thus facilitating more strategic decision-making.

Harnessing Technological Advances to Broaden Horizons

The ongoing integration of technological advancements continually redefines the landscape of quantitative finance. High-performance computing enables analysts to process vast volumes of data at remarkable speeds, while cloud computing offers scalable infrastructures for running complex simulations. Additionally, big data technologies enhance the management and analysis of diverse data sets, significantly boosting the predictive power of quantitative models and contributing to more informed investment strategies.

As we navigate the multifaceted domain of quantitative finance, it becomes increasingly evident that the field represents a dynamic confluence of precision and innovation. The methodologies derived from quantitative finance are not static scripts; they evolve in tandem with technological progress and fluctuations in market environments. A deep understanding of its definition and scope reveals that quantitative finance is much more than a collection of mathematical tools; it is a comprehensive framework that informs strategic decisions, nurtures innovation, and ultimately plays a vital role in the financial success of those who adeptly leverage its capabilities. With its analytical depth and precision, quantitative finance stands as both a guiding force and a catalyst for financial innovation, setting the stage for future discoveries in the pursuit of alpha generation.

Tracing the Evolution and Influence of Quantitative Finance on Investment Practices

To truly appreciate the significance of quantitative finance in today's investment landscape, we must explore its remarkable evolution—from theoretical beginnings to its essential role in modern investing. This journey is characterized by technological breakthroughs, shifting market dynamics, and a lasting influence on investment strategies worldwide.

Early Foundations and Theoretical Innovations

Quantitative finance's origins can be traced to the mid-20th century, when financial economists like Harry Markowitz first laid the groundwork for its development. His introduction of Modern Portfolio Theory (MPT) revolutionized the way investors approached risk and return.

With the increasing importance of quantitative analysis, the Capital Asset Pricing Model (CAPM) emerged in the 1960s, further embedding quantitative methodologies into financial practices. CAPM provided a systematic approach for evaluating the relationship between an asset's risk and its expected return, fundamentally reshaping asset pricing and investment strategies. This empirical framework enabled investors to assess risk-adjusted performance, propelling the field of quantitative finance into the mainstream.

The Quantitative Revolution of the 1970s and 1980s

The 1970s heralded a significant leap forward with the development of the Black-Scholes option pricing model. Spearheaded by Fischer Black, Myron Scholes, and Robert Merton, this groundbreaking work established a structured methodology for accurately pricing options. The adoption of the Black-Scholes model not only transformed derivatives trading but also solidified quantitative finance as a vital component of market operations. Its widespread acceptance catalyzed the rapid expansion of derivative markets, inspiring firms and investors to embrace sophisticated quantitative approaches for risk exploration and management.

This period also witnessed a remarkable surge in computational power, paving the way for an increased reliance on quantitative methods. The 1980s, in particular, saw hedge funds like Renaissance Technologies at the forefront of this transformation, utilizing mathematical models to anticipate market behavior. Under the leadership of Jim Simons, Renaissance harnessed high-frequency data and advanced algorithms, marking a new era in which computers conducted investment analyses at innovative speeds and complexities.

The Rise of Algorithmic and High-Frequency Trading

The 1990s and early 2000s ushered in the dominance of algorithmic trading, spurred by advances in computing technology and the advent of electronic trading platforms. During this time, quantitative strategies broke into the mainstream of finance, fundamentally challenging traditional trading paradigms. Hedge funds and investment banks began investing heavily in data analytics and algorithm development, recognizing the competitive advantages that could be gained from executing trades in milliseconds.

Consider the transformation observed in the foreign exchange markets, where the speed of algorithmic trading reshaped currency trading strategies. Quantitative models that analyze historical trends alongside real-time data streams enabled traders to execute trades with unprecedented speed, significantly reducing the influence of human error and emotional decision-making.

Impact on Modern Investment Strategies

Today, the influence of quantitative finance is omnipresent, permeating a diverse array of investment strategies and fundamentally shaping the financial landscape. Approaches such as factor investing, which organizes stocks based on characteristics like size, value, and volatility, utilize quantitative techniques to construct portfolios aimed at optimizing risk-adjusted returns.

Moreover, advancements in machine learning and AI-driven models represent the forefront of quantitative finance's evolution. These cutting-edge technologies analyze vast datasets to uncover previously hidden patterns, refining investment strategies and enhancing the ability to predict market trends with greater accuracy.

Studying Historical Impact for Future Success

The historical trajectory of quantitative finance highlights its profound influence on investment practices. Today's investors, equipped with insights from this rich history, are increasingly poised to utilize quantitative methods to navigate the complexities of contemporary markets.

Reflecting on this historical evolution, it is evident that quantitative finance is far more than an academic pursuit; it is a dynamic and transformative force driving financial innovation. The lessons derived from its development provide invaluable guidance for future endeavors, underscoring its crucial role in shaping the investment strategies of tomorrow. Armed with a deeper understanding of its historical impact, investors and strategists alike can better harness the full potential of quantitative finance in the quest for alpha generation.

The Crucial Role of Data in Quantitative Strategies

Data stands as the foundational pillar of all quantitative strategies in finance, supplying the essential raw material from which insightful financial models emerge. In an industry where accuracy can spell the difference between prosperity and failure, the significance of having robust and comprehensive datasets cannot be overstated. To truly grasp the vital role that data plays in quantitative finance, one must consider how it informs decision-making, shapes model development, and facilitates the extraction of actionable intelligence from the complexities of the market.

Data as the Engine of Insights

At the heart of quantitative strategies lies the ability to leverage data to uncover patterns, trends, and anomalies within market behavior. This transformational process turns raw data into actionable insights, fundamentally guiding financial decision-making. For instance, when examining historical price data, quantitative analysts can evaluate potential stock investments based on empirical insights rather than mere speculation. Past performance data serves not only as a reference point but as a crucial component in developing predictive models that enable investors to anticipate future price movements.

A Closer Look at Equity Market Analysis

Consider the dynamic nature of equity markets. A quantitative analyst may dive into time-series data, examining daily closing prices, trading volumes, and measures of volatility to construct sophisticated forecasting models. For example, in a mean-reversion strategy, an analyst could scrutinize historical prices to identify instances when a stock's current price deviates significantly from its historical average. This analysis triggers buy or sell decisions based on the expectation of a short-term correction. The validity and precision of these trading signals hinge upon the quality and richness of the data utilized.

Elevating Data Quality Through Rigorous Preprocessing

The effectiveness of any quantitative strategy heavily relies on data quality. Inaccurate or incomplete data can lead to flawed models and misguided conclusions. Hence, diligent data cleaning and preprocessing are indispensable initial steps in the analytical workflow. Techniques such as outlier filtering, normalization, and thorough checks for missing values are essential to preserve data integrity.

Take the scenario of an investment firm swamped with extensive price feeds marred by sporadic data anomalies. Furthermore, regular data audits can ensure ongoing dataset accuracy, reinforcing the strength and dependability of the quantitative strategies at play.

Embracing Alternative Data for Enhanced Insights

In recent years, the emergence of alternative data sources has dramatically enriched traditional datasets, broadening the scope of quantitative analysis. This new frontier includes diverse information, such as social media sentiment, geolocation data, satellite imagery, and transaction-level retail data. Hedge funds, for instance, increasingly utilize sentiment analysis derived from platforms like Twitter to gauge public perception of specific stocks, effectively enhancing their trading models. This multi-faceted approach empowers analysts to capture nuanced market dynamics and adjust strategies proactively, ultimately leading to more informed decision-making.

Case Study: Harnessing Sentiment Analysis in Trading Models

Let's consider an innovative trading model that harnesses sentiment analysis from news articles and social media to anticipate stock movements. For example, a surge in negative sentiment concerning a company's leadership could prompt immediate reassessment of its stock holdings, allowing for early intervention to mitigate potential losses.

Navigating Data Management Challenges

While the wealth of insights that data can provide is invaluable, managing extensive datasets introduces significant challenges. Chief among these are ensuring data security and adhering to regulatory standards, especially as global data privacy concerns intensify. It is imperative for firms to implement secure data storage solutions and stringent compliance protocols to safeguard sensitive information, thereby protecting their strategies and sensitive data from unauthorized access and potential legal repercussions.

In essence, data is the lifeblood of quantitative strategies, providing the necessary foundation for financial innovation and performance. This commitment to data-driven insights paves the way for informed decision-making and effective alpha generation.

As technology continues to advance, the ability to harness and interpret data will remain a defining characteristic of success in quantitative finance.

A Comprehensive Insight into Alpha Generation

In the intricate landscape of finance, the concept of alpha serves as the holy grail for investors—a coveted metric that signifies superior investment performance, surpassing the benchmarks such as the S&P 500. The essence of alpha generation is woven into the fabric of quantitative finance, where ingenious strategies and sophisticated models are meticulously crafted to uncover avenues for achieving these excess returns. However, the pursuit of alpha is not just a technical challenge; it encompasses a strategic blend of innovative modeling, astute market insight, and disciplined execution.

Defining Alpha: Its Impact and Importance

At its core, alpha represents an investment's performance on a risk-adjusted basis, reflecting the additional returns garnered beyond a benchmark. For investors, alpha is not merely a statistic; it embodies the validation of an investment strategy's effectiveness. A positive alpha signals that an investment has outperformed the market due to the skillful application of a manager's strategy, while a negative alpha typically indicates underperformance. Thus, capturing alpha stands as a testament to a manager's expertise and market acumen—a distinction that transcends mere chance in the unpredictable terrain of financial markets.

Laying the Framework for Alpha: From Design to Execution

The journey of alpha generation commences with the creation and validation of strategic models that anticipate market behavior. This process merges statistical methodologies, extensive data analysis, and financial intuition to design strategies aimed at exploiting specific market inefficiencies or predicting price shifts. Fundamental tools, such as factor analysis, become critical in helping analysts identify and leverage factors that historically drive returns—such as momentum, value, size, or volatility.

Consider a strategy built on momentum investing—where the historical tendency of winning stocks to maintain their upward trajectory in the short term is harnessed. Analysts can develop quantitative models that screen stocks based on their recent price performance relative to market averages. Such models aspire to generate alpha by capitalizing on continuation patterns in stock price movements before these trends become widely recognized within the marketplace.

Backtesting: Essential Validation of Alpha Strategies

Transitioning from theoretical constructs to practical applications involves thorough backtesting. This process evaluates strategies against historical data to gauge their potential viability. Analysts can utilize this analytical lens to identify weaknesses and confirm the robustness of their models across different market environments.

For example, imagine a quantitative team creating a pairs trading strategy that identifies two correlated stocks exhibiting occasional divergence in their price relationship. Through backtesting, the team can analyze the strategy's hypothetical performance under various historical scenarios, continually refining parameters to enhance alpha generation while mitigating risk.

Harnessing Technology: The Frontier of Alpha Capture

In the fast-paced world of hedge funds and proprietary trading firms, technology plays an essential role in the execution of alpha-generating strategies. With the rise of advanced computing and big data analytics, quantitative analysts have access to unparalleled amounts of data and processing power, enabling them to refine their models with exceptional accuracy and speed.

For instance, employing machine learning algorithms allows a fund to dynamically adjust its trading signals based on real-time market data, social media sentiments, and macroeconomic indicators. This adaptive approach enables strategies to remain responsive to shifting market conditions, significantly enhancing the probability of capturing alpha while ensuring rigorous risk management.

Navigating Challenges: A Balanced Approach

However, the pursuit of alpha is not without its hurdles. Theories of market efficiency contend that as more traders implement sophisticated quantitative models, the availability of alpha opportunities declines. Additionally, the rise of high-frequency and algorithmic trading has compressed the windows for capitalizing on market inefficiencies, intensifying competition in this domain.

In such a dynamic environment, continuous innovation and model adaptation become crucial. Successful alpha generation necessitates a delicate equilibrium between generating returns and managing systemic risk. This involves continually reassessing strategies in light of unforeseen economic events, regulatory changes, and liquidity challenges, thus ensuring both robustness and sustainability in an ever-evolving market landscape.

Looking Ahead: Reflecting on Outcomes

In conclusion, alpha generation stands as a multi-dimensional challenge that requires a harmonious synthesis of data expertise, strategic insight, and operational precision. Yet, the pursuit of sustained alpha is more than a quest for profit—it symbolizes a firm's ability to adeptly navigate the complexities of global financial markets with creativity and rigor.

As practitioners delve deeper into the realm of quantitative finance, the quest to master the art of alpha generation remains the pinnacle of financial skill. It invites finance professionals to build on existing knowledge while daring to explore new and uncharted domains in their quest for investment excellence.

Unveiling the Landscape of Quantitative Strategies

Quantitative finance is a fascinating domain defined by its ability to blend rigorous mathematical models with data-driven analysis, all aimed at navigating financial markets. Understanding this rich tapestry of strategies is vital for investors seeking to develop resilient investment methodologies that react adeptly to market dynamics.

Momentum and Trend-Following Strategies

At the heart of many quantitative approaches lies the momentum strategy, premised on the idea that assets exhibiting positive performance trends are likely to continue on that trajectory. This approach is underpinned by behavioral finance theories, where investor sentiment and psychological biases reinforce the momentum. Practitioners may, for example, target stocks with robust gains over the past six months, anticipating that these winners will continue their upward climb while underperformers will drift lower.

In practice, a sophisticated quantitative model can be deployed to scan the universe of stocks daily, flagging those in the top decile for momentum based on historical performance metrics. Algorithmic trading enhances this strategy, allowing traders to swiftly execute buy and sell orders in response to evolving market indicators, thus positioning their portfolios to capitalize on identified trends.

Mean Reversion Strategies

In contrast to momentum strategies, mean reversion posits that asset prices will ultimately revert to their historical averages, suggesting that deviations from the norm are temporary. A popular application of this principle is pairs trading, where two correlated securities—sharing a historical price relationship—are traded based on their divergence.

For example, consider two companies in the same industry, which typically move in tandem. If a sudden market shock causes a price spike in one while the other remains stable, a savvy investor might short the overvalued stock and buy the undervalued one, betting on a return to their historical correlation. This requires careful statistical analysis to identify effective pairs and monitor their price movements, ensuring that the identified anomalies genuinely represent short-term trading opportunities.

Arbitrage Strategies

Arbitrage strategies thrive on price discrepancies found in different markets or related assets, with the aim of securing risk-free profits. These strategies may take various forms, including statistical arbitrage, convertible bond arbitrage, and merger arbitrage. Statistical arbitrage, in particular, employs intricate algorithms to pinpoint fleeting mispricings between assets that historically maintain a strong correlation.

Consider a basic instance of spatial arbitrage: a trader might purchase a commodity in one exchange where it is undervalued, simultaneously selling it in another where it is overvalued. The key to success in this endeavor lies in rapid execution, as the market tends to correct these discrepancies swiftly. Thus, the ability to react promptly is indispensable.

Factor-Based Strategies

Factor investing revolves around the assembling of portfolios based on specific attributes or "factors" that have consistently yielded returns over extended periods. Common factors include value—investing in stocks with low price-to-earnings ratios—size, where small-cap stocks often outperform their larger counterparts, and quality, which encompasses companies with strong financial metrics like high returns on equity.

A skilled portfolio manager might develop a multi-factor model that emphasizes stocks demonstrating high scores across these dimensions, thereby diversifying risk while striving for enhanced returns. Continuous analysis and adjustment are essential, as market conditions evolve and factors may shift in their predictive power, requiring diligence in managing these strategies effectively.

Machine Learning and Artificial Intelligence Strategies

The advent of machine learning and artificial intelligence has revolutionized quantitative finance, enabling the development of models that can identify complex nonlinear patterns within vast datasets. These advanced approaches allow for real-time adaptations based on incoming data and adaptive learning, offering significant improvements over traditional methodologies.

One innovative application involves sentiment analysis through natural language processing (NLP), which assesses market sentiment by parsing vast quantities of information from news articles, financial reports, and social media. This capability not only aids in informed decision-making but also helps fine-tune strategies in line with prevailing market sentiment, aligning investment actions dynamically as conditions shift.

Tail Risk Hedging Strategies

In a world of uncertainty, tail risk hedging strategies become vital, focusing on protecting investments from rare yet potentially devastating market events. Often characterized by fat-tailed distributions, these events may have disproportionate impacts on portfolios.

For instance, purchasing out-of-the-money put options can serve as a hedge against severe declines in asset prices. Such strategies may appear costly in stable markets but provide essential protection against black swan events, ensuring that long-term wealth remains safeguarded through prudent risk management practices.

Building a Cohesive Investment Framework

Success in the world of quantitative finance necessitates a deep understanding of the myriad strategies available and a clear articulation of investment objectives. Each strategy, rich in its own benefits and challenges, must fit coherently within a comprehensive investment framework.

Effective implementation hinges on not just a thorough grasp of these diverse approaches but also the skillful integration of technology and rigorous performance monitoring. This ongoing evaluation allows professionals to remain proactive, adjusting strategies in response to the ever-changing landscape of financial markets.

The Dichotomy of Quantitative Investing:
An In-Depth Exploration

In the vast and complex world of financial markets, quantitative investing emerges as a powerful testament to modern innovation. Nevertheless, like any advanced method, quantitative investing possesses both remarkable strengths and notable limitations. Gaining insight into these intricacies is essential for investors and fund managers seeking to navigate the evolving landscape of investment strategies effectively.

Advantages of Quantitative Investing

1. Systematic and Objective Framework: At the foundation of quantitative investing is its unwavering commitment to a systematic approach, where decisions are made based on numerical data rather than the sway of human emotions. This objectivity helps mitigate biases— such as overconfidence or emotional reactions— that can cloud decision-making. Through algorithm deployment, quant strategies ensure consistent execution, fostering a disciplined framework that often outperforms discretionary methods.

For example, consider a quantitative strategy that identifies undervalued stocks by analyzing historical earnings data.

This model operates independently of volatile market news, maintaining a steady course and seizing opportunities that may elude emotion-driven investors.

1. Expertise in Handling Large Data Sets: The strength of quantitative strategies lies in their unparalleled ability to process and analyze immense volumes of data, from historical asset prices to economic indicators and even alternative data streams like social media sentiment. This proficiency enables quants to unveil complex patterns and correlations that might escape traditional analysis.

For example, an algorithm could effectively correlate surges in social media activity with subsequent stock price movements, pinpointing lucrative trading opportunities that might otherwise go unnoticed by conventional methods.

1. Robust Backtesting Capabilities: A standout benefit of quantitative investing is the ability to rigorously backtest strategies against historical data. This process allows investors to assess the viability of models prior to real-world application, offering invaluable insights into potential risks and returns.

Take, for instance, a trend-following model: by simulating its performance across various market conditions—both bull and bear—investors can evaluate its robustness, fine-tuning parameters to ensure its practical efficacy and resilience when implemented.

1. Rapid Trade Execution: The inherent design of quantitative models enables swift execution of trades, a critical advantage in fast-paced markets. Algorithmic trading systems can swiftly capitalize on fleeting price inefficiencies or exploit short-term arbitrage opportunities, often before they dissipate, thus enhancing competitiveness in time-sensitive environments.

A prime illustration of this is high-frequency trading (HFT), where algorithms execute thousands of trades per second, constantly recalibrating positions in response to minute fluctuations in market prices.

Disadvantages of Quantitative Investing

1. The Peril of Model Overfitting: One of the most significant risks associated with quantitative investing is overfitting, where a model becomes excessively tailored to historical data, compromising its effectiveness in live markets. While such models may excel in backtests, they often falter in real-world conditions due to their reliance on noise-driven patterns instead of fundamental market dynamics.

For instance, an overfitted model might generate stock movement predictions based solely on arbitrary, historical correlations that crumble when faced with unforeseeable real-world events.

1. Dependence on Data Quality: The efficacy of quantitative strategies hinges upon the quality, accuracy, and availability of data. Poor or inaccurate data can lead to misguided decisions and errant forecasts, underscoring the necessity of thorough data cleaning and preprocessing—a labor-intensive yet crucial aspect of the investment process.

Picture a machine learning model operating on flawed datasets, riddled with inconsistencies or gaps. The outcome becomes inherently unreliable, and any resulting investment strategies could yield disappointing returns.

1. Challenges of Market Adaptation: Given that markets are inherently dynamic, conditions can shift rapidly. Models that fail to adapt regularly may become obsolete, struggling to meet new market realities. Maintaining the competitiveness of quantitative

strategies necessitates ongoing monitoring and recalibration, which can be resource-intensive.

For instance, an algorithm optimized for a stable economic environment may find itself ill-equipped to handle abrupt shifts, such as a sudden interest rate hike, highlighting the importance of continuous model reassessment.

1. Ethical and Regulatory Dilemmas: As technology and automation advance, quantitative investing raises ethical concerns and attracts regulatory scrutiny. Issues such as market manipulation, data privacy, and the implications of high-frequency trading practices on overall market stability necessitate adherence to stringent compliance standards.

Events like the infamous 2010 Flash Crash accentuate the systemic risks associated with algorithmic trading, leading to increased regulatory oversight and compliance expectations for those engaged in quantitative strategies.

Striking a Balance in Investment Strategy

While quantitative investing offers a wealth of benefits, it is imperative to approach it with diligence to navigate its inherent challenges. The synthesis of robust model development, ongoing evolution, and prudent application of quantitative techniques is paramount in unlocking sustainable returns, all while adhering to ethical and regulatory frameworks. Prepared to confront the complexities of the financial landscape, the decision to incorporate quantitative methodologies should stem from a deep understanding of these dynamics, ensuring a competitive edge in the continual quest for alpha generation.

The Essential Role of Mathematical Models in Finance

Mathematical models are the bedrock of contemporary quantitative finance, serving as vital tools that enable financial professionals to navigate the complexities of vast datasets. These frameworks are pivotal in analyzing myriad aspects of investing, including risk management and portfolio optimization, fundamentally reshaping the approach to market analysis.

Precision and Predictability

One of the foremost advantages of employing mathematical models in finance is their capacity to inject precision and predictability into markets characterized by volatility. This clarity fosters a degree of predictability, allowing investors to strategize more effectively and respond promptly to market shifts.

A prime example is the Black-Scholes model, a groundbreaking tool for options pricing. It revolutionized the derivatives market, empowering investors to make informed decisions based on reliable valuations.

Models for Risk Management

Risk management is another critical domain where mathematical models exert a profound impact. Utilizing stochastic models—like Value at Risk (VaR) and Conditional Value at Risk (CVaR)—investors can estimate the potential loss within a portfolio under normal market conditions over a defined timeframe. These models are indispensable for setting risk parameters and ensuring that exposure aligns with risk tolerance.

For instance, a financial analyst may leverage the VaR model to gauge the minimum expected loss for a trading day, operating within a 95% confidence interval. This estimation not only aids in the development of hedging strategies but also serves to protect capital and enhance portfolio resilience.

Optimization and Asset Allocation

The role of mathematical models extends seamlessly into the optimization of portfolios and asset allocation strategies.

Techniques such as the Capital Asset Pricing Model (CAPM) and the Markowitz Portfolio Theory harness mathematical constructs to balance risk against expected returns. Such models guide investors in creating efficient portfolios, ideally positioned along the efficient frontier.

The Markowitz model is particularly noted for its innovative use of covariance matrices, allowing investors to minimize variance for a targeted expected return. Its widespread adoption underscores its significance within the toolkit of quantitative finance.

Limitations and Requirements

Despite their myriad advantages, mathematical models are not without limitations and assumptions. They typically rely on various premises—such as market efficiency and the normal distribution of returns—which, if inaccurate, can compromise their reliability. Moreover, the necessity for high-quality data and substantial computational resources can strain the infrastructure available to finance professionals.

Consider the Gaussian models that dominate the financial landscape. These models assume that market returns follow a normal distribution—a condition that frequently fails, especially during periods of market turbulence or unforeseen events. This discrepancy highlights the importance of employing a diverse array of models and cultivating a robust understanding of the scenarios that could challenge their applicability.

Adaptation to Dynamic Markets

To remain effective, the application of mathematical models must be accompanied by continuous adaptation and recalibration. The financial landscape is perpetually evolving, influenced by shifting participant behaviors and underlying economic variables. Successful implementation of these models demands regular evaluations and adjustments to align with emerging trends and anomalies.

Take, for example, the Elliott Wave Theory, which posits that investor psychology oscillates through predictable cycles. While the model boasts historical validation, its practical use requires sensitivity to changing market sentiments. As new trading behaviors or financial instruments emerge, the model's application must be updated accordingly to ensure relevance.

Mathematical models lie at the intersection of innovation and practicality within the realm of quantitative finance. They transform complex financial principles into structured, actionable insights that drive informed decision-making. Ultimately, the effective utilization of these models depends on a seamless blend of theoretical understanding, empirical evidence, and the agility to adapt to the ever-changing market landscape.

Through disciplined application of mathematical models, financial strategists are equipped with the necessary tools to navigate complexity and uncertainty. This blend of structured innovation fosters not only a competitive edge but also significant contributions to our evolving financial ecosystem. It is through this lens that financial leaders endeavor to forge pathways to sustainable success and insight-driven strategies.

The Dynamic Interplay of Theory and Practice in Quantitative Finance

Quantitative finance is an exhilarating field characterized by the intricate dance between theoretical concepts and practical applications. This relationship goes beyond a simple transaction; it is an ongoing dialogue where real-world challenges stimulate theoretical innovation and theoretical insights inform pragmatic solutions, resulting in robust and actionable investment strategies.

Bridging the Gap: From Concept to Implementation

To effectively bridge the divide between theory and

practice, financial professionals must first acquire a deep understanding of the foundational theories that guide quantitative models. Take, for example, the Efficient Market Hypothesis (EMH). This theory suggests that asset prices always incorporate all available information, leading to the notion that consistently outperforming the market without additional risk is virtually impossible. Nonetheless, in reality, market inefficiencies offer savvy investors opportunities to exploit temporary price discrepancies through well-crafted quantitative models.

Algorithmic trading systems serve as a prime illustration of this dynamic. These systems are built on theoretical principles such as statistical arbitrage, which posits that asset prices tend to revert to their historical mean. A firm grasp of these theoretical frameworks enables practitioners to devise sophisticated algorithms that capitalize on fleeting price anomalies, executing trades with a speed and precision unattainable by manual trading methods.

Selecting the Right Tools: Appropriate Model Selection

Choosing the right models is crucial for translating theoretical insights into effective practical applications. Innovative models, like the Black-Litterman model, enhance traditional mean-variance optimization by incorporating investor perspectives.

Consider a hedge fund portfolio manager utilizing the Black-Litterman model. Armed with a mix of historical data and market forecasts, they can optimize the weightings of their diverse portfolio. This model's adaptability allows for the melding of quantitative analysis with qualitative insights, facilitating the transformation of theoretical constructs into concrete investment strategies designed to optimize returns while maintaining prudent risk exposure.

Empirical Testing and Continuous Adjustment:
Validating Theoretical Constructs

Empirical testing is paramount for validating and refining theoretical models. The efficacy of these constructs must be rigorously evaluated against real-world data, ensuring that they stand the test of practical application. This often involves backtesting strategies on historical datasets to measure potential performance before actual capital is deployed.

For instance, a financial analyst may backtest a momentum-based trading strategy against previous market conditions to assess its viability. The results yield critical insights, revealing areas for model enhancement and adjustment.

Navigating Market Challenges: Adapting to Anomalies

The transition from theory to practice is not without its hurdles; notably, models must adeptly account for unexpected market anomalies. Many theoretical frameworks operate on assumptions of market stability and rational behavior, conditions that can quickly crumble in the face of stress or during black swan events. Crafting models capable of navigating these complexities necessitates both sophistication and flexibility.

The evolution of risk management practices post-2008 financial crisis exemplifies this need for adaptability. Prior models, which relied on historically normal conditions, fell short during the crisis. Thus, risk management frameworks were transformed to incorporate stress testing and scenario analysis, tools that better capture the inherent variability of real-world markets.

Cultivating Practitioner Skills: A Holistic Development Approach

The successful application of theoretical models hinges not only on numerical acumen but also on the practitioner's intuition and market understanding. While mastering complex algorithms and models is essential, a comprehensive grasp of market dynamics and behavioral finance is equally important. Professionals must actively pursue continuous learning and skill enhancement to remain at the forefront of rapidly evolving financial theories and technologies.

For instance, financial professionals often utilize simulation techniques, like Monte Carlo simulations, to project potential future market scenarios.

In essence, the interplay between theory and practice in quantitative finance is akin to a symphony, where precision harmonizes with intuition and structured frameworks meet the realities of the market. Core mathematical models and theories serve as the foundation, while practical experiences provide the context and flexibility necessary for their effective application.

This symbiotic relationship calls for a mindset that values adaptability, keen insight, and a genuine enthusiasm for continuous learning. As financial strategies advance, the enduring dialogue between theory and practice not only grounds innovation in empirical realities but also encourages transformative approaches. This balance empowers financial professionals not only to anticipate shifts in the market landscape but also to actively drive change, forging a future informed by evidence and inspired by theoretical possibilities.

Navigating Regulatory Considerations in Quantitative Finance

In the fast-paced realm of quantitative finance, where sophisticated mathematical models and high-frequency trading algorithms reign supreme, navigating the intricate regulatory landscape is both a necessity and a strategic imperative. Compliance is not merely about meeting legal requirements; it's a foundational pillar upon which sustained success and innovation can be built.

The Evolving Regulatory Landscape

The financial crisis of 2008 marked a watershed moment in regulatory oversight, triggering a wave of reforms aimed at curbing systemic risk and safeguarding investors.

These regulatory measures have significantly influenced the operations of quantitative finance, where the speed and sophistication of trading strategies often present unique challenges to compliance. Key regulatory frameworks, including the Securities and Exchange Commission (SEC) regulations in the United States, the European Markets in Financial Instruments Directive (MiFID II), and the Basel III accords for financial institutions, each address critical facets of financial operations—ranging from market transparency and capital requirements to comprehensive risk assessment protocols.

For example, MiFID II mandates heightened transparency in both pre-trade and post-trade activities, imposing rigorous reporting obligations on firms engaged in high-frequency trading. As a result, quantitative trading systems must be meticulously designed to log and report vast quantities of data with both accuracy and speed, ensuring compliance while maintaining efficiency in execution.

Innovating Within the Compliance Framework

Firms operating at the cutting edge of quantitative finance frequently pioneer advancements in machine learning and complex data analytics. However, as innovation surges, the need for robust compliance mechanisms becomes paramount.

Consider a hedge fund deploying algorithmic trading strategies across diverse asset classes. To satisfy requirements framed by regulations such as the SEC's Rule 15c3-5—which mandates pre-trade risk controls for direct market access—the fund will incorporate pre-trade compliance measures within its algorithms. These safeguards ensure that all trades fall within authorized limits, acting as a bulwark against excessive risk exposure. This proactive approach not only ensures regulatory compliance but also enhances overall operational integrity, cultivating trust with both investors and regulators.

Upholding Ethical Standards

In today's digital finance ecosystem, compliance transcends mere adherence to regulations; it involves a steadfast commitment to ethical standards. The intersection of regulatory compliance and ethical considerations, both of which aim to promote transparency, fairness, and market integrity, is critical for quantitative finance professionals. Vigilance against ethical pitfalls such as market manipulation and unfair trading practices is essential, as these may breach both regulatory and moral guidelines.

To navigate these complexities, firms should establish a strong internal policy framework. Periodic audits of trading algorithms along with ongoing education and training in regulatory and ethical standards can serve as effective practices. These preventative strategies not only minimize the risk of regulatory infringements but also help cultivate a culture of compliance within the organization.

Harnessing Technology for Compliance

The role of technology in navigating and achieving regulatory compliance cannot be overstated. The advent of RegTech (Regulatory Technology) is revolutionizing how firms manage compliance risks, equipping them with tools that leverage artificial intelligence for monitoring and reporting.

Imagine a quantitative trading firm utilizing a RegTech platform for trade surveillance. This advanced system employs machine learning algorithms to identify anomalous trading behavior and potential compliance issues, generating real-time alerts for compliance officers. Such integration of technology empowers firms to preemptively address regulatory infractions, significantly reducing the need for extensive manual oversight.

Striking a Balance Between Innovation and Regulation

The ongoing challenge for financial institutions lies in balancing the pursuit of innovation in quantitative finance with the demands of regulatory compliance. As new regulations emerge, firms must remain agile, adapting not only to compliance requirements but also to the bounds of technological potential. This dynamic necessitates an organizational culture that encourages collaboration between compliance teams and quantitative strategists. This proactive stance could lead to the development of industry-leading solutions that not only meet compliance standards but set new benchmarks for regulatory excellence.

In the world of quantitative finance, where rapid innovation often surpasses the pace of regulatory adaptation, a vigilant approach to compliance is indispensable. Regulations should not be viewed merely as constraints; rather, they are integral to cultivating sustainable and ethical financial practices. Within this regulatory framework lies the potential for authentic innovation—where technology, finance, and compliance converge to propel the industry forward in a responsible manner.

Successfully navigating this landscape requires strategic insight, adaptability, and an ethical commitment to preserving market integrity. As financial markets continue to evolve, those firms that master the intricacies of regulatory compliance will not only safeguard their interests but also pave the way for groundbreaking advancements in the field of quantitative finance.

As we gaze toward the future of quantitative finance, we're on the brink of a transformative era, driven by innovative trends that not only promise to redefine established strategies but also challenge long-standing paradigms. The convergence of cutting-edge technology, diverse data sources, and shifting market dynamics heralds a plethora of opportunities for those ready to embrace the change. Within this dynamic landscape, we delve into the key trends set to shape the quantitative strategies of tomorrow.

The Integration of Artificial Intelligence and Machine Learning

The infusion of artificial intelligence (AI) and machine learning (ML) into quantitative finance is already significantly altering the industry. However, we have only scratched the surface of what these advanced technologies can achieve. As computational capabilities advance at an unprecedented pace, AI algorithms are evolving to become increasingly intricate, enabling them to detect nuanced patterns that conventional methods may overlook. Take deep learning models, for example; these powerful tools can analyze vast datasets in real-time, allowing traders to respond almost instantaneously to market fluctuations and optimally adjust portfolios with remarkable accuracy.

Imagine the implications of an AI-driven trading model that constantly learns from high-frequency trading data, dynamically adjusting strategies based on the latest insights. Picture a system leveraging reinforcement learning to refine execution strategies by systematically evaluating millions of transactions to reduce market impact and slippage. This level of seamless adaptability not only enhances strategy performance but also significantly mitigates the risk of human error.

The Ascendance of Alternative Data

The rapid expansion and democratization of alternative data sources are revolutionizing the methods quants use for model construction. Moving beyond traditional metrics and historical price information, alternative data encompasses a wide spectrum—from satellite imagery and social media sentiment analysis to transaction logs and outputs from Internet of Things (IoT) devices. These unconventional datasets provide unparalleled insights that were once difficult, if not impossible, to obtain, laying the groundwork for novel alpha generation strategies.

Consider how hedge funds might leverage satellite imagery to monitor parking lot traffic at retail locations, allowing them to forecast consumer behavior and potential revenue trends long before quarterly earnings reports are published. Alternatively, by analyzing sentiment on platforms like Twitter, traders can gauge public perception surrounding a company's major announcements, equipping them to anticipate subsequent price fluctuations. As the variety and volume of available data expand, so too does the potential to craft innovative strategies founded on a nuanced understanding of market dynamics.

The Promise of Quantum Computing

We stand on the threshold of a revolutionary shift with the advent of quantum computing. While still nascent in its application within finance, the potential ramifications for quantitative strategies are staggering. Quantum computers possess the capability to execute complex calculations much faster than classical computers, enabling them to address problems that are currently considered intractable. In fields such as risk parity portfolio construction or Monte Carlo simulations, quantum computing could provide instantaneous solutions to optimization challenges that traditional systems may take hours or even days to resolve.

Imagine a quantum algorithm working to optimize a vast asset portfolio, considering thousands of variables and constraints, and delivering an ideal solution in mere moments. Though we still await full-scale practical applications, the opportunities in areas such as cryptography, risk management, and derivative pricing promise to reshape the landscape of finance.

The Shift Toward Sustainable and Ethical Investing

A significant trend influencing the evolution of quantitative strategies is the increasing focus on sustainable and ethical investing. As investors progressively seek strategies that align with environmental, social, and governance (ESG) principles, quants are challenged to weave these considerations into both model development and execution. This shift not only addresses changing societal values but also reflects a critical reassessment of risk and opportunity landscapes with a long-term perspective.

Incorporating tools and metrics that evaluate a company's ESG performance into quantitative models enables more informed investment decisions, balancing financial returns with ethical considerations. For instance, using machine learning to analyze ESG data in conjunction with traditional financial metrics may uncover intersections that suggest a firm's potential for sustainable growth, thus providing a more holistic view of both risk and reward.

The Evolution of Natural Language Processing

Natural language processing (NLP) represents one of the most exciting advances within AI, providing powerful tools for extracting meaningful insights from unstructured data sources. This technology empowers quantitative analysts to process and analyze large volumes of textual data—ranging from news articles and financial reports to conference call transcripts—at scale, converting qualitative information into actionable quantitative signals.

Consider how traders might leverage NLP to quantify sentiment from financial news during earnings season, integrating these sentiment scores into predictive models that anticipate immediate stock volatility. The ongoing refinement of NLP capabilities opens new avenues for sentiment analysis, offering deeper insights into market psychology and behavior.

The future of quantitative strategies is inextricably linked to technological advancements and the evolving demands of investors. Each emerging trend—from AI and alternative data to quantum computing and sustainable investing—ushers in a wave of possibilities, compelling finance professionals to refine their approaches while balancing innovation with ethical responsibility. As we diligently navigate and adapt to these trends, the role of quantitative finance will undoubtedly become increasingly integral and transformative, shaping the market landscape for years to come.

CHAPTER 2: DATA ACQUISITION AND MANAGEMENT

Historical data offers a treasure trove of insights from past market behaviors, enabling analysts to identify recurring patterns, trends, and seasonal cycles. This data typically encompasses a wealth of information, including historical pricing, trading volumes, corporate financial statements, and macroeconomic indicators. The significance of historical datasets comes to light particularly during the backtesting phase, where strategies and models are rigorously tested against past performance to validate hypotheses before live implementation.

Imagine a quantitative analyst tasked with constructing a trend-following strategy for the equity markets. Time series analysis techniques, such as moving averages or Bollinger Bands, heavily leverage this historical data, allowing for informed predictions about future market activities.

However, reliance on historical data is not without its pitfalls. The assumption that past market behaviors will repeat can be misleading, especially in the face of structural changes or new variables that impact market dynamics. Despite these limitations, historical data remains a cornerstone of quantitative strategies, serving as a critical baseline for many analytical approaches.

Real-Time Data: Capturing the Moment

Real-time data acts as the heartbeat of quantitative finance, essential for those strategies that capitalize on immediate market opportunities. This category includes live market prices, order book information, transaction volumes, and news feeds, providing a vivid snapshot of current market conditions. High-frequency trading (HFT) firms, for instance, rely heavily on real-time data to execute trades within fractions of a second, seizing upon fleeting discrepancies across various exchanges.

Consider an algorithm designed for pairs trading—a technique centered on identifying correlated securities to profit from temporary deviations in their price relationship. This dynamic responsiveness ensures sustained strategy performance in an environment where timing is everything.

However, real-time data comes with its own set of challenges. The sheer volume and speed of incoming data necessitate robust technological infrastructure and advanced data processing capabilities. Innovations such as pipelined architectures and data processing frameworks like Apache Kafka or MQTT are essential to navigate this complex landscape efficiently.

Alternative Data: The New Frontier of Insights

In today's highly competitive markets, alternative data sources are increasingly recognized for their potential to generate alpha through innovative insights. This category diverges from traditional financial metrics, encompassing unconventional datasets such as social media sentiment, satellite imagery, logistics data, and environmental reports.

For instance, hedge funds might employ sophisticated sentiment analysis algorithms to parse Twitter data, gauging consumer sentiment about a new product launch and subsequently adjusting their investment strategies based on these insights. Similarly, satellite imagery can yield valuable information for agricultural strategies, helping analysts estimate crop yields by assessing farmland conditions across different regions.

The primary appeal of alternative data lies in its capacity to provide a more nuanced and comprehensive understanding of market dynamics, enabling investors to identify opportunities that traditional datasets might overlook. Yet, the integration of alternative data requires advanced data science techniques to clean, normalize, and interpret these diverse datasets effectively, transforming them into actionable intelligence.

The intricate interplay between historical, real-time, and alternative data underscores the multifaceted nature of data within quantitative finance. The growing complexity and plethora of available datasets present both exciting opportunities and formidable challenges, pushing the boundaries of data management and analytic innovation. As quantitative strategies evolve, the emphasis on harnessing diverse data types will be paramount in unlocking new avenues for alpha generation and risk management. This dynamic environment ensures that finance professionals must continually refine their skills to adeptly navigate the ever-evolving landscape of the financial markets.

Unveiling the Power of Data Sources and Platforms in Quantitative Finance

Delving into the intricate realm of quantitative finance requires more than just sophisticated algorithms and thoughtful trading strategies; it necessitates a deep understanding of diverse data sources and the robust trading platforms that support them. These essential tools form the foundation of any successful quantitative operation, providing vital streams of information that empower professionals to make well-informed investment decisions. For modern quantitative strategists, familiarizing themselves with prominent data sources—such as Bloomberg, Refinitiv (formerly Reuters), and a host of emerging platforms—is crucial. Each platform boasts its unique advantages, offering distinct datasets and analytical capabilities that play a pivotal role in designing and executing effective market strategies.

Bloomberg: The Comprehensive Powerhouse

As a premier leader in the financial technology space, Bloomberg sets an industry benchmark for extensive data coverage and sophisticated analytical tools. The Bloomberg Terminal, celebrated for its iconic dual-screen design, serves as an unparalleled resource, granting users access to real-time and historical data spanning a diverse array of asset classes. Whether you're analyzing equities, fixed income, commodities, currencies, or derivatives, Bloomberg's expansive datasets are indispensable for any quantitative analysis.

But the true strength of Bloomberg lies beyond its impressive data repository. The platform offers a suite of advanced analytical tools that allow users to dissect data with remarkable precision. The Bloomberg Query Language (BQL), for instance, empowers analysts to conduct custom queries, enabling them to extract complex datasets tailored to specific analytical needs. Imagine a financial analyst exploring the relationship between macroeconomic indicators and bond yields; with Bloomberg's detailed economic calendar and advanced modeling tools, they can efficiently conduct their research and unearth actionable insights.

Despite its unparalleled offerings, Bloomberg's premium pricing can be a significant barrier for smaller firms and individual traders. However, for major financial institutions and hedge funds, investing in a Bloomberg subscription often yields substantial returns, delivering a competitive edge that can be pivotal in today's fast-paced market.

Refinitiv: The Agile Contender

Refinitiv, evolving from the respected Reuters lineage, stands as another cornerstone in the financial data landscape.

Building on its history of delivering reliable news, Refinitiv seamlessly integrates high-quality data feeds with real-time news analytics—an essential combination for making timely investment decisions. Its flagship product, Eikon, competes strongly with Bloomberg, offering a suite of tools specifically designed for asset managers, analysts, and traders.

One of Refinitiv's key advantages is its incorporation of artificial intelligence and machine learning capabilities, which deliver predictive analytics and sophisticated data visualizations. For example, the StarMine suite provides users with advanced equity research tools that evaluate stock valuation, analyst forecasts, and market momentum. A trader might harness these tools to refine their stock selection process, using StarMine's insights to identify investment opportunities with expected favorable returns.

While Refinitiv is often perceived as a cost-effective alternative to Bloomberg, the choice between these platforms frequently hinges on user preferences, specific data needs, and the nature of investment strategies employed.

Other Emerging Platforms: Exploring New Horizons

In addition to Bloomberg and Refinitiv, a multitude of other platforms cater to the diverse demands of quantitative professionals. FactSet, with its emphasis on data integration and modeling capabilities, excels in offering corporate financial information and alternative datasets. Meanwhile, platforms like QuantConnect and Quantopian (now integrated with Robinhood) focus on algorithmic trading, attracting independent quants and smaller trading firms looking to innovate without heavy resource expenditure.

Quandl, specializing in alternative datasets, provides access to unconventional data such as sentiment analysis, web traffic statistics, and environmental metrics. This can be particularly advantageous for quantitative analysts seeking fresh insights beyond traditional data lenses. For instance, an investment firm might leverage Quandl to enrich their models with consumer traffic data, allowing them to anticipate retail sales trends ahead of quarterly earnings releases.

The Convergence of Data and Strategy

The choice of data platform profoundly influences both the breadth and effectiveness of quantitative strategies. It's essential for quantitative experts to continuously evaluate platform capabilities to ensure their tools align with evolving strategic goals and regulatory frameworks.

This fusion of traditional and alternative data sources represents a broader trend in which data-driven decision-making enhances the quantitative approach. In the competitive landscape of finance, staying ahead requires not only selecting the right platforms but also creatively harnessing their potential to uncover alpha and adeptly navigate market complexities.

Ultimately, mastering leading data sources and platforms transcends mere technical necessity; it becomes a strategic imperative. Those who can skillfully navigate these powerful tools will carve out an advantage in the ever-evolving financial landscape, guided by insightful data analytics and innovative frameworks.

Mastering Data Cleaning and Preprocessing Techniques in Quantitative Finance

In the world of quantitative finance, the transition from raw data to actionable insights hinges crucially on one often-overlooked phase: data cleaning and preprocessing. This phase serves as the foundation for robust quantitative models—without meticulous attention to this step, analysts risk basing their strategies on flawed, biased, or incomplete data. Such missteps can undermine even the most sophisticated analyses. Join us as we delve into the nuances of data refinement, revealing how this critical endeavor sharpens financial decision-making and drives successful outcomes.

The Indispensability of Data Cleaning

Far from being a mere housekeeping chore, data cleaning is a strategic imperative that significantly impacts the reliability of quantitative strategies. Financial datasets are frequently riddled with discrepancies, including missing values, outliers, and inconsistencies—each posing a potential threat to analytical integrity and decision-making accuracy.

For instance, consider an analyst collecting equity price data from various sources over several years. Variations in vendor formats, mismatched timestamps, and erroneous entries can complicate the analysis. A missing price point for a highly liquid stock on a pivotal trading day could skew a volatility model, leading to misguided trading decisions.

Fundamental Techniques for Data Cleaning

1. Identifying and Handling Missing Values: Missing data is a common challenge in financial datasets. Analysts have several approaches to tackle this, including imputation (filling gaps with statistical estimates like mean or median), deletion (removing incomplete records), or interpolation (estimating values based on adjacent data points). For time series data, techniques such as forward or backward filling can maintain continuity without distorting trends.

2. Managing Outliers: Outliers can dramatically affect analytical outcomes, leading to skewed results. Techniques like Z-score analysis can help identify these anomalies. However, in finance, where outliers might indicate genuine market events, context matters. For instance, a stock price surge following a major corporate announcement may not be an anomaly but a critical market signal that needs careful consideration.

3. Standardizing Formats: Uniformity in data formats

—such as dates, currencies, and text encodings— is vital for merging datasets from diverse sources. Financial software tools are invaluable in this regard, as they often provide functionalities for format standardization, easing the integration process. An analyst dealing with multinational trading data, for example, must harmonize currency formats to ensure coherent and comparable analyses.

Advanced Preprocessing Techniques

1. Feature Scaling and Transformation: In quantitative models, especially those leveraging machine learning, scaling and normalization of data are crucial. Techniques like min-max scaling or z-score standardization bring various features onto a uniform scale, preventing any single feature from disproportionately influencing outcomes. Additionally, log transformations can stabilize variance in skewed datasets, aiding in clearer pattern recognition.

2. Encoding Categorical Variables: Many financial datasets include categorical variables—like market sectors or credit ratings—that require transformation into numerical formats for computational analysis. One-hot encoding and label encoding are common methods for such conversions, allowing for more effective model processing. For instance, categorizing different industries for a stock portfolio often necessitates these transformations to harness the full potential of machine learning algorithms.

3. Feature Engineering: Beyond mere cleaning, the art of identifying and constructing relevant features can significantly enhance predictive models. Creating derived metrics—such as moving averages, returns

over selected periods, or liquidity ratios—can add valuable insights and improve model sophistication. For instance, integrating a momentum indicator can enhance the accuracy and performance of a trading algorithm.

Data Cleaning in Practice: A Real-World Case Study

Imagine a hedge fund implementing a systematic trading strategy based on macroeconomic indicators and market sentiment. Upon gathering data from a myriad of sources, including government statistics and sentiment analyses, the team encounters inconsistencies in temporal granularity and sentiment scoring. To bolster their strategy, they employ preprocessing techniques—synchronizing datasets to weekly intervals and standardizing sentiment scores—thereby strengthening their predictive model and ultimately achieving a higher success rate in trading signals.

The Critical Role of Preprocessing in Strategy Development

As quantitative strategists explore the depths of alpha generation, the significance of data cleaning and preprocessing techniques becomes increasingly evident. These foundational processes enable analysts to build models on reliable, high-quality data, thereby amplifying the effectiveness of advanced quantitative strategies. Consequently, refining data through thorough cleaning and preprocessing is not merely a preliminary step; it is a strategic launchpad for uncovering superior financial insights.

Mastering these techniques empowers finance professionals to tackle the inherent challenges of raw financial data head-on, transforming potential obstacles into opportunities for innovation and strategic growth. Through diligent groundwork, modern finance specialists can reveal profound market truths, which are essential for thriving in today's data-driven landscape.

In the dynamic world of quantitative finance, the accuracy and reliability of the data that fuels sophisticated models are of utmost importance. As we delve deeper into the process of refining these datasets, we confront pivotal challenges —namely, missing data and outliers. If not addressed thoughtfully, these issues can compromise the integrity of our analyses, introduce biases, skew results, and ultimately hinder sound strategic financial decision-making.

Navigating the Waters of Missing Data: Strategies for Excellence

Dealing with missing data is an almost universal challenge in financial datasets. The sources of missing entries can vary widely—from collection errors and system limitations to simple human oversight. Yet, the implications of neglecting these gaps can ripple through trading strategies, adversely affecting the accuracy of insights derived.

1. Imputation Techniques: Imputation serves as a cornerstone strategy for estimating missing values and preserving the integrity of datasets. While methods like mean or median substitution are straightforward to apply, they risk diluting variance and obscuring meaningful patterns in the data. More sophisticated techniques, such as multiple imputation, leverage relationships among variables to predict missing values, fostering a richer dataset. For instance, when trade volume data is lacking for specific days, imputing based on historical trends helps maintain continuity in volatility analyses, facilitating more reliable predictive evaluations.

2. Data Interpolation: Particularly beneficial for time series datasets, interpolation estimates missing values between existing data points to create seamless transitions. Linear interpolation is widely favored in finance due to its simplicity; however, polynomial or spline interpolation can capture

more intricate patterns, making them invaluable for datasets like stock prices, where trading halts can create gaps.

3. Machine Learning Models: The advent of machine learning techniques ushers in an innovative approach to predicting missing values. Algorithms such as k-nearest neighbors or regression trees analyze observed data to identify underlying patterns, enabling accurate estimations for missing entries. This methodology shines particularly in complex multi-asset portfolios, where variable relationships can be intricate and highly interdependent.

Addressing Outliers: Identification and Strategic Treatment

Outliers can be a double-edged sword in financial analysis. While they may point to data entry errors or exceptional occurrences, they can also signify significant market movements that warrant attention.

1. Detection Methods: Accurately identifying outliers is crucial. Statistical tools like Z-scores or the Interquartile Range (IQR) method provide clear criteria for locating entries that deviate from the norm. Visualization tools, such as boxplots and scatter plots, can offer intuitive insights into outlier distributions. For example, a sudden surge in trading volume for a security might indicate potential market manipulation or a significant news event, necessitating careful analysis rather than arbitrary exclusion.

2. Contextual Analysis: Assessing the relevance of an outlier to the broader market context is vital. Quantitative analysts may find that retaining genuine outliers enhances their insights. For example, a significant drop in bond prices could

signal a shift in fiscal policy or evolving political circumstances. Discarding such outliers might strip models of crucial, profitable signals.

3. Transformation Techniques: When an outlier fails to present substantial value, transformation techniques such as winsorizing can provide a solution. This approach adjusts extreme values to reduce their influence without outright elimination, ensuring that data points remain well within a chosen percentile range.

Real-World Application: Striking the Proper Balance

Imagine a quantitative analyst working on a predictive model for foreign exchange rates. Historical data may reveal gaps during weekends and erratic price spikes due to geopolitical events. Retaining these outliers ultimately enhances model precision and relevance, ensuring that the framework delivers actionable trading signals.

Reaching a Harmonious Balance

The interaction between missing data and outliers in quantitative finance necessitates a balanced approach—one that values data integrity while also recognizing the potential insights outliers may offer.

Implementing rigorous control measures during data preprocessing empowers quantitative professionals to construct reliable datasets effectively, laying the foundation for well-informed strategy development. Proficiently managing missing data and outliers advances the credibility of financial models and safeguards against the pitfalls that can lead to skewed interpretations of market behavior.

In summary, adeptly handling missing and anomalous data transcends mere technicality; it requires a nuanced understanding of market dynamics and the strategic implications of each dataset irregularity.

In the fast-paced, data-driven world of finance, constructing effective frameworks for data storage and retrieval is not just important; it's essential for the smooth functioning of quantitative models. As the quantity, diversity, and speed of financial data continue to grow exponentially, strategists are challenged to devise robust systems capable of not only efficiently housing vast amounts of information but also ensuring swift and accurate access for insightful analysis. Let's explore the intricacies of developing these frameworks, where strategic foresight and precision converge to unlock new avenues for alpha generation.

Architecting Robust Storage Systems

The backbone of any advanced analytical operation is its data storage architecture. Selecting the appropriate structure tailored to an organization's specific needs is vital. Financial data infrastructures must be scalable and adaptable, efficiently handling fluctuating volumes and various data types.

1. Relational Databases: Despite the rise of newer technologies, relational databases (RDBMS) such as MySQL and PostgreSQL remain foundational elements in the finance industry. Their well-defined structures are perfectly suited for storing transactional and historical data where clear relationships among datasets exist. For instance, a database that relates stock prices, trading volumes, and corporate events facilitates seamless cross-referencing, which is crucial for conducting fundamental quantitative analyses.

2. NoSQL Databases: In contrast, NoSQL solutions like MongoDB and Cassandra excel at accommodating unstructured or semi-structured data through their flexible, schema-less setups. These databases are particularly adept at managing alternative data sources such as social media feeds

or sentiment analysis, increasingly leveraged in modern investment strategies where agility in data processing is key.

3. Data Lakes: For institutions eager to store data in its raw format, data lakes present an appealing option. Utilizing platforms like Amazon S3 or Azure Data Lake, financial strategists can preserve an extensive range of information for future exploration. This methodology enables diverse analytical processes, from historical retrospectives to machine learning initiatives, without the need for premature structuring or processing.

Efficient Data Retrieval Strategies

Swift retrieval of relevant data transforms a well-designed storage system into a vital tool for strategic decision-making. Financial datasets are often dynamic, and without prompt access methodologies, valuable insights may slip away.

1. Indexing Mechanisms: Leveraging effective indexing strategies can drastically enhance query performance. Incorporating composite indexing— where indices are created on multiple columns—can significantly expedite complex queries. For example, an index on a table recording security trades that incorporates both security identifiers and trade dates can make time-sensitive analytical queries much faster and more efficient.

2. Caching Solutions: Caching is essential for minimizing retrieval delays, allowing frequently accessed data to be stored closer to processing units. Innovative technologies like Redis and Memcached enhance access speed, particularly during unpredictable market conditions where immediate responses are critical.

3. API Integrations: Application Programming Interfaces (APIs) enable seamless integration between storage solutions and analytical platforms, eliminating cumbersome manual data extraction. This connectivity is essential for multi-strategy operations, allowing real-time data streams to feed automated trading algorithms. For instance, Bloomberg's API provides direct access to financial data, facilitating its integration into analytical environments for enhanced operational efficiency.

Practical Application: Real-World Scenarios

Imagine a quantitative analyst navigating a vast repository of both historical and real-time stock data. Coupling effective indexing and caching strategies to accelerate querying processes means retrieval times are significantly reduced, while API integrations allow for effortless filtration and search operations, enabling precise data extraction on demand.

Building Future-Proof Data Systems

As technological advancements continue to accelerate, the frameworks built for data storage and retrieval must be agile enough to accommodate future innovations. Cloud-based solutions like Google Cloud's BigQuery and AWS's Redshift empower firms with the scalability and flexibility necessary to efficiently meet rising data demands. Adopting cloud architectures not only enhances operational capacity to manage data surges but also facilitates integration with emerging technologies, such as blockchain and the Internet of Things (IoT).

Effective data management orchestrates the convergence of storage, retrieval, and processing into a cohesive and reliable system that uplifts the efficacy of quantitative strategies.

In summary, robust frameworks for data storage and retrieval lie at the heart of intelligent financial analysis.

The Cornerstone of Quantitative Finance: A
Deeper Dive into Data Analysis

In the dynamic world of quantitative finance, data analysis is not just an auxiliary tool; it is the bedrock upon which strategic decision-making is built. Two prominent methodologies—time series and cross-sectional data analysis —each offer their own distinctive lenses through which to examine market data. Understanding the nuances and applications of these techniques is vital for developing sophisticated models that not only generate alpha but also enhance overall market performance.

Time Series Data Analysis: Capturing the
Rhythm of Financial Markets

At its core, time series analysis is concerned with the examination of data points collected over specified intervals —be they seconds, days, months, or years. This methodology excels in unveiling patterns inherent to the data, such as trends, seasonality, and cyclical movements, making it an essential tool for forecasting future market behavior.

1. Trend Analysis: By scrutinizing long-term data movements, trend analysis reveals sustained directional shifts in asset prices. For example, a comprehensive review of a major stock index over the past decade might uncover a steady upward trend, indicating a bullish market sentiment that savvy portfolio managers can leverage to optimize their investment strategies.

2. Seasonal Patterns: Certain markets are characterized by predictable seasonal behaviors. A time series analysis of retail stocks may uncover consistent price surges around the holiday season, positioning investors to capitalize on anticipated demand spikes.

3. Autocorrelation and Stationarity: Integral to time

series analysis is the evaluation of a dataset's autocorrelation—how current values are related to past values—and the assessment of its stationarity, or the stability of its statistical properties over time. Tools like the Augmented Dickey-Fuller (ADF) test measure stationarity, while autocorrelation functions (ACF) clarify relationships between different time intervals.

Cross-Sectional Data Analysis: A Snapshot of Market Dynamics

In contrast, cross-sectional analysis zeroes in on data from multiple entities at a single point in time. This approach provides invaluable insights into the factors influencing asset performance without the influence of temporal changes, allowing for nuanced comparisons across diverse entities.

1. Comparative Analysis: By examining key financial metrics across various entities, cross-sectional analysis reveals vital insights into relative valuations. For instance, analyzing the price-to-earnings (P/E) ratios of several firms within the same sector can spotlight undervalued stocks ripe for investment.

2. Factor Models: Cross-sectional techniques are often utilized in factor analysis, where the relationship between asset returns and characteristics like size, value, or momentum are explored. Conducting a cross-sectional regression helps pinpoint the most significant factors influencing performance, thus guiding investment strategies.

3. Diversification and Risk Assessment: This approach is also pivotal in evaluating risk and portfolio diversification.

Bridging the Gap: The Synergy of Both Approaches

In practice, the strengths of time series and cross-sectional analyses can be seamlessly integrated for enhanced financial insight. For instance, a quantitative strategist tasked with forecasting stock returns could begin with time series techniques to identify specific trends and seasonal patterns for each asset, thus shaping strategic timing for trades. Following that, they could employ cross-sectional analysis to compare stocks within a sector, revealing those that show favorable factor characteristics or advantageous valuations.

Case Study: Pair Trading Strategy

A practical illustration of integrating both methodologies can be observed in a pairs trading strategy, which entails trading two historically correlated assets simultaneously. This strategy operates under the premise that their price relationship will revert to its historical mean. Time series analysis is utilized to monitor historical correlations and price deviations, while cross-sectional analysis aids in selecting which asset pairs are most likely to converge. This fusion of insights enables traders to exploit temporary market inefficiencies, aiming for alpha generation while mitigating risk.

Navigating Challenges and Enhancements

Despite the distinct advantages each methodology presents, they come with their own set of challenges. Time series models may necessitate adjustments for issues like non-stationarity or volatility clustering, whereas cross-sectional models face hurdles such as multicollinearity among variables. Advanced analytical techniques—such as ARIMA models for time series and sophisticated regression or machine learning techniques for cross-sectional analysis—can enhance both accuracy and robustness.

In today's fast-paced financial landscape, the ability to combine insights from time series and cross-sectional analyses delivers unprecedented flexibility and depth. Together, they empower financial strategists with a comprehensive toolkit for deciphering market dynamics and crafting advanced models aimed at alpha generation amidst complexity. Through meticulous application and ongoing refinement, these methodologies pave the way for innovative strategies that challenge conventional market paradigms and drive superior performance.

The Intricacies of Scale and Granularity in Quantitative Finance

In the dynamic and complex arena of quantitative finance, the notions of scale and granularity are not merely technical terms; they are fundamental concepts that shape the accuracy and relevance of financial models. Understanding these dimensions is essential for developing robust alpha-generating strategies and for achieving informed decision-making in financial contexts.

Scale: Navigating the Depths of Financial Data

Scale encompasses the extent and scope of data points employed in financial modeling and analysis. Thus, determining the right scale becomes paramount for uncovering actionable insights.

1. Macro vs. Micro Scale: Financial analysis oscillates between macroeconomic and microeconomic perspectives. At a macro level, analysts examine overarching trends reflected in economic indicators like GDP growth and inflation rates, providing a foundation for strategic market assessments. In contrast, the micro scale hones in on the specifics of individual securities or asset classes—such as tick-by-tick price movements—that illuminate the intricacies of high-frequency trading strategies.

2. Time Horizons: The choice of time horizons significantly influences data analysis. Short-term analyses may capture noise within the market's microstructure, making them vital for

day traders, while longer-term evaluations reveal enduring market trends. For example, weekly stock fluctuations can inform swing trading decisions, whereas examining decades of historical data may unveil broader secular trends advantageous for long-term investment strategies.

3. Geographical Scale: The geographic scope of data is another critical factor. Global strategists may integrate data from various international markets to exploit diversification opportunities, while those focusing on localized markets can gain insights into regional economic behaviors and phenomena.

Granularity: The Precision in Data Analysis

Granularity concerns the level of detail contained in a dataset, resembling the microscope's capacity to reveal hidden intricacies. A higher granularity indicates a keen dive into finer details, while lower granularity may obscure vital insights.

1. Data Resolution: Data resolution refers to the level of detail captured in analysis. High-resolution data, such as intraday trading information, serves as the backbone for developing high-frequency trading algorithms, while aggregated daily prices may suffice for conventional portfolio management practices.

2. Categorization: Granular categorization of data—such as by asset sector, geographic region, or risk factor—enables a nuanced understanding of financial instruments. Portfolio managers often classify a diverse range of investments into distinct asset classes or sectors to enhance risk allocation and optimize returns in varying market conditions.

3. Dimensionality Reduction: While increased granularity can enrich insights, it can also introduce

complexity. Techniques like Principal Component Analysis (PCA) can aid in managing this complexity, balancing the richness of detailed data with the computational efficiency required for analysis.

Synergizing Scale and Granularity: A Strategic Approach

The optimal interaction between scale and granularity is most effectively realized in customized data models tailored to specific financial objectives. For instance, an asset manager formulating a global investment strategy might first aggregate comprehensive macroeconomic data to form a high-level market view. Subsequently, granular analyses could be employed to pinpoint sector-specific opportunities within individual markets, allowing for more targeted strategies.

Practical Example: A Multi-Layered Approach to Risk Management

Imagine a risk management strategy that adeptly leverages both scale and granularity. At the macro level, insights garnered from global economic indicators, market indices, and geopolitical events help establish foundational risk assessments. Simultaneously, a closer examination of granular transaction-level data reveals volatilities and anomalies within the portfolio's constituent securities. This dual approach ensures a comprehensive risk management framework that factors in broad market trends while addressing specific risk characteristics.

Navigating Challenges in Balancing Scale and Granularity

Achieving the ideal balance between scale and granularity presents challenges, such as the need for effective data integration and the proper allocation of computational resources. Higher granularity typically demands extensive storage and processing capabilities, while broader datasets can create challenges in synthesizing disparate data sources. Tackling these challenges necessitates innovative data engineering solutions and methodological precision to ensure that financial models retain their integrity and utility.

The interplay between data scale and granularity reflects a delicate balancing act that requires a thoughtful approach specific to each financial application. Mastering the assessment and optimization of these dimensions empowers quantitative finance professionals to enhance the depth and precision of their models and to refine their strategies with clarity and foresight. This integrated approach fuels the pursuit of alpha generation in an increasingly data-driven financial landscape, paving the way for success in an ever-evolving market environment.

Harnessing Big Data Technologies in Finance:
The Power of Hadoop and Spark

In today's fast-paced financial landscape, the explosion of big data has fundamentally transformed how organizations manage and analyze information. Leveraging vast amounts of data effectively opens up unparalleled opportunities for extracting actionable insights. At the forefront of this technological revolution are Hadoop and Spark, two pivotal platforms that are now essential tools in the toolkit of quantitative analysts and data scientists. Mastery of these technologies is critical for developing sophisticated financial models and achieving exceptional alpha generation in an increasingly competitive market.

Hadoop: The Cornerstone of Distributed Data Processing

Hadoop has become synonymous with big data solutions, renowned for its capacity to manage and process massive datasets across distributed computing clusters. This framework is built on two essential pillars: the Hadoop Distributed File System (HDFS) and the MapReduce programming model, both of which are indispensable for handling financial data at scale.

1. HDFS (Hadoop Distributed File System): HDFS is designed for storing vast quantities of data across numerous machines, offering both fault tolerance and high availability. For example, in a financial institution dealing with petabytes of transaction data, HDFS guarantees that data is replicated and remains accessible, even in the event of hardware failures, thus safeguarding against the risk of data loss.

2. MapReduce: This powerful programming paradigm enables the parallel processing of data by breaking down tasks into smaller, manageable sub-tasks distributed across multiple nodes. In the realm of financial analytics, MapReduce can be employed to process extensive datasets, such as sorting historical price records or aggregating transactions from different regions, significantly enhancing processing speeds and operational efficiency.

Example in Action: Take a financial firm examining customer transaction trends. Insights gained from this analysis could inform credit risk assessments and lead to more tailored product offerings.

Spark: Turbocharging Big Data Analytics in Finance

While Hadoop provides a strong foundation for data storage and processing, Apache Spark elevates this framework by enabling faster and more versatile computations. Through its innovative in-memory processing architecture, Spark supports a wider array of data processing workloads, including machine learning and real-time analytics.

1. In-Memory Processing: Spark's ability to keep data resident in memory minimizes disk I/O operations, which greatly accelerates processing speed. This capability is particularly crucial in scenarios like real-time trading, where every millisecond can

have significant financial implications. Algorithmic trading strategies, for instance, can utilize Spark to swiftly process streaming data, executing trades almost instantaneously based on live market conditions.

2. Machine Learning with MLlib: Spark's MLlib, a comprehensive machine learning library, simplifies the integration of various models into financial applications. An asset management firm could leverage MLlib to conduct predictive analytics, assessing stock price movements based on historical data and macroeconomic indicators, thereby refining portfolio strategies.

3. Structured Streaming and Real-Time Analytics: Spark's support for real-time data processing is essential for applications like fraud detection and high-frequency trading.

Illustrative Case: Imagine a hedge fund using Spark's streaming capabilities to aggregate data on market sentiment from news outlets and social media. This real-time analysis of sentiment could empower traders to adjust their positions dynamically, optimizing returns while managing risks effectively.

Integration and Synergy: The Combined Force of Hadoop and Spark

Utilizing Hadoop and Spark together can create a powerful synergy, where Hadoop's robust storage capabilities seamlessly complement Spark's rapid processing. Financial analysts can use Hadoop to store and manage extensive datasets, while harnessing Spark for agile data analysis and model training.

Practical Workflow: A typical workflow might involve consolidating and preprocessing historical market data in Hadoop, which is then analyzed using Spark for computationally intensive tasks, such as backtesting complex quantitative strategies on selected data segments. This integrated approach fosters an efficient data processing ecosystem, allowing for seamless transitions from data storage to insightful analysis.

Navigating Challenges and Ensuring Compliance

Despite the advantages that Hadoop and Spark bring to the table, their implementation within the finance sector is not without challenges, particularly concerning data security, privacy, and regulatory compliance. Financial institutions must bolster their big data infrastructures with stringent security protocols and maintain comprehensive audit trails to meet regulatory requirements.

Security Measures: Employing advanced encryption techniques for both stored and transmitted data, alongside stringent access controls, can significantly mitigate potential security risks. Additionally, regular audits are essential for ensuring compliance with regulations such as the General Data Protection Regulation (GDPR) and other relevant financial standards.

The integration of Hadoop and Spark into the financial sector signifies a revolutionary change in how data is processed and analyzed. These powerful technologies enable financial institutions to derive deeper insights, improve operational efficiency, and foster innovation in quantitative strategies. For finance professionals eager to unlock the full potential of big data, mastering these platforms is a gateway to outperforming the market through enhanced analytical capabilities and strategic agility.

As the financial landscape continues to evolve, the ongoing adoption and refinement of big data technologies like Hadoop and Spark will remain crucial, paving the way for new avenues of alpha generation and setting the stage for the future of finance.

Navigating Ethical Considerations in Data Usage

In the dynamic landscape of quantitative finance, the relentless quest for alpha is intrinsically tied to the effective use of data. As data-driven algorithms and models increasingly shape market behaviors, the importance of ethics in data acquisition and application cannot be overstated. The journey toward alpha generation is not solely about mastering sophisticated techniques; it also hinges on a principled commitment to ethical standards that prioritize both integrity and societal welfare.

The Foundations of Ethical Data Acquisition

The ethical framework governing data usage is complex and multifaceted, beginning with how data is collected. The explosion of big data technologies has created numerous opportunities, but it also introduces ethical dilemmas. Financial institutions frequently gather data from diverse sources—ranging from social media and transaction histories to public databases—each necessitating careful consideration of privacy and consent. For instance, the acquisition of personal data without explicit permission or exploiting loopholes in data-sharing agreements directly contravenes ethical finance principles. These actions not only jeopardize public trust but can also result in severe regulatory penalties and long-term reputational damage.

A notable case exemplifying the ramifications of unethical data practices involved a prominent financial conglomerate that utilized customer transaction data for model training without obtaining explicit consent. The fallout from this incident was immediate and profound: a wave of public indignation, intense regulatory scrutiny, and substantial fines prompted a complete reevaluation of their data handling protocols. This case serves as a potent reminder of the vital importance of ethical data practices in maintaining trust and credibility.

Ensuring Integrity in Data Usage

Once data has been responsibly acquired, the integrity of its application becomes paramount. Quantitative models depend on both historical and real-time data to predict market patterns and inform investment strategies. Upholding data integrity demands meticulous attention to accuracy and impartiality. The use of biased datasets or the strategic exclusion of relevant outliers to "produce" favorable model results is not only unethical but also dangerously misleading. Such practices can have significant financial repercussions, distorting market analysis and potentially resulting in costly investment blunders.

Imagine a scenario where a machine learning model built on incomplete historical pricing data reflects existing market biases, leading to skewed predictions. If investors make decisions based on this flawed analysis, the consequences can be disastrous, further underscoring the critical importance of maintaining data accuracy and conducting comprehensive preprocessing.

Protecting Sensitive Information

In the financial sector, the protection of sensitive data stands as another cornerstone of ethical data usage. Due to the high value of financial information, it often becomes a target for cyber threats. Upholding ethical standards necessitates not only compliance with legal requirements but also proactive measures to safeguard confidential information from unauthorized breaches. Financial institutions are thus required to implement rigorous security protocols—including encryption and regular audits—to defend against potential cyber risks, affirming their ethical duty to protect client data.

The Ethics of Data Sharing

The ethical paradigms governing data sharing are equally

vital. Collaborative efforts between corporations or between academia and industry often involve exchanging data for mutual advantage. In such scenarios, maintaining transparency about how data will be utilized and ensuring that datasets are anonymized to protect individual identities is imperative. Any failure to ethically manage shared data can result in grave ramifications, including the unlawful exposure of personal information, thus undermining both trust and compliance.

Industry Standards for Ethical Data Usage

Ethical responsibility extends beyond individual organizations; it permeates the entire financial landscape. Establishing industry-wide guidelines and standards can foster uniform compliance and help rebuild public confidence in data usage within the sector. These standards emphasize a culture of accountability and transparency, providing a framework for ethical behavior that can guide practitioners across the field.

As the realm of quantitative finance continues to expand and evolve, prioritizing ethical considerations in data usage is essential. Adhering to these principles not only enhances the integrity of financial practices but also enriches the pursuit of alpha, transforming it into a mission that aligns profit-driven goals with broader societal ideals. Through steadfast commitment to ethical standards, practitioners can forge a future that transcends mere financial gain, fostering innovation that resonates with the values of the communities they serve.

Safeguarding Data: Enhancing Security and Compliance in Quantitative Finance

In the dynamic realm of quantitative finance, data serves as the heartbeat of investment strategies and analytical models. As such, the imperative to protect this critical asset cannot be overstated. The intersection of cutting-edge data security measures and rigorous compliance with legal standards is crucial, as the effectiveness of algorithms hinges on the integrity of the data they process. Lacking these essential protections, the longevity and success of any quantitative strategy become precariously vulnerable.

The Critical Nature of Data Security

In finance, data security encompasses a comprehensive strategy designed to shield sensitive information from unauthorized access, cyberattacks, and other malicious activities. The inherent value of financial data makes it a prime target for cybercriminals. As incidents of fraud and data breaches escalate, institutions depend on predictive algorithms that are only trustworthy if the underlying data remains secure. A failure in data integrity can result not only in financial penalties but can also irreversibly damage stakeholder trust—an invaluable commodity in a sector where reputation is paramount.

Consider the case of a global asset management firm that suffered a catastrophic data breach, where hackers accessed confidential client information and proprietary investment strategies. The fallout was significant, resulting in financial losses and a mass exodus of clients who were understandably shaken by the firm's inability to safeguard their sensitive data. This situation vividly illustrates the absolute necessity of implementing comprehensive security protocols, including advanced encryption, multi-factor authentication, and regular vulnerability assessments to preempt similar incidents.

Navigating the Complex Compliance Landscape

The regulatory framework governing data security in finance is multifaceted and continually evolving. Compliance mandates that financial institutions adhere to an array of stringent laws and guidelines, which regulate the storage, processing, and sharing of data. Authorities recognize the imperatives of data protection, leading to the establishment of sophisticated security regulations aimed at mitigating risks. For instance, the General Data Protection Regulation (GDPR) enacted in the European Union has reverberated across global borders, prompting firms to rigorously re-evaluate their data handling practices.

For firms engaged in quantitative trading across multiple jurisdictions, the challenge of complying with diverse regulatory requirements—such as the GDPR in Europe, the California Consumer Privacy Act (CCPA) in the U.S., and Singapore's Personal Data Protection Act (PDPA)— is formidable. Noncompliance can result in hefty fines and regulatory scrutiny, which can disrupt operations and tarnish reputations. Thus, a proactive compliance strategy is crucial; teams must stay informed about regulatory updates and seamlessly integrate these requirements into their data governance frameworks.

Adapting to Technological Advancements

As technology evolves, the landscape for maintaining data security and compliance necessitates constant adaptation. The rise of cloud computing offers scalable storage options but also introduces new security risks. Effective cloud security strategies must include strict access controls, encryption of data both at rest and during transit, and advanced monitoring systems capable of detecting and mitigating threats in real-time.

Moreover, firms harnessing big data technologies should embrace Secure DevOps—an approach that integrates security into every phase of software development and operational processes.

Fostering a Culture of Security Awareness

An effective data security and compliance framework requires a cultural shift within organizations, promoting security awareness across all levels of staff. Employees must be educated about the critical importance of data protection and remain vigilant against evolving threats. Regular training sessions focusing on recognizing phishing attempts and other social engineering tactics, along with updates on regulatory changes, are essential components of this initiative.

One practical method of strengthening this awareness is through simulated phishing exercises. For example, a financial institution that implemented such simulations found that a notable percentage of employees failed to identify suspicious links. Targeted training following this revelation drastically reduced susceptibility to phishing attempts, demonstrating the effectiveness of proactive education in minimizing risks.

Strategic Governance and Oversight

Integrating data security and compliance into the overarching governance structure of the organization is vital. This includes appointing dedicated leadership, such as a Chief Information Security Officer (CISO), responsible for overseeing the execution of data protection initiatives. Conducting regular audits and penetration testing ensures that governance frameworks remain robust and can adapt to the ever-changing threats and regulatory challenges that characterize the financial landscape.

As the field of quantitative finance increasingly relies on data as its backbone, establishing a resilient framework for data security and compliance is not merely a best practice; it is an absolute necessity. The future of data security in finance requires a balanced approach that combines tactical defenses with strategic oversight, ensuring that finance professionals can confidently navigate the evolving digital landscape with agility and integrity.

CHAPTER 3: STATISTICAL FOUNDATIONS FOR QUANTITATIVE MODELS

The world of quantitative finance thrives on statistical principles that provide a robust analytical framework for parsing financial data and crafting investment strategies. Key concepts such as mean, variance, and correlation form the backbone of this discipline, equipping quantitative strategists with the essential tools needed to interpret market behaviors and achieve alpha in their portfolios. Grasping these fundamental ideas is vital for any aspiring quantitative analyst seeking to navigate financial complexities.

The Role of Mean: Central Tendency in Finance

At the heart of statistical analysis lies the mean, often termed the average, which serves as a fundamental measure of central tendency. It reveals the typical value around which data points cluster, offering crucial insights for financial decision-making. In finance, the mean can signify average returns, establishing a benchmark against which investors can measure actual performance.

For example, consider a stock with daily returns over a month that yields figures like 1%, 0.5%, -0.2%, and 2%. To find the mean return, you would sum these daily returns and divide by the number of days, resulting in:

[Mean = ((1 + 0.5 - 0.2 + 2) / 4) = 0.825\% per day.]

This average not only provides a reference point for assessing whether an asset consistently exceeds expectations but also acts as a foundational element for advanced quantitative strategies. Analysts can leverage this benchmark to evaluate the potential for growth and to refine risk models, driving more informed investment decisions.

Variance: A Measure of Risk and Volatility

While the mean offers a glimpse into average performance, variance delves deeper, quantifying the dispersion of data points around the mean. This measurement is essential for understanding the risk and volatility associated with financial assets. A higher variance signifies greater volatility, indicating that returns can fluctuate significantly from the mean, leading to increased risk.

Variance is calculated by averaging the squared differences between each data point and the mean, expressed mathematically as:

[^2 = ((X_i -)^2 / N),]

where (^{2}) represents variance, (X_i) denotes individual returns, () is the mean, and (N) is the number of observations.

In practical scenarios, envision two portfolios: one with daily returns that closely hover around the mean, resulting in low variance, and another characterized by significant daily fluctuations and high variance. This latter portfolio would require a more comprehensive risk management strategy. A deep understanding of variance equips analysts not only to measure risk but also to develop effective hedging techniques and diversification strategies, crucial for maintaining portfolio stability.

Correlation: Understanding Variable Relationships

Correlation is a vital statistical measure that indicates how two variables move in relation to one another. Ranging from -1 to 1, the correlation coefficient reveals the strength and direction of their relationship: values near 1 denote a strong positive correlation, values close to -1 suggest a strong negative correlation, and values around 0 indicate no relationship.

In the context of portfolio management, a thorough grasp of correlation mechanics is indispensable for effective diversification. Consider a portfolio comprised of assets that showcase low or negative correlations; this structure can lead to a reduction in overall volatility, as losses in one area may be mitigated by gains in another. If two stocks, A and B, exhibit a correlation coefficient of -0.3, this negative relationship implies they typically move inversely, thereby balancing each other and reducing overall risk.

To illustrate, suppose we calculate the correlation between the returns of Stock A ([5%, 6%, 7%]) and Stock B ([3%, 2%, 4%]). The correlation coefficient can be determined using the formula:

[Correlation(A, B) = ((A_i - A)(B_i - B) / sqrt((A_i - A))^2 (B_i - B))^2,]

where (A_i) and (B_i) represent individual returns for stocks A and B, while (A) and (B) denote their respective means.

Practical Application in Quantitative Models

Equipped with insights from mean, variance, and correlation, quantitative analysts can formulate predictive models and fine-tune investment strategies. These statistical underpinnings inform critical decisions in portfolio construction, risk assessment, and strategic asset allocation. When designing trading algorithms, a comprehensive understanding of these concepts empowers analysts to create models capable of dynamically adjusting to ever-changing market conditions, ultimately optimizing returns while managing risk effectively.

Integrating these foundational statistical measures into their analytical toolkit allows finance professionals to navigate the intricate landscape of quantitative investing confidently. This essential knowledge serves as a springboard for exploring more advanced statistical methodologies, such as regression analysis and machine learning, all of which play pivotal roles in the quest for sustainable alpha generation and consistent outperformance.

Probability Distributions and Their Applications in Quantitative Finance

Probability distributions are fundamental to quantitative finance, serving as essential tools for understanding and analyzing market dynamics. They provide a structured way to explore how probabilities spread across various outcomes, enabling analysts to assess risk, model asset behavior, and extract valuable insights from complex data. A comprehensive grasp of the various types of distributions and their implications is indispensable for developing effective quantitative models that can navigate the intricacies of today's financial markets.

The Normal Distribution: The Financial Bell Curve

At the heart of financial modeling lies the normal distribution, often visualized as the classic bell curve. This distribution posits that returns on assets are typically symmetrically distributed around a central mean, which holds significant implications for financial prediction and risk assessment.

For example, if the annual returns of a stock follow a normal distribution with a mean of 5% and a standard deviation of 2%, analysts can confidently infer that about 68% of returns will land within one standard deviation of the mean— between 3% and 7%. This property plays a critical role in risk assessment and portfolio management, aiding strategists in evaluating the likelihood of extreme gains or losses.

However, it is essential to approach the normal distribution with caution. Financial markets frequently exhibit behaviors that deviate from this model due to fat tails or skewness, where extreme outcomes occur more frequently than predicted. This reality prompts analysts to explore alternative distributions, ensuring that models remain accurate and reflective of actual market conditions.

The Lognormal Distribution: A Realistic Approach to Asset Prices

When it comes to modeling stock prices, the lognormal distribution often takes precedence. Unlike the normal distribution, which can yield negative values, the lognormal distribution recognizes that asset prices cannot fall below zero, aligning more closely with the realities of financial markets.

A vivid application of the lognormal distribution is found in option pricing models, such as the Black-Scholes model. Imagine an analyst forecasting a stock price with an expected annual growth of 8% and a volatility of 15%.

Mastering the use of the lognormal distribution empowers financial strategists to capture realistic price behaviors, ultimately crafting strategies that are intuitive and aligned with the inherent characteristics of asset price dynamics. This reduces the risk of miscalculations based on unrealistic assumptions.

The Exponential Distribution: Timing and Risk Assessment

The exponential distribution plays a vital role in modeling time-related risks, particularly in scenarios like default risk or the time between market transactions. Its defining property of being memoryless—where the probability of an event occurring is independent of past events—makes it particularly suitable for various financial applications.

For instance, in high-frequency trading, the exponential distribution can predict the intervals between trades, aiding in the optimization of execution strategies and minimizing market impact.

In credit risk analysis, the exponential distribution is instrumental in quantifying the time until default.

The Pareto Distribution: Addressing Extreme Outcomes

In financial contexts, the Pareto distribution is crucial for modeling phenomena that display heavy tails, where extreme events, although infrequent, hold significant impact. This distribution becomes particularly relevant during financial crises or other market disruptions, as these are instances where outcomes diverge drastically from the norm.

Analysts often leverage the Pareto distribution to assess income distribution, optimize insurance portfolios, and understand the tail risks associated with equity returns. In a hedge fund environment, identifying assets whose return distributions align with a Pareto model can inform strategic decisions that hedge against infrequent but severe losses— ultimately safeguarding the portfolio's integrity.

Integrating Distributions in Quantitative Models

The vast applications of probability distributions in quantitative finance underscore their critical importance. In portfolio optimization, for instance, strategists blend insights from different distributions to model returns and correlations, ensuring that risk management frameworks align with investment objectives. Moreover, the pricing of derivatives relies on these statistical foundations, bridging theoretical robustness with empirical accuracy. This knowledge goes beyond theory; it translates into actionable strategies that enhance performance while effectively mitigating potential risks in an ever-evolving financial landscape.

Hypothesis Testing and Confidence Intervals
in Quantitative Finance

In the fast-paced world of quantitative finance, hypothesis testing and confidence intervals are invaluable tools that help analysts differentiate between authentic market signals and random fluctuations. This not only informs model development and risk assessment but also enhances the execution of trading strategies.

Understanding Hypothesis Testing

Hypothesis testing is a fundamental statistical method that allows analysts to draw conclusions about a population parameter based on sample observations. This process starts with the formulation of two opposing statements: the null hypothesis (H0) and the alternative hypothesis (H1). The null hypothesis generally posits that there is no significant effect or relationship, while the alternative hypothesis contends that a noteworthy effect or relationship exists.

In a practical finance scenario, consider an analyst who wants to evaluate whether the mean return of a recently developed trading strategy surpasses that of an established benchmark or target. For instance, if the goal is to determine whether the new strategy achieves an average return exceeding 5%, the hypotheses would be structured as follows:

- H0: μ = 5% (The average return of the new strategy is equal to 5%.)
- H1: μ > 5% (The average return of the new strategy is greater than 5%.)

The analyst would then compute a relevant test statistic, such as a t-statistic, from the sample data and identify the corresponding p-value. If this p-value falls below a pre-defined significance level, typically set at 0.05, the null hypothesis is rejected, suggesting that the new strategy indeed offers a statistically significant improvement in returns.

Confidence Intervals: Assessing the Precision of Estimates

While hypothesis testing functions as a binary decision framework, confidence intervals provide a broader view by estimating a range of plausible values for an unknown parameter. A confidence interval represents an estimated range that, with a specified confidence level (for example, 95%), is likely to encompass the true value of the parameter being evaluated.

In the financial landscape, confidence intervals are particularly useful for gauging the reliability of estimated returns, volatility, or risk metrics. For example, take an analyst who predicts the average return of an asset to be 6%, with a standard error of 1%. The calculation for a 95% confidence interval would follow:

$$[6\% \ 1.96 \ 1\%]$$

This yields a range between 4.04% and 7.96%. This interval indicates that, should the analysis be repeated across various samples, the true mean return is expected to fall within this range 95% of the time.

Practical Applications and Implications in Finance

The integration of hypothesis testing and confidence intervals in finance extends across various domains, significantly enhancing decision-making processes and the credibility of models:

1. Backtesting Trading Strategies: Quantitative strategists utilize hypothesis testing during the backtesting of trading strategies by comparing actual returns with a zero mean or benchmark, thereby validating profitability assumptions. Additionally, confidence intervals can provide insights into the performance consistency of these strategies under diverse market conditions.

2. Risk Assessment: In managing risk, analysts can test hypotheses related to volatility changes in response to economic shifts. This ensures that financial models effectively capture market dynamics. Confidence intervals further illuminate the range of potential risk exposures, facilitating sound hedging strategies.

3. Comparative Analysis: Finance professionals frequently employ hypothesis testing to assess whether performance differences among various investment options are statistically significant, thereby guiding informed decisions about asset allocation and diversification.

4. Evaluating Portfolio Performance: Fund managers often scrutinize whether their active management strategies yield genuine value compared to passive benchmarks. With hypothesis testing, they can rigorously assess whether observed alpha is a real outcome or simply a product of market variability.

A thorough understanding of hypothesis testing and confidence intervals equips finance professionals with robust statistical tools essential for interpreting market data and enhancing strategic initiatives.

Incorporating these analytical techniques into daily practice fosters a disciplined approach that can withstand the unpredictable nature of financial markets, cultivating a culture of continual improvement and well-informed decision-making. The capacity to rigorously evaluate assumptions and quantify uncertainty lies at the very core of successful quantitative finance, steering the quest for sustainable alpha generation across a range of investment horizons.

Regression Analysis in Finance

Regression analysis serves as a foundational element in the realm of quantitative finance, providing sophisticated tools to uncover the relationships between financial variables. Its predictive capabilities make regression a crucial instrument for everything from market forecasting to risk assessment. As analysts and strategists navigate the complexities of financial markets, regression analysis illuminates the intricate connections that influence market dynamics, equipping them with insights essential for informed decision-making.

Understanding the Basics of Regression Analysis

At its core, regression analysis seeks to establish a functional relationship between a dependent variable and one or more independent variables. The most prevalent form is linear regression, which assumes a linear correlation between these variables, expressed through the equation:

$$[Y = \beta_0 + \beta_1 X_1 + \beta_2 X_2 + + \beta_n X_n +]$$

In this equation, (Y) typically signifies the dependent variable, often a critical financial metric such as asset returns. The ($X_1, X_2, , X_n$) represent independent variables, which could include market indices, economic indicators, or other pertinent metrics. The coefficients ($\beta_0, \beta_1, ,$ β_n) reflect the impact of each independent variable, while ( ) accounts for the error term, capturing any variance not explained by the independent variables.

Diverse Applications of Regression Analysis in Finance

Regression analysis demonstrates its versatility across a variety of financial applications:

1. Asset Pricing Models: One of the most recognized models utilizing regression is the Capital Asset Pricing Model (CAPM). CAPM leverages regression to evaluate the relationship between an asset's expected return and its market risk, yielding valuable insights:

[Expected Return = Risk-Free Rate + (Market Return - Risk-Free Rate)]

Here, () indicates the asset's systematic risk compared to the market, derived through regression analysis of historical return data.

1. Investment Analysis and Portfolio Management: Analysts apply regression to assess how individual securities contribute to overall portfolio performance. Multi-factor models, such as the Fama-French three-factor model, expand upon CAPM by including additional factors like company size and book-to-market ratios. This enriched approach enhances risk adjustment during portfolio construction, enabling more robust investment strategies.

2. Risk Management: Through regression, analysts can investigate how various economic indicators influence financial risk measures, such as Value at Risk (VaR). This analysis is pivotal for developing effective hedging strategies and improving overall risk mitigation efforts.

3. Evaluation of Historical Performance: By regressing historical price data against time or other economic variables, analysts uncover insights into price trends and cyclical behaviors. This practice can reveal the implications of specific market events or broader economic shifts on asset valuations.

The Nuances of Model Selection and Validation

Effective regression analysis hinges on the careful selection of the appropriate model and rigorous validation of its results.

- Choosing Variables: Selecting the right independent variables is crucial. Analysts must strike a balance between underfitting (omitting essential factors) and overfitting (introducing irrelevant variables). Techniques such as stepwise regression and leveraging domain expertise help refine the selection process.

- Validating the Model: After model specification, it's essential to test its assumptions and predictive capabilities. Residual analysis may identify issues like heteroscedasticity or autocorrelation, prompting adjustments with techniques like Generalized Least Squares (GLS) to enhance predictive accuracy.

- Out-of-Sample Testing: To ensure robustness, analysts should validate their models using out-of-sample data. This approach confirms that the model's predictive strength remains intact beyond the initial dataset, reducing the risks associated with overfitting.

A Practical Example: Forecasting Stock Prices with Regression

Consider an analyst tasked with forecasting short-term stock prices using daily closing prices and trading volume data from the past year. The analyst opts for a linear regression model with stock returns as the dependent variable and trading volume as the independent variable.

- Data Preparation: The initial step involves gathering closing prices and trading volumes, calculating daily returns, and examining data for potential correlations or structural breaks.

- Model Specification: A simple regression model is structured as follows:

[Stock Return = \beta_0 + \beta_1 Volume +]

- Model Fitting: The analyst utilizes statistical software, such as Python's SciPy or R's lm() function, to fit the model. Summary statistics are analyzed to evaluate variable significance and overall model fit, while diagnostic plots reveal any multicollinearity or violations of regression assumptions.

- Insight Derivation: If trading volume emerges as a significant predictor, opportunities for contrarian trading strategies might be examined. Conversely, if the model displays unexpected variability, further modeling techniques or additional variables may be needed for a comprehensive forecast.

In summary, regression analysis offers an essential framework for deciphering financial patterns, enhancing decision-making capabilities across diverse financial domains. It adeptly balances simplicity and complexity, providing clarity amid the uncertainties of financial markets and fostering strategic insights.

The Fundamentals of Time Series Analysis

In the dynamic world of financial markets, time series analysis serves as a fundamental methodology essential for uncovering the intricate temporal dependencies and cyclical patterns that exist within financial data. As market conditions shift and evolve, the capacity to model and predict these temporal sequences becomes increasingly critical, enabling stakeholders to make informed decisions and strategic plans.

Understanding Time Series Data

At its core, time series data comprises observations collected sequentially over time – whether daily stock prices, quarterly earnings reports, or annual GDP figures. Unlike cross-sectional data, where the observations are independent of one another, time series data exhibit temporal dependencies that present unique analytical challenges and opportunities. These observations can reflect various characteristics, such as trends, seasonality, cyclical changes, and irregular fluctuations, all of which time series analysis seeks to model and understand meticulously.

Core Components of Time Series Analysis

1. Trend Analysis: A trend signifies the long-term trajectory of a time series, indicating consistent upward or downward movements over time. Identifying these trends is vital for capturing the overall direction of the market. Analytical methods like moving averages or exponential smoothing are valuable tools for distilling this underlying trend from the surrounding noise in the data.

2. Seasonality: Seasonality encompasses periodic fluctuations that occur at regular intervals, influenced by predictable seasonal factors such as fiscal quarters or holidays. Seasonal Decomposition of Time Series (STL) allows analysts to dissect the data into its core components—trend, seasonal, and residual—thus enabling a clearer analysis of these seasonal influences.

3. Cyclical Patterns: In contrast to seasonality, cyclical patterns refer to fluctuations that do not adhere to a fixed periodicity but occur across more extended time frames tied to economic cycles or business conditions. Techniques like spectral analysis or business cycle models can help identify and analyze these cycles, offering deeper insight into market behavior.

4. Stationarity: A stationary time series possesses statistical properties—such as constant mean and variance—over time. Stationarity is crucial because many time series models rely on the assumption of a stable structure. When non-stationary data are present, analysts can employ techniques like differencing or transformations (e.g., logarithmic

transformation) to stabilize the data for effective modeling.

Key Methods and Techniques

1. Autoregressive Integrated Moving Average (ARIMA) Models: ARIMA combines three components— autoregression (AR), differencing (I for integrated), and moving averages (MA)—to forecast future values based on past observations and forecast errors. Selecting the optimal ARIMA model involves determining appropriate orders for AR, I, and MA components, often guided by criteria like the Akaike Information Criterion (AIC).

2. Example: Imagine a financial analyst tasked with modeling monthly unemployment rates that display observable trends and some cyclical patterns. An ARIMA(1,1,1) model might be selected, where '1' signifies the orders of the autoregressive, integrated, and moving average components, respectively.

3. Exponential Smoothing State Space Models: These models utilize a smoothing approach that places greater emphasis on recent observations. Methods such as Holt-Winters exponential smoothing are adept at breaking down data into its level, trend, and seasonal components, facilitating efficient forecasting for complex datasets.

4. Vector Autoregression (VAR) Models: In situations where multiple time series variables influence one another, VAR models become invaluable. They allow for a comprehensive analysis by enabling each variable to be expressed in terms of its own past values and those of other variables in the dataset, capturing the dynamic interactions within interconnected datasets.

5. Example: Consider an economist examining the relationship between GDP growth and inflation rates.

Practical Application: Forecasting Financial Indices

Imagine a trader responsible for forecasting the closing prices of a financial index. The process typically unfolds through several key steps:

- Data Exploration: Start by visually plotting the time series data to identify patterns in trends and seasonality. Conduct statistical tests, such as the Augmented Dickey-Fuller test, to evaluate data stationarity.

- Model Selection: Based on the preliminary examination, choose an appropriate ARIMA model. In this case, an ARIMA(2,1,2) model may be deemed suitable, particularly if statistical tests indicate a non-stationary structure that stabilizes following differencing.

- Model Fitting: Utilize tools such as Python's statsmodels library to fit the ARIMA model, subsequently analyzing fit metrics. Perform residual diagnostics to confirm the absence of autocorrelation, validating the model's appropriateness.

- Forecasting: Generate future forecasts through the model, extending predictions into the anticipated timeframe. Visual comparisons of actual and predicted values serve to assess forecast accuracy.

- Performance Evaluation: Lastly, evaluate forecast performance using out-of-sample testing and error metrics, such as Mean Absolute Percentage Error (MAPE), to refine model parameters and enhance predictive capability.

Proficiency in time series analysis empowers financial strategists to transform historical market behaviors into actionable insights and predictions, forming a pivotal element of quantitative finance. As markets increasingly embrace data-driven approaches, mastery of time series methodologies equips analysts with the foresight necessary to navigate market trends and fine-tune strategic decisions effectively.

In the quest for alpha, the disciplined application of time series analysis cultivates a nuanced understanding of market rhythms, establishing it as an indispensable tool in the repertoire of modern financial professionals. The journey through the complexities of time series not only enhances predictive capabilities but fortifies the foundation for sustainable investment strategies in an ever-evolving financial landscape.

Advanced Statistical Techniques: ARIMA and GARCH

In the realm of quantitative finance, successful decision-making hinges on our ability to understand and predict the unpredictable nature of financial markets. To this end, advanced statistical models such as ARIMA (Autoregressive Integrated Moving Average) and GARCH (Generalized Autoregressive Conditional Heteroskedasticity) serve as invaluable tools. These models not only enhance our forecasting capabilities but also allow for a sophisticated analysis of volatility and uncertainty within financial time series data.

ARIMA: Capturing Time Dependencies

At the heart of time series forecasting, the ARIMA model is essential for analyzing and predicting trends based on the intrinsic relationships between current and historical data points. Its effectiveness stems from its unique composition of three key components: autoregression (AR), integration (I), and moving averages (MA).

1. Autoregressive (AR) Component: This component seeks to determine how today's observations are influenced by previous values. Through a careful examination of correlations among lagged data points, analysts can discern the significant impact that history bears on present outcomes.

2. Integrated (I) Component: Integration involves transforming non-stationary series into stationary ones by applying differencing techniques. This step is vital when dealing with data that exhibit trends or irregular fluctuations, as it stabilizes the series, paving the way for reliable analysis.

3. Moving Average (MA) Component: The moving average aspect assesses how current observations relate to past errors.

Example: Imagine an analyst assigned to forecast weekly sales for a retail brand. Upon observing trends and seasonal patterns, they select an ARIMA(1,1,1) model. This choice combines one lag for autoregression, a first-order difference to manage the upward trend, and one lag for the moving average, resulting in a well-rounded prediction model.

GARCH: Addressing Volatility Clustering

After establishing forecasts with ARIMA, the challenge of managing volatility surfaces prominently — that's where GARCH techniques come into play. Unlike ARIMA models that predominantly focus on predicting the mean of a time series, GARCH models delve into the dynamics of conditional variance, allowing analysts to develop comprehensive volatility forecasts.

1. Recognizing Volatility Clustering: In financial markets, it is common to witness episodes of high volatility followed by calms, a behavior known

as volatility clustering. GARCH effectively captures these phenomena, modeling the variance as a function of both past variances and past squared innovations.

2. GARCH Model Structure: The quintessential GARCH model integrates previous squared residuals (representing volatility shocks) with past variances into a sophisticated equation for conditional variance. This adaptable framework ensures that analysts can accurately capture prolonged phases of market calm or turbulence.

Example: Consider a portfolio manager striving to assess risk through the lens of daily return volatility.

Application and Implementation: A Practical Walkthrough

Successfully deploying ARIMA and GARCH models necessitates a systematic approach, beginning with thorough data exploration and culminating in confident forecasting.

1. Data Preprocessing:
2. Stationarity Assessment: Conduct tests such as the Augmented Dickey-Fuller to confirm stationarity or to ascertain the necessary order of differencing.
3. Volatility Visualization: Utilize rolling variance plots to uncover volatility patterns, indicating whether GARCH models are appropriate.
4. Model Specification and Fitting:
5. For ARIMA, leverage autocorrelation (ACF) and partial autocorrelation (PACF) plots to identify optimal parameters (p, d, and q).
6. For GARCH, begin with initial parameter estimates, calibrate the model on historical data through maximum likelihood estimation, and evaluate the fit.
7. Validation and Forecasting:

8. Implement out-of-sample testing to verify the model's predictive accuracy.

9. Generate forecasts with confidence intervals that extend beyond the trailing data, effectively juxtaposing predictions against actual outcomes for reliability assessment.

10. Performance Evaluation:

11. For ARIMA, use metrics such as the Root Mean Squared Error (RMSE) to assess the model's fit.

12. For GARCH models, compare realized volatility against predicted values, making adjustments to parameters as required to ensure accuracy.

The strategic application of ARIMA and GARCH models equips financial professionals with the tools necessary to navigate the complexities of market dynamics. While ARIMA shines in establishing and forecasting mean trends, GARCH addresses the intricate and fluctuating nature of volatility.

Together, these advanced statistical techniques empower analysts to forecast with precision and deftly maneuver through the complexities inherent in financial decision-making.

The Role of Exploratory Data Analysis (EDA) in Quantitative Finance

In the realm of quantitative finance, where decisions hinge on precise data insights, Exploratory Data Analysis (EDA) stands out as a vital phase in the analytical journey. This initial stage is not merely a precursor to more complex modeling; it is a rich process dedicated to unveiling hidden patterns, anomalies, and structures within the data. EDA lays the groundwork for robust quantitative strategies, ultimately enhancing the accuracy and effectiveness of subsequent analyses.

Uncovering the Narrative Within the Data

EDA is more than a routine process; it is the art of storytelling through data. Before embarking on intricate modeling efforts, analysts engage in EDA to foster a deep understanding of their data, thus tailoring future approaches to its unique characteristics.

1. Initial Data Assessment: The EDA process begins with a broad examination of the dataset, utilizing fundamental statistics—such as means, medians, and standard deviations—to establish a solid baseline for understanding data distribution.

Example: Imagine working with a dataset containing daily stock prices over a year.

1. Visualization Techniques: Visualizing data is a cornerstone of EDA. Effective visualization illuminates insights that might be obscured when relying solely on numerical data. Tools such as histograms, box plots, and scatter plots empower analysts to easily recognize patterns and irregularities.

Example: A histogram illustrating daily returns could reveal an unexpected frequency of sizable losses, hinting at a potential heavy-tailed distribution. Similarly, scatter plots might expose non-linear relationships between variables, prompting further exploration.

Addressing Data Challenges Proactively

One of the critical advantages of EDA is its ability to identify and diagnose data challenges early in the analysis. Issues like missing values, anomalies, and the need for transformations are tackled proactively, ensuring that subsequent statistical models are built on a stable foundation.

1. Handling Missing Values: A vital aspect of EDA is identifying and managing missing data—whether through imputation techniques or by excluding

incomplete records. This careful approach ensures a cleaner dataset, enhancing the dependability of future models.

Example: In financial datasets, missing values often stem from unreported trading days. Analysts might opt to address these gaps using historical averages or interpolation methods, preserving the dataset's integrity.

1. Identifying Outliers: Outliers can distort analytical results and lead to misguided interpretations. EDA plays a crucial role in pinpointing these anomalies, enabling analysts to discern whether they are errors or authentic deviations deserving further investigation.

Example: A time series plot revealing an unusual spike in asset returns could indicate either a data entry mistake or a significant market event—an important distinction clarified through EDA's insights.

1. Data Transformations: Certain datasets might require transformations to better align with the assumptions of subsequent statistical models. Techniques such as log transformations or differencing can stabilize variance and shift a dataset into a stationary state.

Example: An analyst could apply a log transformation to excessively skewed stock price data, creating a more favorable environment for robust modeling.

Guiding Informed Modeling Decisions

Through EDA, analysts establish criteria that guide their modeling choices, selecting statistical techniques tailored to the data's distinctive characteristics. This informed approach optimizes both accuracy and relevance in model development.

1. Feature Selection: EDA assists in pinpointing significant variables that contribute to predictive

models, allowing analysts to reduce noise and focus only on influential features. Correlation matrices, for instance, can illuminate issues of multicollinearity that require attention.

Example: An exploration of a dataset containing various economic indicators might reveal strong correlations between GDP growth and market returns, signaling GDP as a key predictor for financial modeling endeavors.

1. Deciding on Model Complexity: Insights gained from EDA also inform analysts about the necessary complexity of their models. In some instances, a straightforward linear regression may suffice, while in others, advanced models like ARIMA or GARCH might be warranted to address series with autocorrelation or conditional heteroscedasticity.

Example: An analyst might forego a complex model after EDA reveals that a singular factor primarily drives most of the variance observed in an asset's returns.

EDA in Practice: A Structured Workflow

Implementing EDA involves a structured yet iterative process, blending creativity with analytical insight. The following outlines a typical workflow adopted by practitioners:

1. Data Collection and Preprocessing:
2. Collect relevant data from credible sources.
3. Clean the dataset, addressing missing values, duplicate entries, and any inaccuracies right from the start.
4. Descriptive Statistics and Visualizations:
5. Generate summary statistics, offering a concise overview of the dataset's key features.
6. Utilize visualization tools to create graphs that reveal data distributions and highlight potential trends.

7. Pattern Identification:

8. Seek out emerging trends and seasonalities, utilizing time series decomposition as necessary.

9. Analyze relationships between variables through pairwise scatter plots and correlation matrices.

10. Anomaly Detection:

11. Employ both visual and quantitative methods to identify potential outliers.

12. Investigate these anomalies, rationalizing their existence to determine appropriate treatment.

Exploratory Data Analysis stands as the cornerstone for informed statistical modeling, serving as the bridge to advanced techniques such as ARIMA and GARCH. EDA is foundational in equipping analysts with the insights necessary to navigate the complexities of data, transforming chaos into clarity and fostering predictable, favorable financial outcomes.

Non-parametric methods occupy a vital and distinctive niche in the realm of quantitative finance. Unlike parametric methods, which rest on specific assumptions regarding the underlying statistical distributions of data, non-parametric techniques reject the notion of a predetermined data form. This inherent flexibility transforms them into powerful tools for modeling the complexities of real-world financial markets, which often defy the overly simplistic or inaccurate assumptions of normality and specific distribution shapes.

Embracing Flexibility in Complex Environments

The true strength of non-parametric methods lies in their remarkable adaptability. They create a robust framework for analyzing diverse datasets that may not adhere to conventional distributional assumptions. This capability is especially relevant in the unpredictable world of finance, where market behaviors are punctuated by irregular cycles, sudden shifts, and outlier events. Analysts frequently navigate scenarios where traditional models struggle, making non-parametric approaches increasingly appealing for capturing the intricacies and irregularities inherent in financial data.

A prime example of a non-parametric technique is Kernel Density Estimation (KDE), which helps analysts elucidate the underlying probability density of a random variable. KDE circumvents the need for data to fit a specific distribution by estimating the likelihood of various outcomes based on the data's natural distribution.

Here's a practical illustration of using KDE in Python:

``` python import numpy as np import matplotlib.pyplot as plt from scipy.stats import gaussian_kde

\#\# Simulated financial instrument returns
returns = np.random.normal(0, 1, size=1000)  \# Illustrative normal data

\#\# Performing Kernel Density Estimation
kde = gaussian_kde(returns)
x_grid = np.linspace(-4, 4, 1000)
plt.plot(x_grid, kde.evaluate(x_grid), label='Kernel Density Estimate')
plt.hist(returns, density=True, alpha=0.5, bins=30, label='Histogram')
plt.title('Kernel Density Estimation of Returns')
plt.xlabel('Returns')
plt.ylabel('Density')
plt.legend()
plt.show()
```

In this example, the code demonstrates how KDE aids in estimating the density of a financial returns dataset.

Addressing the Challenges of Diverse Datasets

Non-parametric methods truly excel in scenarios marked by high variability and limited sample sizes. A notable example is the Wilcoxon signed-rank test, an essential non-parametric instrument for evaluating trading strategy performance. This test effectively assesses datasets that deviate from the normal distribution, enabling hypothesis testing regarding median-based differences under less stringent conditions than conventional t-tests require.

Furthermore, in financial applications where the assumption of homoscedasticity—constant variance of errors—is frequently violated, robust non-parametric methods such as bootstrapping and permutation tests come to the fore. These methods generate sampling distributions through repeated resampling of the data, facilitating more reliable inferences when traditional assumptions of normality and equal variance break down.

A Case Study: Enhancing Portfolio Diversification

In practice, non-parametric methods are invaluable for crafting robust portfolio diversification strategies, particularly during periods of extreme market behavior. In scenarios where conventional Mean-Variance Optimization (MVO) falters due to its reliance on normal distribution assumptions, non-parametric approaches can augment this process. For instance, employing nearest-neighbors resampling techniques can more accurately estimate asset return distributions, yielding portfolios that are more adaptable and responsive to unpredictable market fluctuations.

A quantitative analyst might leverage non-parametric resampling techniques to model asset return distributions under historically stressing conditions. This approach provides a realistic foundation for estimating future risks and returns, which in turn informs the calibration of portfolio allocations resilient to unforeseen market liquidity shocks or economic downturns.

The incorporation of non-parametric methods in quantitative finance presents an array of possibilities driven by their adaptability, robustness, and capacity to manage datasets that resist traditional parametric approaches. As critical complements to various financial models, these techniques empower strategists and analysts to devise more precise and relevant solutions. This nuanced approach ultimately champions a more rigorous and effective exploration of financial data, facilitating better-informed decision-making in an increasingly intricate landscape.

Multivariate Analysis in Financial Contexts

In the intricate landscape of quantitative finance, multivariate analysis stands out as a crucial tool for deciphering the multifaceted relationships between various financial variables. The ability to analyze multiple interconnected factors can be transformative—revealing hidden patterns and delivering strategic insights that shape high-stakes decisions.

Unraveling Interconnected Financial Variables

The dynamics of financial markets are inherently complex, with numerous variables influencing outcomes in a symbiotic manner. For instance, the performance of a particular stock is not simply an isolated event; it is intricately affected by market indices, economic indicators, interest rates, and more. Each of these elements interacts continually, shaping the market's behavior and influencing investor sentiment. Multivariate analysis provides a structured approach to explore these interactions, enabling analysts to understand how different variables co-evolve over time and impact each other.

A prime example of multivariate analysis in action is Principal Component Analysis (PCA). This technique reduces the dimensionality of large datasets without compromising their essential characteristics. This is particularly advantageous in portfolio optimization, where minimizing the number of variables can reduce computational burdens while preserving essential information.

Example: PCA Application Using Python

```python
``` python import numpy as np from sklearn.decomposition import PCA import matplotlib.pyplot as plt

\#\# Simulating financial data for three correlated assets
np.random.seed(42)
assets_returns = np.random.normal(0, 1, (1000, 3)) \# Replace with actual financial returns

\#\# Applying PCA
pca = PCA(n_components=2)
components = pca.fit_transform(assets_returns)

\#\# Visualizing the results
plt.scatter(components[:, 0], components[:, 1], alpha=0.5)
plt.title('Projection of Asset Returns onto Principal Components')
plt.xlabel('Principal Component 1')
plt.ylabel('Principal Component 2')
plt.grid()
plt.show()
```

This code snippet illustrates how PCA can streamline the analysis of financial returns, highlighting discernible patterns by projecting them onto a reduced set of components.

Exploring Deeper with Factor Analysis

Factor analysis further advances the capabilities of multivariate analysis by helping identify latent variables that succinctly capture underlying data patterns. In finance, this technique is fundamental for developing factor models which explain asset returns through exposure to specific risks, or "factors." Such models are vital for constructing multifactor portfolios that seek to optimize risk-adjusted returns.

For instance, factor analysis can elucidate the impact of
```

macroeconomic dynamics on asset performance. This layered understanding equips portfolio managers to align their strategies with overarching economic trends and the unique characteristics of various assets, enhancing both strategic precision and performance.

Correlation and Causation: A Multivariate Perspective

A significant advantage of multivariate analysis is its ability to distinguish between correlation and causation—an essential consideration in finance. Gaining insights into causal relationships among variables can greatly influence trading strategies and risk management practices. Techniques such as Vector Autoregression (VAR) enable analysts to model temporal dynamics and predict the behavior of interrelated time series variables.

For instance, an investor monitoring exchange rates, interest rates, and commodity prices can leverage a VAR model to unravel the dynamic interactions between these variables, gaining valuable forecasts about future movements. This analytical framework fosters a deeper understanding of interconnected systems, thus anticipating potential vulnerabilities and informing strategic decisions more effectively.

Example: VAR Model Implementation in Python

```python
```python import numpy as np import pandas as pd from statsmodels.tsa.api import VAR

\#\# Simulating time series data for three financial metrics
np.random.seed(0)
time_series_data = np.random.normal(size=(100, 3))

\#\# Creating a DataFrame for the data
df = pd.DataFrame(time_series_data, columns=['Metric1', 'Metric2', 'Metric3'])

\#\# Fitting a VAR model
```
```

```
model = VAR(df)
results = model.fit(maxlags=15)

\#\# Displaying summary of results
print(results.summary())

` ` `
```

This example showcases how a VAR model can capture and forecast interdependencies among time-related financial variables, equipping analysts with robust tools for strategic forecasting.

Crafting Holistic Financial Strategies

Ultimately, multivariate analysis serves as a cornerstone for developing comprehensive financial strategies that are both nuanced and resilient to the complexities of the market. The applications of these analytical techniques extend across portfolio management, risk assessment, and economic forecasting, ensuring that financial strategies are well-informed and robust.

When harnessed effectively, these methodologies empower financial professionals to transcend simplistic analyses, embracing a more interconnected perspective that mirrors the nature of financial markets. With multivariate analysis as an integral toolkit, finance experts can craft strategies that extract meaningful insights from the intricate web of market variables—ultimately paving the way for superior financial performance and stewardship.

Exploring Monte Carlo Techniques in Quantitative Finance

In the dynamic realm of quantitative finance, simulation methods—particularly Monte Carlo techniques—are essential for navigating the inherent uncertainties of financial markets. These methods empower analysts and strategists to create detailed models of complex systems, leveraging randomness and statistical sampling to predict variability in market behavior.

The Power of Stochastic Processes

At the heart of Monte Carlo simulation lies the principle of harnessing stochastic processes to analyze the behavior of financial instruments. Unlike deterministic models, which yield a single forecast, Monte Carlo simulations generate a spectrum of possible outcomes. Each outcome reflects different scenarios in the multifaceted interplay of market dynamics, making these techniques particularly vital for assets characterized by volatility or influenced by various external factors.

Take, for instance, the process of pricing a complex derivative like an option. Monte Carlo simulation facilitates an in-depth evaluation of potential payoffs by simulating numerous trajectories for the underlying asset's price movement, informed by assumed volatility and market conditions. Each trajectory illustrates a plausible future scenario, enabling analysts to assess risk exposure and anticipate potential gains or losses comprehensively.

A Practical Implementation: Pricing a European Call Option

To illustrate the power of Monte Carlo simulation, let's walk through an example of pricing a European call option using Python code. This example encapsulates the broad methodology:

```python
``` python import numpy as np

\#\# Simulation parameters
S0 = 100  \# Initial stock price
K = 110   \# Strike price
T = 1     \# Time to maturity in years
r = 0.05  \# Risk-free interest rate
sigma = 0.2  \# Volatility
simulations = 10000  \# Number of simulations

\#\# Generate random end-of-period asset prices
np.random.seed(42) \# For reproducibility
```
```

```
Z = np.random.standard_normal(simulations)
ST = S0 * np.exp((r - 0.5 * sigma**2) * T + sigma * np.sqrt(T) * Z)

\#\# Calculate payoffs and determine the average present
value
payoff = np.maximum(ST - K, 0) \# Call option payoff
option_price = np.exp(-r * T) * np.mean(payoff)

print(f"The estimated price of the European call option is:
option_price:.2f")
```

` ` `

In this example, we simulate potential future stock prices to calculate the payoffs for the option based on those prices. This approach, involving repeated sampling over various potential paths, yields a robust estimate of the option's price in continually changing market conditions.

Risk Management Through Value-at-Risk (VaR)

Beyond derivative pricing, Monte Carlo techniques are indispensable in the field of risk management. One noteworthy application is the assessment of Value-at-Risk (VaR), a metric that quantifies the potential loss in portfolio value over a specified period at a given confidence level. Unlike traditional VaR models that presume a normal distribution of returns, Monte Carlo VaR simulations allow analysts to capture complex distributions and interdependencies, thereby enhancing the accuracy of risk assessments.

For example, to establish the daily VaR at a 95% confidence level, a financial institution can simulate daily portfolio returns to construct a comprehensive distribution of outcomes. The VaR is determined by identifying the loss threshold below which 5% of the outcomes occur, thus providing a probabilistic estimate of potential financial loss in adverse scenarios.

Broadening the Horizon: Diverse Applications

of Monte Carlo Techniques

The versatility of Monte Carlo simulations extends far beyond derivatives and risk assessment; their applications encompass investment strategy testing, retirement planning, and asset-liability management. In investment strategy analysis, simulations utilize historical price data to project the outcomes of various trading or allocation strategies under different market conditions. Similarly, when planning for retirement, these techniques help estimate the sustainability of investment portfolios, accommodating diverse future market conditions and withdrawal strategies.

The true strength of Monte Carlo methods lies in their flexibility and capacity to model real-world uncertainties.

Empowering Proactive Decision-Making

As financial markets continue to evolve in complexity and uncertainty, the necessity for reliable analytical tools becomes increasingly critical. Monte Carlo simulations offer a profound means of addressing these challenges, transforming potential chaos into structured insights.

In an ever-changing quantitative finance landscape, mastering these simulation methods is essential for achieving alpha in the marketplace. The intrinsic value of Monte Carlo techniques lies in their ability to convert uncertainty into opportunity, paving the way for innovative financial solutions that are both informed and resilient. Through these methodologies, finance professionals can navigate uncertainties with confidence, ultimately fostering a more stable and prosperous financial environment.

CHAPTER 4:
BUILDING ALPHA
MODELS

Navigating the intricate world of financial markets can often resemble a complex labyrinth characterized by volatility and fierce competition. At the heart of this dynamic environment lies the relentless pursuit of "alpha," a term that encapsulates the excess return that an investment portfolio generates above its benchmark index. Alpha is more than just a figure; it embodies the value added through a manager's astute investment decisions—decisions that are distinct from wider market trends. This concept is fundamental to active management and highlights the noble quest to achieve consistent outperformance—an endeavor that juxtaposes difficulty with potential reward.

The Foundations of Alpha

The foundation of alpha is rooted in the belief that markets are not perfectly efficient. If they were, all available information would be instantly reflected in asset prices, rendering the quest for alpha nearly impossible. Yet, real-world market anomalies provide fertile ground for investment strategies that seek to identify and exploit inefficiencies. This can involve tactics like detecting mispriced assets, understanding market timing, or utilizing volatility to deviate from theoretical return expectations.

Alpha springs from a portfolio manager's ability to perceive these inefficiencies, exercising skilled asset management to capture emerging opportunities. Whether through sophisticated algorithmic trading, nuanced risk assessments, or meticulous portfolio construction, the journey to generate alpha hinges on a blend of market insights and innovative strategies.

Quantitative Methods in Pursuing Alpha

In the realm of quantitative finance, professionals utilize systematic mathematical and statistical models to predict price movements and uncover alpha. These models can range from straightforward rule-based systems to sophisticated algorithms that incorporate elements of machine learning and artificial intelligence. Two prominent quantitative approaches stand out: factor models and arbitrage strategies.

Factor Models

Factor models are essential tools for dissecting and quantifying sources of alpha. They break down asset returns into common and idiosyncratic risk factors, allowing investors to exploit statistically significant correlations between security characteristics and their returns. The Fama-French Three-Factor Model, for instance, enhances the traditional Capital Asset Pricing Model (CAPM) by incorporating size and value factors alongside market risk.

Imagine a skilled portfolio manager using factor models to target alpha through strategic investments in small-cap stocks that have historically outperformed during specific economic cycles.

Arbitrage Strategies

Arbitrage strategies further highlight the quantitative quest for alpha by enabling investors to pinpoint risk-free profit opportunities through simultaneous asset transactions. A common example is index arbitrage, where a manager capitalizes on price discrepancies between a stock index and its associated futures contracts.

Practical Examples: Realizing Alpha

In practical terms, actualizing alpha demands not just robust model development but also rigorous testing and validation. A compelling illustration is the use of momentum strategies within equity markets. These strategies hinge on identifying stocks demonstrating strong historical performance, leveraging the tendency of securities to display prolonged rising prices due to investor sentiment or market momentum.

Consider a quantitative hedge fund that crafts a momentum-based trading algorithm. Continual refinement of this model using advanced statistical techniques and contemporary market insights positions the fund favorably on the path to alpha generation.

Evaluating and Sustaining Alpha

The journey to alpha does not end with the implementation of models; it requires ongoing evaluation and adaptability. Financial markets are in a state of constant flux, influenced by evolving market conditions, regulatory changes, and technological innovations. As such, sustaining alpha mandates a rigorous cycle of model evaluation and recalibration. Utilizing backtesting methods, strategists can refine their approaches to adapt to volatile environments and maintain a competitive edge.

Furthermore, accurately measuring alpha necessitates careful performance attribution to discern whether returns are a product of true managerial skill or merely reflect market exposure.

Understanding alpha and devising effective strategies to achieve it reflects both analytical skill and perceptive market insight. This pursuit signifies the unwavering ambition for financial outperformance and underscores the necessity for continuous adaptation amid shifting market landscapes.

For the astute strategist, the quest for alpha transcends mere investment; it evolves into an ongoing journey that intertwines quantitative precision with the art of investment.

As one integrates sophisticated models with an adaptable mindset, the pathway to alpha generation becomes clearer —revealing the profound synergy between theoretical frameworks and practical implementation. Embarking on this journey provides a unique opportunity to explore methodologies that align quantitative strategies with consistent market success—a pursuit that is as challenging as it is essential in today's competitive financial arena.

Factor Models in Finance: Unlocking the Secrets of Investment Strategies

To truly grasp the intricacies of factor models, one must explore the underlying components that shape sophisticated investment strategies. At their essence, factor models break down the fluctuations in asset returns into distinct forces—or factors—that actively influence the performance of individual securities or entire portfolios. These models provide a crucial framework for comprehending, forecasting, and optimizing financial behavior by linking identifiable characteristics with expected returns.

The Foundation of Factor Models

The theoretical foundations of factor models emerge from a desire to distill the complex realities of asset markets into manageable variables that represent overarching influences. These factors can come from a wide array of sources, from macroeconomic indicators like GDP growth and inflation rates to more specific traits such as a company's operational efficiency. Notably, factor models suggest that a significant portion of investment returns can be traced back to certain key factors, rather than mere market sentiment volatility.

Among the various factor models, the single-factor Capital Asset Pricing Model (CAPM) is one of the most recognized.

It streamlines investment decisions by proposing that a security's expected return is a linear function of its systematic risk—measured by beta, which gauges sensitivity to market movements. Although CAPM provides valuable insights, its simplicity can often be limiting, leading investors to adopt multifactor models that capture a broader array of return-driving influences.

Multifactor Models: Expanding the Narrative

Multifactor models—such as the renowned Fama-French Three-Factor Model—enhance our understanding of Market dynamics by introducing additional dimensions like the size and value factors. These models account for market anomalies, where smaller firms and companies with attractive book-to-market ratios frequently outperform larger counterparts. The Carhart Four-Factor Model builds on this by incorporating a momentum factor, acknowledging the tendency for stocks with strong recent performance to maintain momentum in the near term.

Consider a practical scenario: an investment manager employing a multifactor approach might scrutinize historical return data to pinpoint instances when small-cap stocks or high-value equities surpassed market performance.

Practical Implementation of Factor Models

The successful implementation of factor models demands both meticulous analysis and a profound understanding of financial markets. Identifying relevant factors, quantifying their impacts, and integrating them into asset allocation strategies are critical steps in this process. Utilizing quantitative tools alongside economic theories and empirical research serves as a compass for factor selection and model construction.

One exemplary application of factor models can be found in the realm of index creation. Exchange-Traded Funds (ETFs) frequently employ multifactor strategies to align their holdings with specific factor premiums. An ETF targeting low-volatility stocks may focus on companies with historically lower price fluctuations—leveraging the low-volatility anomaly, which suggests that these less volatile portfolios often achieve superior risk-adjusted returns.

Navigating Challenges with Factor Models

Despite their numerous advantages, factor models come with inherent challenges. One significant concern pertains to the risk of overfitting—a situation in which a model appears statistically significant when evaluated against historical data, yet fails to perform in varying market conditions. The constantly evolving nature of financial markets means that factors once deemed reliable may suffer from reduced efficacy as market dynamics shift.

Moreover, distinguishing genuine factors—systematic sources of risk and return—from mere statistical anomalies necessitates rigorous testing and validation. This may involve employing cross-validation techniques and constantly reassessing model assumptions. A backtest may reveal an enticing dividend yield factor, but further scrutiny could unveil that its apparent strength stems from a hidden correlation with another asset class, limiting its standalone validity.

The Role of Factor Models in Risk Management

Beyond their potential for alpha generation, factor models play a critical role in effective risk management. Utilizing stress tests and scenario analyses, investors can utilize factor models to predict how economic changes—ranging from interest rate fluctuations to sudden market disruptions—might impact their portfolios.

For illustration, an asset manager anticipating inflation might strategically realign the portfolio's factor exposures to minimize sensitivity to rising interest rates.

As financial markets continue to evolve, so too must the factor models that underpin them. The emergence of new factors—such as ESG (Environmental, Social, and Governance) considerations—highlights the field's adaptability and responsiveness to contemporary issues.

The true elegance of factor models lies in their ability to distill intricate market data into actionable insights, empowering investors to navigate systematic patterns for strategic advantages. In the consistently competitive quest for alpha, these models serve as guiding lights, steering investors through the multifaceted landscape of financial markets with both precision and foresight. Ultimately, the success of factor models relies on practitioners striking a balance between theoretical foundations and practical application— an equilibrium that epitomizes the artistry and science of quantitative investing.

Risk-Adjusted Return Metrics: Harmonizing Risk and Reward

In the sophisticated world of quantitative finance, the relentless pursuit of exceptional investment returns must be tempered by a profound understanding of the risks involved. Risk-adjusted return metrics serve as indispensable tools for investors, offering valuable insights into the delicate interplay between potential rewards and associated risks.

Why Risk Adjustment Matters

When assessing investments, relying on raw return figures often paints an incomplete picture of performance. Consider two portfolios that generate identical returns over the same period: one might experience high volatility while the other remains stable. In such cases, the risk-reward balance can be disproportionately skewed. Adjusting returns for risk is essential, particularly when making comparisons across various assets or investment classes.

Portfolio managers and investors leverage these metrics to

design portfolios that optimize returns while maintaining risk within acceptable boundaries. In an era of market volatility, where unexpected fluctuations challenge the status quo, risk-adjusted return metrics empower investors to adopt strategies that prioritize sustainable growth.

Key Risk-Adjusted Return Metrics

Several metrics have emerged to elucidate the relationship between risk and return, each offering unique perspectives on performance dynamics.

The Sharpe Ratio

One of the most widely recognized metrics is the Sharpe Ratio, which quantifies the excess return—or risk premium—per unit of risk that a portfolio achieves above a risk-free asset. It is calculated using the formula:

[Sharpe Ratio = ((R_p - R_f) / \sigma_p)]

In this equation, (R_p) denotes the portfolio's return, (R_f) is the risk-free rate, and (\sigma_p) represents the standard deviation of the portfolio's excess return. A higher Sharpe Ratio indicates more efficient risk-adjusted performance.

For example, consider a portfolio with a 10% annual return and a standard deviation of 5%, juxtaposed against a risk-free rate of 2%. The Sharpe Ratio would be:

[Sharpe Ratio = ((0.10 - 0.02) / 0.05) = 1.6]

This suggests that the portfolio yields 1.6 units of return for every unit of risk taken—an appealing reflection of risk efficiency.

The Sortino Ratio

A nuanced refinement of the Sharpe Ratio, the Sortino Ratio focuses specifically on downside risk by excluding upside volatility from its calculations. It is formulated as:

[Sortino Ratio = ((R_p - R_f) / \sigma_downside)]

This metric is particularly beneficial for assessing investments where minimizing loss potential is just as critical as maximizing returns. For instance, a pension fund manager, tasked with protecting assets for future payouts, may rely on the Sortino Ratio to identify investments that align with a strategy of protective growth.

The Treynor Ratio

In contrast to the Sharpe and Sortino Ratios, the Treynor Ratio employs beta—a measure of systematic risk—to assess performance. With a focus on market risk, it provides insights into a portfolio's returns relative to its exposure to market fluctuations:

[Treynor Ratio = ((R_p - R_f) / \beta_p)]

This metric proves especially valuable for investors managing portfolios with distinct exposures to market risk. For example, hedge funds employing market-neutral strategies often utilize the Treynor Ratio to gauge their risk-adjusted performance against broader market movements.

Practical Applications in Portfolio Management

The implementation of risk-adjusted return metrics blends quantitative analysis with strategic intuition. Portfolio managers routinely apply these metrics to:

1. Compare Investment Opportunities: Before committing capital to new investments, managers analyze Sharpe, Sortino, and Treynor ratios across various asset classes to assess relative efficiency.

2. Optimize Asset Allocation: By aligning allocations with desired risk-reward profiles, these metrics help tailor portfolios to meet specific return objectives within acceptable risk parameters.

3. Monitor Performance: Regular evaluation of risk-adjusted returns enables managers to adapt

strategies in response to changing market conditions and volatility levels.

Challenges and Considerations

Despite their utility, risk-adjusted return metrics come with limitations. A significant challenge lies in their predictive power, which can wane during extreme market conditions, where historical volatility may fail to capture future risk dynamics. Additionally, selecting an appropriate risk-free rate—especially in environments where rates hover near zero or become negative—can significantly influence metric calculations.

Moreover, overreliance on a single metric can oversimplify the complexities of investment decisions. A holistic evaluation often requires employing a combination of metrics to capture the full spectrum of risk-adjusted performance.

The effective application of risk-adjusted return metrics extends beyond merely enhancing portfolios; it represents the art of reconciling ambition with caution. As the financial landscape becomes increasingly intricate, these metrics offer the analytical foundation necessary to navigate uncertainties with precision.

In the ongoing quest for alpha generation, proficient investors blend these metrics with sharp judgment, understanding that true portfolio success is measured not just by returns earned, but by how well risks were identified, managed, and consciously embraced. This intricate dance between balance and foresight illuminates the path toward enduring financial mastery, enabling investors to thrive in an unpredictable world.

Valuation Metrics and Their Applications:
Unveiling Investment Potential

In the multifaceted realm of quantitative finance, astute investors tirelessly probe to uncover the true value of their assets, crafting well-informed strategies that facilitate alpha generation. At the core of this analytical process lies valuation metrics, indispensable tools that empower investors to discern intrinsic value, assess investment attractiveness, and seize opportunities in the ever-evolving financial landscape. Effectively leveraging these metrics goes beyond mere calculation; it involves a sophisticated understanding of complex market dynamics and a keen eye for identifying lucrative avenues for investment.

Understanding the Framework of Valuation

Valuation serves as a vital function that unravels the intricate relationship between a company's market price and its actual worth. These metrics act as diagnostic instruments, essential for informed portfolio construction, prudent risk management, and strategic asset allocation.

Diverse Array of Valuation Metrics

Given the complexity of valuation, a multitude of metrics has emerged, each tailored to evaluate different dimensions of financial performance. A comprehensive understanding of these tools is crucial for sophisticated portfolio management.

Price-to-Earnings Ratio (P/E)

One of the most widely recognized metrics is the Price-to-Earnings (P/E) ratio, which juxtaposes a company's current share price against its per-share earnings:

[P/E Ratio = (Market Price per Share / Earnings per Share (EPS))]

The P/E ratio acts as a litmus test for market expectations and investor sentiment. A high P/E often indicates optimistic growth projections, while a low P/E may suggest undervaluation or market skepticism. This metric is especially useful in evaluating growth potential among companies within a particular sector.

Example: Let's compare two firms in the tech industry—

Company A, boasting a P/E ratio of 30, and Company B, with a P/E of 15. Investors might interpret Company A's elevated P/E as indicative of anticipated robust growth, yet understanding the industry norms is crucial for a rounded perspective.

Price-to-Book Ratio (P/B)

The Price-to-Book (P/B) ratio offers a contrast between a firm's market capitalization and its book value, providing insights into how the market perceives the company's net assets:

[P/B Ratio = (Market Value / Book Value)]

A P/B ratio below one may hint at potential undervaluation or operational challenges, whereas a higher P/B reflects market confidence in the company's asset base. This metric is especially relevant in capital-intensive sectors, where accurate asset valuation is paramount.

Example: In the banking sector, it is not uncommon to see institutions trading at a P/B ratio below one, signaling market apprehension about asset valuations or external regulatory pressures.

Discounted Cash Flow (DCF) Analysis

Though more sophisticated, Discounted Cash Flow (DCF) analysis presents a well-rounded methodology for valuing a company based on anticipated future cash flows, which are then discounted to their present value. This approach integrates intrinsic value assessment via projected financial performance and relevant market conditions.

The DCF formula can be expressed as follows:

[DCF = ((Cash Flow_t / (1 + r)^t))]

Here, each cash flow is discounted using a rate (r), which represents the cost of capital or required return.

Example: For a tech firm projecting substantial growth, DCF analysis involves forecasting free cash flows over several years and suitably adjusting these estimates based on an assumed discount rate.

Strategic Applications in Investment

Valuation metrics form the bedrock of sophisticated investment strategies, equipping managers with the insights necessary to navigate complex decisions and align with their financial goals.

1. Identifying Market Opportunities: Investors harness valuation metrics to detect undervalued stocks or sectors that may be poised for growth.

2. Risk Assessment and Diversification: A solid grasp of asset valuation allows portfolio managers to evaluate risk exposure and fine-tune their holdings to achieve optimal diversification. For instance, a focus on P/B ratios may guide managers toward firms with substantial tangible assets, offering a cushion during volatile market conditions.

3. Performance Benchmarking: Valuation metrics serve as essential tools for tracking investment performance against industry peers and benchmarks, facilitating timely adjustments aimed at maximizing returns.

Challenges and Dynamic Considerations

While invaluable, valuation metrics necessitate careful interpretation to avoid misjudgments. The flexibility of financial models must adapt to ongoing macroeconomic shifts and sector-specific nuances. Fluctuations in market conditions, such as changing discount rates or evolving earnings expectations, can subtly influence valuations.

Additionally, over-reliance on any single metric can obscure a holistic understanding of a company's financial health. A multi-metric approach fosters a balanced perspective, blending quantitative insights with strategic considerations.

Achieving mastery over valuation metrics provides a significant competitive advantage, transforming raw financial data into actionable intelligence ready for strategic application. As the race for alpha intensifies, valuation retains its essential role, illuminating the path through financial uncertainty.

For the discerning investor, engaging with valuation transcends anchoring decisions in numbers; it represents an exploration of the narratives that drive market dynamics, allowing for informed actions that contribute to genuine wealth creation.

Designing a Systematic Trading Strategy:
Crafting the Blueprint for Success

Designing a systematic trading strategy is akin to engineering a complex machine, where every component must work in harmony to capture the oscillations of the financial markets. This multifaceted task blends rigorous analysis, creative problem-solving, and meticulous execution. A systematic trading strategy serves not merely as a static blueprint; rather, it evolves into a dynamic mechanism within the realm of quantitative investing, turning market volatility into structured opportunities for alpha generation.

Defining the Objective and Scope

At the core of every successful trading strategy is a crystal-clear objective—whether it's aimed at capital appreciation, risk mitigation, or a carefully curated balance of both, tailored to specific market conditions. This clarity of purpose establishes a solid foundation upon which the entire strategy can be built.

For example, a strategy might focus on capitalizing on momentum, identifying and trading within short-term price trends, or exploiting mean reversion by pinpointing overbought and oversold conditions.

The Role of Rules and Algorithms

A successful systematic strategy hinges on a set of predetermined rules that dictate trading decisions, effectively removing the emotional biases that can cloud judgment. Crafting these rules requires a thoughtful synthesis of financial theory, empirical research, and insights from experienced practitioners.

Take, for instance, a moving average crossover strategy for equity trading:

1. Define Entry and Exit Signals: Establish a shorter-term moving average alongside a longer-term one. A buy signal is generated when the short-term moving average moves above the long-term average, while a sell signal is triggered by the opposite crossover.

2. Determine Position Sizing: Outline guidelines for how capital is allocated to each trade, utilizing risk management techniques designed to mitigate exposure.

3. Set Execution Algorithms: Develop algorithms to automatically identify and act on these signals in real time, ensuring decisions are based on the most current market data.

4. Integrate Market Conditions: Adjust criteria to consider broader market volatility, allowing your strategy to remain adaptable in an ever-changing environment.

Backtesting for Validation

The strength of a systematic trading strategy is rigorously assessed through backtesting, which simulates its performance against historical market data. This critical phase allows you to validate the proposed rules and optimize parameters before moving the strategy into the live trading arena.

Example of Backtesting Implementation:

Utilizing the Python backtrader library, you can easily implement your strategies for testing. Below is a simplified example of how you might backtest the moving average crossover strategy:

```python
``` python import backtrader as bt

class MovingAverageCross(bt.SignalStrategy):
def __init__(self):
self.sma1 = bt.ind.SMA(period=10)
self.sma2 = bt.ind.SMA(period=30)
self.signal_add(bt.SIGNAL_LONG, self.sma1 > self.sma2)
self.signal_add(bt.SIGNAL_SHORT, self.sma1 < self.sma2)

if __name__ == '__main__':
cerebro = bt.Cerebro()
cerebro.addstrategy(MovingAverageCross)
data    =    bt.feeds.YahooFinanceData(dataname='AAPL',
fromdate='2020-01-01', todate='2021-01-01')
cerebro.adddata(data)
cerebro.run()
cerebro.plot()

```
```

In this example, the effectiveness of the strategy—utilizing a 10-day and 30-day simple moving average—is evaluated against historical data for Apple Inc., allowing you to gauge its performance under varying market conditions.

Continuous Refinement and Adaptation

As market dynamics shift, so too must trading strategies evolve. Ongoing refinement—based on live performance and continual scenario analysis—establishes a robust feedback loop that enhances the resilience of your strategy.

Employing machine learning techniques can also facilitate the dynamic adjustment of strategies by identifying predictive patterns within expansive and growing datasets. This ability to adapt is crucial as markets become increasingly complex, and similar algorithmic strategies vie for the same opportunities.

Risk Management Integration

A comprehensive strategic framework is not complete without an integral focus on risk management. This involves setting stop-loss orders, defining position limits, and vigilantly monitoring risk metrics like Value-at-Risk (VaR) to safeguard against unforeseen downturns.

Example of Risk Management Application:

If a trading strategy delivers a high Sharpe ratio during backtesting yet suffers significant drawdowns once live, recalibration may be necessary. This could involve tightening risk constraints or enhancing diversification to bolster overall stability.

Performance Review and Strategic Iteration

Regularly assessing the performance of your strategy against pre-established objectives and benchmarks provides critical touchpoints for strategic iteration. Important evaluation metrics should encompass not only traditional measures of return but also risk-adjusted metrics, such as the Sortino ratio, which focuses specifically on downside risk.

The creation of a systematic trading strategy represents a harmonious blend of precision and intuition, merging the art of finance with the scientific rigor of quantitative analysis. It requires steadfast dedication to methodological discipline and the agility to adapt in response to innovations in the market. As participants in this sophisticated ballet of strategy design, traders emerge not only as architects of their financial futures but also as artisans of a legacy built on disciplined innovation.

Backtesting Frameworks and Considerations:
The Crucible of Strategy Validation

Backtesting acts as a vital crucible where systematic trading strategies are meticulously tested, refined, and validated before they are set loose in the unpredictable realm of live markets. This critical process enables quantitative strategists to scrutinize the viability of their models against historical data, offering profound insights into potential future performance. The art of backtesting harmoniously fuses rigorous data analysis with innovative hypothesis testing, forming a cornerstone of strategy development.

Establishing a Robust Framework

The bedrock of effective backtesting resides in a well-structured framework capable of mimicking real market conditions. To achieve accurate simulations, strategists must focus on data integrity, algorithm precision, and proper parameter selection. It's imperative to craft a framework that not only reflects real-time trading challenges but also circumvents the pitfalls of over-optimization.

Key Elements of a Backtesting Framework:

1. Historical Data Integrity: Ensure the use of clean, high-quality datasets that encapsulate realistic trading scenarios. Address survivorship bias by incorporating historical data from delisted securities, thereby ensuring a comprehensive and unfiltered dataset.

2. Transaction Cost Modeling: Realistically model transaction costs, including bid-ask spreads, slippage, and commissions. Underestimating these factors can create an illusion of superior strategy performance, ultimately skewing results.

3. Execution Simulation: Simulate various market conditions via advanced execution models. Acknowledge that delays, partial fills, and other market anomalies can significantly alter the actual

returns of your strategy.

4. **Risk and Return Metrics:** Employ an array of metrics such as the Sharpe Ratio, Sortino Ratio, and drawdown analysis to critically evaluate the risk-adjusted returns, ensuring that strategies demonstrate resilience under pressure.

Methodological Considerations

An effective backtesting process not only serves as a profitability check but also uncovers weaknesses, providing invaluable opportunities for enhancement. Here are essential methodological considerations to improve the reliability and validity of your backtesting results:

- **Walk-Forward Analysis:** A robust method for statistical validation, this approach involves segmenting historical data into training and testing phases. Train your models on in-sample data, and then test them on out-of-sample data to minimize the risks associated with overfitting, a common pitfall where a model excels in training but falters in real-world application.

- **Sensitivity Analysis:** Systematically explore variations in key parameters to assess their impact on performance outcomes. This process reveals which parameter sets yield consistent results across diverse market conditions, thereby fortifying predictability and reliability.

- **Monte Carlo Simulations:** Utilize these simulations to encapsulate randomness and variability in performance outcomes.

Hands-On Backtesting Example

Engaging with backtesting may seem daunting, but user-friendly tools like the Python library zipline streamline the evaluation process for systematic strategies. Below, we present a straightforward example of testing a simple moving average crossover strategy:

```python
import zipline from zipline.api import order_target, record, symbol import pytz from datetime import datetime

def initialize(context):
context.asset = symbol('AAPL')
context.short_mavg = 30
context.long_mavg = 100

def handle_data(context, data):
short_mavg     =     data.history(context.asset,     'close',
context.short_mavg, '1d').mean()
long_mavg      =     data.history(context.asset,     'close',
context.long_mavg, '1d').mean()

if short_mavg > long_mavg:
order_target(context.asset, 100)
elif short_mavg < long_mavg:
order_target(context.asset, 0)

record(AAPL=data.current(context.asset, 'price'),
short_mavg=short_mavg,
long_mavg=long_mavg)

if __name__ == '__main__':
start = datetime(2019, 1, 1, tzinfo=pytz.UTC)
end = datetime(2020, 1, 1, tzinfo=pytz.UTC)
result     =     zipline.run_algorithm(start=start,     end=end,
initialize=initialize,
capital_base=10000, handle_data=handle_data,
bundle='quantopian-quandl')
result.plot()
```

This script initiates a backtesting endeavor by trading Apple

HAYDEN VAN DER POST

Inc. stock (AAPL) based on the crossover of two moving averages. Using zipline, you can effortlessly navigate the complexities of backtesting, yielding valuable insights from historical performance with minimal overhead.

The Significance of Realism

To ensure that backtesting results have practical applicability, it's crucial to recognize and mitigate potential biases, such as "look-ahead" bias, where future data inadvertently informs trading decisions. Additionally, acknowledging and planning for "black swan" events—unexpected occurrences that significantly impact market behavior—is vital for fostering resilience in your analysis.

Regularly reassess your assumptions and account for various market conditions, including both volatile and stable periods. This approach will help protect your strategy from becoming overly optimized for a specific environment.

Integrating Feedback Loops

Successful strategies born from meticulous backtesting require an ongoing cycle of adaptation and refinement. Incorporate live feedback loops and track performance against the dynamic realities of the market.

Backtesting is the lifeblood of developing systematic trading strategies—it not only guides informed investment decisions but also serves as a rigorous testing ground for market hypotheses. When conducted thoughtfully, it transcends mere validation, transforming theoretical constructs into market-ready solutions. This proactive approach fosters a culture of continuous learning, adaptation, and improvement, equipping strategists to not only withstand historical scrutiny but to navigate a future brimming with financial opportunity.

Developing quantitative trading strategies is an intricate art that demands keen insight and unwavering attention to detail. The desire to build a successful model that consistently

120

delivers alpha can be captivating, yet many practitioners encounter pitfalls that can derail even the most promising initiatives. Recognizing these traps is essential on the path to creating resilient strategies capable of withstanding the challenges of shifting markets and economic landscapes.

Misinterpretation of Data

One prevalent pitfall is the misinterpretation of data, often driven by the temptation to unearth patterns where none exist. This phenomenon, commonly referred to as overfitting, occurs when a model becomes overly tailored to historical data, inadvertently capturing noise rather than genuine market signals. For example, a strategist might develop a model grounded in extensive historical price data across diverse equities. If they incorporate an excessive number of variables or rely on data from an atypical period, they risk crafting a model that excels in retrospective evaluations but falters dramatically in real-world conditions.

To avoid this trap, it is crucial to implement rigorous data validation and employ out-of-sample testing. Dividing data into training and test sets, along with utilizing cross-validation techniques, can bolster the reliability of findings, ensuring they are truly predictive rather than merely descriptive. For instance, employing a rolling window methodology allows the model to continuously adapt and be tested against new data segments, thereby reinforcing its robustness over time.

Neglecting Market Dynamics

Another significant hazard is the failure to account for the dynamic nature of markets. Markets are continually influenced by a multitude of factors, ranging from economic policies to geopolitical developments. Ignoring these influences can lead to the creation of strategies that lack flexibility and become obsolete. A telling illustration is the persistence of models crafted before the 2008 financial crisis, which often failed to incorporate the seismic shifts in risk perception that ensued. As a result, strategies that thrived before the crisis could falter drastically when confronted with new realities.

To navigate this challenge, it is vital to institute a system for ongoing model evaluation and recalibration based on the latest market data. Conducting scenario analyses and stress tests against various hypothetical situations prepares a strategy for potential market fluctuations, ensuring that it remains relevant and effective over time.

Ignoring Transaction Costs and Liquidity

Another common oversight is the disregard for transaction costs and market liquidity, which can severely undermine the efficacy of a trading strategy. A model may project high returns on paper, yet these anticipated gains can vanish once transaction costs are factored in. Moreover, strategies that engage in trading within illiquid markets may struggle to execute trades at favorable prices, leading to slippage that erodes expected profits.

Take, for instance, a high-frequency trading strategy designed to generate significant profits through rapid buying and selling. If executed in a market characterized by low liquidity, the costs associated with execution could easily outweigh the theoretical gains. Therefore, integrating a comprehensive cost analysis module into the strategy development process is essential, encapsulating factors such as bid-ask spreads, commissions, and slippage into the model.

Lack of Diversification

Inadequate diversification during strategy development can expose traders to an unacceptable level of concentration risk. Over-reliance on a single asset class, region, or economic sector can render a strategy vulnerable, particularly when specific market conditions disproportionately impact those concentrated areas. A historical example includes hedge funds that heavily invested in technology stocks during the dot-com bubble; when the bubble burst, their lack of diversification resulted in considerable losses.

To bolster resilience, it is imperative to diversify across various dimensions—such as asset classes, geographical regions, and trading strategies. Techniques like mean-variance optimization can aid in constructing well-balanced portfolios that harmonize the pursuit of alpha generation with acceptable risk levels.

Misalignment with Investment Objectives

Finally, a frequent misstep lies in the misalignment of the trading strategy with overarching investment objectives. A well-constructed strategy may falter if it does not align with the investor's risk tolerance, investment timeline, or expected returns. For instance, a pension fund with long-term obligations may find little benefit from a high-risk strategy focused on short-term volatility.

Thoroughly defining and understanding investment objectives is crucial before embarking on strategy development, ensuring that the strategy aligns with the investor's long-term goals. Moreover, regular reassessment of the strategy's alignment with these objectives as market conditions evolve is essential for maintaining its relevance and effectiveness.

In summary, the development of quantitative trading strategies necessitates a delicate balance between innovation and prudent caution. This multifaceted approach will equip practitioners to thrive in the ever-evolving world of quantitative finance, maintaining a forward-thinking mindset amid shifting market dynamics.

Case Studies of Successful Alpha Models

Examining the achievements of successful alpha models provides invaluable insights into their design, adaptability, and the strategic intricacies that drive their performance.

The Renaissance Technologies Case: Statistical Arbitrage at Its Pinnacle

Renaissance Technologies, founded by mathematician James Simons, exemplifies the art of leveraging statistical arbitrage to consistently generate alpha. Their flagship Medallion Fund has achieved remarkable returns by employing sophisticated mathematical models supported by a team of world-class scientists. The model's brilliance lies in its capacity to swiftly identify pricing inefficiencies across diverse markets, executing trades rapidly to capitalize on fleeting opportunities.

A standout feature of the Medallion Fund is its relentless commitment to refining strategies through the analysis of extensive datasets. Leveraging machine learning algorithms, the fund adapts in real time to shifting market conditions, ensuring that the model remains agile and pertinent. This dynamic methodology emphasizes the necessity of ongoing iteration, the integration of new data insights, and a culture of continuous improvement, crucial for long-term success in the markets.

Bridgewater Associates: The All-Weather Strategy

Under the visionary leadership of Ray Dalio, Bridgewater Associates developed the "All-Weather" strategy, which illustrates the critical value of diversification across varying economic environments. This approach is meticulously designed to perform robustly in both inflationary and deflationary contexts, allowing the fund to prosper regardless of macroeconomic fluctuations. The model's success hinges on its careful balancing of risks, ensuring no single economic scenario unduly influences the portfolio's performance.

The principal lesson from Bridgewater's achievement is the value of stress testing models in diverse market conditions. This case serves as a powerful reminder of how strategic diversification, grounded in thorough economic analysis, can create a formidable framework for alpha generation that stands strong in the face of economic adversity.

AQR Capital Management: The Integration of Academic Research

AQR Capital Management, co-founded by Cliff Asness, exemplifies the successful application of academic research in practical investing. The firm skillfully translates theoretical insights into actionable investment strategies, capitalizing on factor investing by employing constructs like value, momentum, and carry across various asset classes. This multifactor approach captures persistent market anomalies, enhancing alpha generation through effective diversification.

AQR's methodologies underscore the significant advantages of combining academic rigor with real-world application. Their commitment to research and a willingness to engage in empirical validation illustrate the importance of grounding models in robust theoretical principles, allowing them to weather market fluctuations and emerge stronger as a result.

GMO: Mean Reversion and Valuation Insights

Grantham, Mayo, & van Otterloo (GMO) has achieved remarkable success through a focus on mean reversion and long-term valuation insights. Led by Jeremy Grantham, GMO's strategies exploit the inefficiencies caused by short-term market movements, positioning investments to benefit as prices revert to their intrinsic values over time. The firm places a strong emphasis on valuation metrics to select assets with the potential for superior returns relative to their risk profile.

This case illuminates the long-term perspective necessary for harnessing valuation-driven alpha. GMO's disciplined approach to valuation, coupled with a commitment to sustainability, highlights the virtues of patience and foresight in strategy development. This steadfast focus on fundamental truths provides a compass for navigating market volatility.

Man AHL: Harnessing Technology in Systematic Trading

Man AHL epitomizes the fusion of technology and systematic trading, employing quantitative models bolstered by advanced computational capabilities. The success of their alpha models is rooted in a comprehensive integration of technology, allowing for continuous live testing and swift adaptability.

This case reinforces the transformative power of technology in shaping effective alpha models.

The analysis of these successful alpha models reveals common themes of adaptability, rigorous validation, and innovative integration of technology and theory. The capacity to respond dynamically to changing market and economic conditions—anchored by a foundation of diversified risk management and well-founded strategic principles—emerges as a fundamental element of success. The lessons embedded within these case studies serve as a guiding light for practitioners aiming to develop models that not only excel at generating alpha but also exhibit resilience and flexibility in the ever-evolving financial landscape.

In the complex world of finance, the continuous pursuit of alpha—an excess return on an investment relative to the return of a benchmark index—is both a daunting challenge and an exhilarating opportunity. In this ever-evolving landscape, effective portfolio construction emerges as a strategic cornerstone. Creating a portfolio that not only aspires to generate alpha but does so consistently requires a masterful blend of both art and science, harmonizing quantitative analysis with intuitive market insight. Building on previous explorations of successful alpha models and theoretical frameworks, let's unpack the principles and methodologies that lay the foundation for a high-performance portfolio.

Strategic Foundations of Portfolio Construction

At the core of alpha generation lies the strategic allocation of assets, guided by a nuanced understanding of the intricate relationship between risk and return. A well-crafted portfolio does not simply chase after returns; it diligently manages risk while optimizing exposure to factors that present sustainable opportunities for alpha generation. Critical to this process is a comprehensive assessment of market conditions, an analysis of historical data, and the identification of the specific factors —such as value, momentum, or size—that are most likely to yield alpha.

To illustrate this balance between risk and return, let's consider a portfolio manager employing a core-satellite strategy. The core of the portfolio might be composed of diversified, broad-market ETFs, providing essential stability and exposure to market beta. Meanwhile, the satellite component consists of more aggressive allocations to individual stocks or sectors that demonstrate a compelling alignment with alpha characteristics. This dual approach allows for the stability of broad market assets while seeking excess returns through selective, targeted investments that are likely to outperform.

The Crucial Role of Factor Models in Alpha Portfolios

Factor models are invaluable tools for dissecting the sources of potential excess returns. For example, a multi-factor model enables a refined approach to stock selection, utilizing essential variables like earnings yield, dividend yield, and sales growth to uncover opportunities within an expansive asset universe.

An exemplary case of effective factor integration can be seen in the practices of quantitative funds, such as those managed by AQR Capital Management. They invest across a spectrum of asset classes—including equities, fixed income, and commodities—employing rigorous factor analysis to highlight valuation-driven opportunities and implement them across diversified asset pools. This disciplined methodology casts a wide net, allowing for the exploitation of factor-based efficiencies that consistently contribute to alpha generation.

Embracing Non-Traditional Assets

In the pursuit of diversification and robust portfolio construction, non-traditional assets—such as real estate, commodities, and emerging market equities or debt—become essential to enhancing alpha potential. These assets frequently exhibit low correlations with traditional stock and bond markets, providing inviting diversification benefits.

Take commodities, for instance. Their unique performance drivers—often influenced by supply-demand dynamics distinct from conventional financial markets—can serve as a hedge against macroeconomic volatility and inflation, thereby enriching overall risk-adjusted returns. A portfolio manager might choose to allocate a portion of the portfolio to commodity-based ETFs or futures contracts that exhibit positive momentum, seamlessly integrating the alpha-generating attributes of these non-traditional investments into the broader strategy.

Risk Management: The Foundation of Sustainable Alpha

No exploration of portfolio construction is complete without addressing the indispensable element of risk management. The ambition to achieve alpha must be underpinned by a robust framework of comprehensive risk assessment techniques. Utilizing strategies like volatility targeting, scenario analysis, and stress testing can help reveal how a portfolio might behave under various market conditions, ensuring resilience against unforeseen shocks.

For example, employing Value at Risk (VaR) as a risk measurement tool can provide insights into the maximum expected loss over a specified period, based on a defined confidence level.

Implementation and Dynamic Rebalancing

The implementation phase—the stage where theoretical strategies translate into actual portfolios—requires precision and care. Leveraging algorithmic trading and automated rebalancing tools can ensure that portfolios remain aligned with strategic objectives, continuously optimizing allocations in response to real-time market signals. Importantly, rebalancing is an ongoing process that adapts to evolving market dynamics and shifts in model inputs.

For instance, a portfolio may initially favor growth stocks in response to strong economic indicators. However, as macroeconomic data begins to suggest a potential downturn, dynamic rebalancing would trigger a reduction in growth exposure, redirecting investments toward quality or defensive stocks that promise more stable returns in times of economic uncertainty.

Constructing a portfolio with the aim of generating alpha is a sophisticated venture that necessitates a disciplined approach to balancing diversification, factor exposure, and rigorous risk management. The success of this endeavor rests on a strategy that is both adaptable and grounded in empirical research, ensuring that decisions remain well-informed, even amid periods of market volatility.

As financial strategists refine their methodologies for portfolio construction, the focus remains on harnessing both traditional and alternative assets, embracing innovative technological tools for implementation, and prioritizing a solid risk management framework.

Continuous Improvement of Financial Models: The Key to Sustained Success in Quantitative Strategies

The Role of Feedback in Model Enhancement

At the core of effective model enhancement lies the feedback loop, a systematic mechanism for integrating lessons learned from past performance into the ongoing development of financial strategies. This iterative process emphasizes not only the importance of understanding mistakes but also recognizing successful elements, which creates a culture of continuous learning and adaptability within the team.

Drawing inspiration from the agile methodologies commonly utilized in software development, financial strategists can adopt a similar ethos. For instance, after executing trades, quantitative analysts can conduct a thorough post-mortem analysis of the results. This transformative practice cultivates models that are not static relics but dynamic systems, adept at responding to the unique challenges posed by an ever-evolving financial environment.

Feedback Collection and Analysis

To implement effective feedback mechanisms, establishing reliable systems for gathering and analyzing performance metrics is paramount. This requires precise and accurate data collection across multiple dimensions, including transaction costs, execution efficiency, and market responses. With advancements in data analytics and machine learning, the ability to sift through intricate datasets has become increasingly streamlined, enabling analysts to derive richer, more actionable insights.

Imagine a scenario where a quantitative strategy underperforms due to unexpected market volatility. Employing machine learning algorithms can further augment this process, enabling the detection of anomalies in trading patterns that highlight elements of the model needing adjustment.

Implementing Model Adjustments

Following the extraction of salient insights from feedback analysis, the challenge becomes translating these discoveries into tangible improvements. This process requires a clear distinction between minor modifications—such as adjusting model parameters—and more significant structural changes.

For example, if performance analysis reveals excessive sensitivity to short-term market noise, quantitative analysts might decide to refine the model's signal-to-entry threshold, allowing it to better filter out inconsequential fluctuations. On the other hand, profound feedback could lead to the introduction of new features or the integration of additional data sources, enriching the model with relevant market signals and enhancing its predictive capabilities.

A compelling illustration of a substantial adjustment could involve incorporating alternative data sources, such as social media sentiment or satellite imagery. This enrichment of the dataset not only broadens the scope of insights but also enables the model to capture nuances that traditional financial indicators may overlook, ultimately increasing its alpha generation potential.

Testing and Validation of Enhanced Models

Once adjustments are made, rigorous testing and validation become critical to ensure that enhancements yield the desired outcomes. Backtesting against historical data provides a vital sandbox environment for evaluating the model's behavior under diverse market scenarios. This phase allows analysts to identify potential pitfalls and rectify them before the model goes live.

Moreover, stress testing with forward-looking scenarios offers invaluable insights into how an enhanced model might perform under extreme market conditions. A model that consistently demonstrates robust performance across these tests not only reinforces confidence in its reliability but also attests to its adaptive capacity.

Continuous Monitoring and Real-Time Adjustments

Integrating real-time monitoring tools significantly bolsters a model's resilience. Sophisticated dashboards that present up-to-the-minute performance metrics enable analysts to make swift adjustments as market conditions evolve. In situations demanding immediate intervention, automated triggers can be programmed to halt trading when variances exceed predetermined thresholds—this proactive approach not only mitigates potential losses but also allows for timely strategic recalibrations.

Cultivating a Feedback-Responsive Culture

The successful implementation of continuous improvement is not solely a technical endeavor; it also requires fostering a culture that values responsiveness to feedback. Encouraging team members—from data scientists to traders—to actively participate in identifying opportunities for enhancement leads to collective growth.

The journey of continuously refining quantitative models through feedback is a dynamic, ongoing process that demands commitment and vigilance. In an environment characterized by perpetual changes, financial professionals who adeptly leverage these feedback mechanisms place themselves at the forefront of alpha generation. Through a dedicated application of feedback-driven development, the pursuit of sustained alpha transcends mere aspiration; it becomes a tangible and achievable reality.

CHAPTER 5: ADVANCED MACHINE LEARNING TECHNIQUES

Machine learning has catalyzed a transformative shift across various sectors, with finance experiencing particularly profound changes. Its integration is revolutionizing quantitative strategies, allowing finance professionals to redefine the way they analyze data and make critical decisions. This capability to harness vast streams of data represents a significant advancement, unveiling efficiencies and insights that traditional methodologies often overlook.

The Foundation of Machine Learning in Finance

The marriage of machine learning and finance is grounded in essential principles from computer science and statistics. Financial markets generate a staggering volume of data daily, including prices, trading volumes, economic indicators, and, increasingly, alternative data sources like web traffic metrics and social media sentiment. Machine learning algorithms excel in parsing through this intricate data maze, facilitating the discovery of correlations, trends, and anomalies that could otherwise remain hidden. This ability to decode complex relationships positions machine learning as a formidable tool in addressing a variety of financial challenges—from fraud detection to predictive analytics and dynamic portfolio management.

At the heart of using machine learning in finance is the capacity to model intricate relationships and interdependencies inherent in the data. Supervised learning techniques train algorithms on historical data paired with known outcomes, allowing them to forecast future market movements with increasing precision. Conversely, unsupervised learning encompasses methods that identify patterns and structures within datasets devoid of pre-existing labels, revealing novel insights about the trading environment.

Practical Applications of Machine Learning in Finance

The proliferation of machine learning technologies has led to the emergence of several practical applications within the financial sector:

1. Algorithmic Trading: Machine learning plays a pivotal role in the development of algorithmic trading strategies capable of executing trades in real-time as market conditions shift. These models analyze historical data to predict stock price movements. For example, the Long Short-Term Memory (LSTM) network—a specialized type of recurrent neural network—demonstrates remarkable competence in capturing sequential dependencies within financial data.

Illustration: Imagine an algorithm that assesses the sentiment surrounding stocks by analyzing social media feeds.

1. Risk Management: Machine learning enhances risk management strategies by predicting potential default rates and evaluating various aspects of market risk. Classification models, such as support vector machines (SVMs), can identify potentially fraudulent transactions by flagging irregular

patterns within payment datasets.

Example: In the realm of credit scoring, machine learning models analyze a range of borrower data to appraise default risk. These advanced models consider a multitude of factors—including historical payment behavior, credit utilization, and prevailing economic conditions—yielding credit scores that more accurately reflect the likelihood of future defaults than traditional methods.

1. Portfolio Management: Machine learning leverages optimization techniques for dynamic asset management. Reinforcement learning—a branch of machine learning that focuses on identifying optimal actions in complex environments—can adapt asset allocations in real-time based on evolving market conditions.

Illustration: A reinforcement learning model could progressively learn from ongoing market interactions to refine a portfolio's Sharpe ratio, striving to maximize returns while minimizing risk exposure.

Challenges and Considerations

Despite its transformative potential, the integration of machine learning in finance faces significant challenges. Overfitting poses a core concern, wherein models excel on historical datasets but falter when confronted with new, unseen data. This risk necessitates rigorous model validation and comprehensive backtesting to assure reliable predictions.

Model interpretability represents another significant consideration. Many advanced machine learning frameworks, especially complex deep neural networks, function as 'black boxes,' providing limited transparency regarding their decision-making processes. This opacity can complicate regulatory compliance, particularly when firms must justify trading decisions to stakeholders.

Furthermore, the integrity of data is paramount. Machine learning models are only as good as the quality of their training data. Therefore, the preprocessing phase—encompassing data cleaning, normalization, and augmentation—plays a critical role in achieving trustworthy results.

Ethical Implications and Future Directions

As the financial industry becomes increasingly reliant on machine learning, ethical considerations draw growing attention. Concerns regarding algorithmic bias and the potential for machine learning systems to inadvertently perpetuate discrimination warrant serious consideration. Ensuring fairness in data and transparency in model operations is essential for cultivating trust in financial practices.

Looking to the future, the combination of machine learning with emerging technologies like quantum computing and blockchain holds tremendous promise for further financial innovation. As we move forward, we can anticipate a surge of sophisticated models that tap into new data sources, including the Internet of Things (IoT) and real-time global information networks.

Machine learning is fundamentally reshaping finance, pushing the boundaries of data analysis, risk management, and strategic decision-making. As the discipline continues to evolve, the techniques that emerge will not only yield superior investment returns but will also redefine the strategies necessary to successfully navigate the unpredictable rhythms of the market.

Exploring the Foundations of Machine Learning in Finance: Supervised and Unsupervised Learning

In the rapidly evolving landscape of finance, machine learning has emerged as a powerful ally, transforming how we analyze and interpret data. Central to this revolution are two primary paradigms: supervised and unsupervised learning. Each offers unique methodologies for extracting insights from data, shaping financial strategies and enhancing decision-making processes.

Supervised Learning in Finance

Supervised learning can be likened to the mentorship relationship between a teacher and a student, where the model learns from a labeled dataset—each input is matched with a corresponding output. This guided approach is particularly effective for prediction tasks, especially when historical data with known outcomes is available.

1. Model Development and Training: The financial sector is rich with historical data, including price movements, trading volumes, and economic indicators, providing a robust training ground for supervised learning algorithms. For instance, when developing predictive models to forecast stock prices, techniques such as linear regression or advanced methods like gradient boosting machines come into play.

For Example: Imagine predicting a stock's closing price. A supervised learning model would analyze various features—daily opening prices, trading volumes, and macroeconomic factors like interest rates and employment statistics—to make predictions. The model refines its accuracy by minimizing the discrepancies between projected and actual closing prices, continually improving its forecasting capability.

1. Classification and Financial Applications: Supervised learning also shines in classification tasks, such as credit risk assessment and fraud detection. Here, algorithms like support vector machines (SVM) and decision trees categorize data points informed by historical examples.

Illustration: Consider the process of evaluating credit risk. In this context, historical borrower data is labeled with outcomes such as repayment or default. A supervised learning model can assess new applicants and classify them as 'low-risk' or 'high-risk' by analyzing key variables like credit history, income stability, and debt-to-income ratios, constantly optimizing its parameters for maximum accuracy.

The Power of Unsupervised Learning

In contrast, unsupervised learning focuses on uncovering patterns without predefined labels. Algorithms sift through datasets, identifying natural groupings and structures, making it a vital tool for exploration and insight generation in complex financial scenarios.

1. Clustering Techniques: Clustering is a fundamental aspect of unsupervised learning that segments data into distinct groups based on inherent similarities. In finance, this can be invaluable for customer segmentation, revealing clusters of investors sharing similar behaviors or reactions to market fluctuations.

Example: Financial institutions might employ clustering techniques to categorize customers according to their transaction behaviors. Using algorithms like k-means, they can distinguish between 'day traders,' 'long-term investors,' and 'retail clients,' enabling tailored marketing strategies or investment recommendations that resonate with each group's preferences.

1. Dimensionality Reduction: Techniques such as principal component analysis (PCA) play a crucial role in reducing the complexity of large datasets, isolating the most significant features that drive financial dynamics. This simplification is particularly important in scenarios like portfolio optimization, where understanding the myriad

factors influencing asset prices is essential.

Illustration: In the high-stakes world of high-frequency trading, vast quantities of data are processed in real time. Dimensionality reduction not only enhances processing speed but also ensures that the decision-making algorithms focus on the most impactful variables, thereby improving performance and responsiveness.

Practical Considerations and Hybrid Strategies

While supervised learning thrives on explicit outcomes, it is susceptible to overfitting, particularly in the volatile realm of finance. Employing regularization techniques can help mitigate this risk, ensuring the model remains robust and adaptable across diverse market conditions.

On the other hand, unsupervised learning, while excellent for exploratory analysis, grapples with challenges in validating the patterns it uncovers since no explicit outcomes guide its path. Nonetheless, it possesses a unique ability to reveal hidden relationships that might otherwise elude traditional supervised methods.

In real-world applications, combining the strengths of both supervised and unsupervised learning frequently leads to enhanced results.

The interplay between supervised and unsupervised learning not only highlights the versatility of machine learning in finance but also underscores its potential to revolutionize decision-making processes. Supervised learning capitalizes on historical data to produce specific predictions, while unsupervised learning uncovers the often subtle structures within data. Together, these methodologies empower financial professionals to harness data-driven strategies, deriving nuanced insights and optimizing decision-making processes.

In the rapidly evolving landscape of quantitative finance,

the integration of advanced machine learning algorithms—such as decision trees, neural networks, and support vector machines (SVM)—plays a pivotal role in shaping modern data-driven strategies. Each of these algorithms offers unique advantages that empower strategists and quantitative analysts to derive critical insights and make informed decisions, solidifying their status as indispensable tools in today's financial sector.

Decision Trees in Financial Modeling

Decision trees serve as an intuitive yet robust approach for modeling decisions, closely mirroring human reasoning processes.

1. How Decision Trees Work: At their essence, decision trees employ a tree-like model to represent decisions and their potential outcomes. They systematically partition the dataset into branches based on well-defined conditions, culminating in 'leaves' that signify decision endpoints.

Illustrative Example: In the context of stock trading, a decision tree could guide the decision to buy, sell, or hold a stock, considering variables such as price movements, historical volatility, and macroeconomic indicators. As the analysis progresses through the branches of the tree, conditional statements adjusted during the training phase refine the algorithm's guidance toward a final decision. This clear visualization facilitates the interpretation of decision paths, empowering practitioners to comprehend the logic behind each prediction easily.

1. Pros and Cons: The primary strength of decision trees lies in their straightforward interpretability, a significant advantage over more opaque models like neural networks. However, they are susceptible to overfitting, especially when tree structures become overly intricate. Utilizing regularization techniques,

such as pruning, is essential to maintain the model's ability to generalize effectively across diverse datasets.

Neural Networks and Deep Learning

Inspired by the intricate architecture of the human brain, neural networks are unparalleled in their ability to capture complex, non-linear relationships within data. Their versatility makes them particularly advantageous for a variety of demanding financial applications, from predictive analytics to algorithmic trading.

1. Structure and Learning Mechanism: Comprising interconnected nodes (neurons) organized into multiple layers, neural networks learn through a process known as backpropagation. This method involves adjusting the weights of the connections among neurons using labeled datasets, all in an effort to minimize prediction errors.

Illustrative Example: When forecasting stock prices, a neural network could incorporate a range of input nodes representing various financial metrics, such as historical prices, trading volumes, and news sentiment. As data is processed through the layers of the network, the model identifies complex patterns and adjusts weights dynamically to enhance prediction accuracy. This iterative adjustment process allows neural networks to uncover nuanced dependencies that conventional linear models may overlook.

1. Applications and Challenges: While neural networks excel in processing vast and intricate datasets, they often demand significant computational resources and are perceived as black boxes, making their insights harder to unpack. Nevertheless, advances such as Deep Learning and Convolutional Neural Networks (CNNs) are revolutionizing areas like sentiment analysis and predictive modeling,

fostering innovation across the financial landscape.

Support Vector Machines (SVM) for Classification

Support vector machines are grounded in solid mathematical principles, adeptly performing classification tasks by identifying the optimal hyperplane that distinguishes data points belonging to different classes. This functionality is particularly crucial in scenarios demanding high precision.

1. How SVM Works: SVMs focus on locating the hyperplane that maximizes the margin between various classes of data points. In finance, this capability proves invaluable for classifying entities based on subtle differences in characteristics.

Illustrative Example: In assessing credit risk, an SVM could differentiate between creditworthy and non-creditworthy clients by analyzing variables like repayment history, loan amount, and income stability.

1. Strengths and Limitations: SVMs are particularly effective for datasets that are not linearly separable, thanks to the application of kernel tricks that handle complex data structures. However, the computational demands can escalate with larger datasets, necessitating careful consideration of scalability and resource allocation.

Integrating Algorithms for Optimal Outcomes

To unlock the full potential of financial data, strategists can harness a blend of these algorithms rather than relying solely on one. This hybrid approach allows for greater adaptability and improved outcomes based on specific data characteristics and strategic objectives.

For instance, enhancing decision trees with boosting techniques like AdaBoost can significantly improve predictive accuracy while reducing bias. In parallel, integrating regularization strategies such as dropout in neural networks can help guard against overfitting. Similarly, fine-tuning SVM kernel functions can optimize performance when confronted with peculiar financial data challenges.

The thoughtful selection and application of algorithms, such as decision trees, neural networks, and SVMs, are critical to achieving alpha generation in finance. Each algorithm offers distinct advantages, and a deep understanding of their nuances allows strategists to make informed choices that enhance predictive accuracy and overall strategy effectiveness.

Feature Selection and Engineering in Quantitative Finance

In the vast and complex world of quantitative finance, the processes of feature selection and feature engineering play a pivotal role in transforming raw financial data into actionable, structured insights that drive the development of high-performing predictive models. These processes are not merely technical; they are essential to unlocking the hidden potential within datasets, significantly enhancing the accuracy and efficiency of machine learning algorithms.

The Role of Feature Selection

Feature selection is the process of identifying the most relevant variables—or predictors—that contribute meaningfully to the outcome variable. This refinement of the dataset helps manage complexity, allowing analysts to eliminate redundant or irrelevant features, which is particularly vital in finance, where datasets can be vast and noisy.

1. Approaches to Feature Selection: A variety of strategies exist to identify an optimal subset of features, achieving a blend of model simplicity and predictive accuracy. Key techniques include filter methods, wrapper methods, and embedded approaches.

2. Filter Techniques: These methods evaluate features

based on statistical measures, assessing the strength of their relationships with the target variable without the influence of a specific model. For example, metrics such as Pearson correlation and the chi-square test can be instrumental in identifying which economic indicators are most closely correlated with fluctuations in bond yields, guiding analysts to prioritize relevant data points.

3. Wrapper Methods: Unlike filter techniques, wrapper methods evaluate the predictive performance of a predefined group of features by training models on various combinations. Techniques such as recursive feature elimination (RFE) progressively train and remove the least impactful features to enhance model accuracy. In the context of portfolio management, RFE could streamline the selection of market factors that most significantly sway portfolio returns, ensuring decisions are data-driven.

4. Embedded Methods: This approach intertwines feature selection with model training, as seen in LASSO regression, which enhances model sparsity by applying penalties to less significant features. In a credit scoring scenario, LASSO may prioritize essential predictors such as credit history while down-weighting irrelevant demographic variables, thereby facilitating a more reliable assessment of creditworthiness.

The Art of Feature Engineering

Feature engineering transcends selection; it comprises the creative processes of developing, transforming, and synthesizing new features that capture the intricate structures within data. The goal is to enable machine learning algorithms to identify and interpret non-linear patterns that are crucial in financial environments.

1. Techniques in Feature Engineering:
2. Transformation and Scaling: Normalizing data is essential for aligning the scales of various inputs. Techniques such as min-max scaling or standardization ensure comparability across features, which is crucial when disparate data points, like stock prices and economic indicators, have vastly different ranges.

3. Encoding Categorical Variables: Converting non-numeric data into numerical formats is vital for algorithmic processing. Methods such as one-hot encoding or label encoding facilitate seamless integration of categorical variables like trading strategies or asset categories into quantitative models. For example, transforming fund performance metrics across sectors into a numerical format allows for more straightforward analytical assessments.

4. Interaction Features: Creating features that illustrate interactions between variables can reveal underlying relationships. For instance, combining a firm's leverage ratio with market volatility to create an engineered feature might highlight specific risks during periods of market turbulence, providing deeper insights into financial dynamics.

5. Temporal Features: Time-related features are indispensable for capturing momentum or seasonal trends pertinent to financial analysis. Metrics such as rolling averages or moving averages help monitor changes in market sentiment over time, which is critical in developing responsive trading strategies.

Balancing Simplicity and Maximization

A pivotal challenge in feature engineering is striking the right balance between simplicity and the depth of information captured. An overabundance of features can lead to overfitting, where a model becomes too tailored to the training data and loses its generalizable power.

1. Regularization and Dimensionality Reduction: Techniques such as principal component analysis (PCA) can mitigate overfitting risks by reducing the number of features while maintaining essential information. In trading models, where hundreds of variables can complicate insights, PCA helps distill the dataset to its most influential components without sacrificing performance.

2. Cross-validation Techniques: Implementing cross-validation during model development ensures that innovations in feature selection and engineering prove effective across multiple data subsets, bolstering their reliability while adapting to various market conditions.

Real-World Example

Imagine we are developing an investment strategy aimed at forecasting sector-specific returns within the S&P 500. Starting with a dataset that includes historical prices, economic forecasts, and sector indices, feature engineering could involve converting historical prices into technical indicators like moving averages, while also incorporating sentiment scores extracted from market news articles.

Simultaneously, applying RFE as a feature selection technique could help isolate the most predictive indicators from the engineered features, thus shaping a robust dataset. Through iterative refinement, the model's ability to pinpoint lucrative investment opportunities consistently improves, demonstrating the dynamic interplay between feature selection and engineering.

In the landscape of quantitative finance, feature selection and engineering serve as foundational pillars for successful machine learning implementations. These techniques empower analysts to transform raw financial data into strategic insights, thereby enhancing decision-making processes and improving performance in pursuit of alpha generation.

Model validation and testing play an essential role in the development of quantitative strategies, acting as the crucial factors that distinguish viable models from those likely to underperform in real market scenarios. Without thorough validation and testing, even the most advanced models may produce unreliable insights, leading to potential financial losses and eroding the credibility of the entire strategy.

Grasping the Concept of Model Validation

Model validation is the first step in this intricate process; it ensures that a model is both correct and robust before it enters the live market. This phase comprises several careful stages, starting with a comprehensive examination of the model's logical framework and theoretical underpinnings. This involves rigorously assessing the foundational assumptions, underlying data, and hypotheses to confirm their alignment with established financial theories.

For example, when developing a predictive model for stock prices using machine learning techniques, one of the core assumptions might be the stationarity of historical data. It's vital to scrutinize time-series data to ensure it is free from trends or seasonal biases that could skew predictions. Techniques such as the augmented Dickey-Fuller test or the evaluation of autocorrelation functions are commonly employed to validate these assumptions effectively.

The Significance of Backtesting

Following initial validation, the next focus is backtesting—

an indispensable method used to evaluate a model's potential by simulating its performance on historical data. Backtesting illuminates the model's predictive strength and highlights potential pitfalls by applying the model to past data, thus assessing its decision-making efficacy without jeopardizing actual capital.

However, backtesting comes with its own set of challenges. A prominent issue is curve fitting, where a model may be overly optimized for historical data, capturing noise instead of inherent trends. This can lead to deceptively high past performance metrics that do not guarantee future success. To mitigate this risk, practitioners often divide historical data into in-sample and out-of-sample datasets. Here, the in-sample data is utilized for model training, while the out-of-sample data serves as a testing ground. This approach helps evaluate the model's adaptability to data it has never encountered before.

The Importance of Forward Testing

Next comes forward testing—or paper trading—where the model undergoes evaluation in real-time market conditions through virtual trades. Unlike backtesting, which solely relies on historical data, forward testing assesses the model's efficacy in a live yet controlled environment. This phase allows strategists to monitor how the model responds to current market dynamics, including transaction costs and liquidity factors that are frequently overlooked during backtesting.

Consider a scenario where a model generates a buy signal based on minute-by-minute price changes. Real market conditions might reveal delays due to processing times or slippage incurred from executing large orders, nuances that are often absent in backtesting. Forward testing is instrumental in uncovering these execution risks, allowing for necessary adjustments to the model, making it more robust in the face of real-world challenges.

Leveraging Statistical Methods in Validation

The realm of quantitative analysis also necessitates a rigorous application of statistical methodologies to enhance model validation. Techniques such as bootstrap aggregating (bagging) and cross-validation are frequently employed to fortify model robustness. Cross-validation is particularly beneficial as it involves dividing the dataset into multiple subsets, allowing for model training and validation across various combinations while calculating the mean validation error. This rigorous approach prevents the model from becoming overly reliant on any single data segment, thereby boosting its generalizability under diverse market conditions.

Additionally, statistical metrics like out-of-sample R-squared and the Sharpe ratio serve as crucial evaluators of model performance. A high out-of-sample R-squared indicates that the model effectively captures variability within the test data, while a positive Sharpe ratio signifies that the model produces returns exceeding the risk-free rate, adjusted for volatility.

The Need for Continuous Improvement Through Testing

Model testing is not a finite process; it must evolve alongside changing market conditions. Regular reviews and recalibrations are essential to ensure that models remain relevant in light of structural shifts in the market or changes in economic paradigms. This involves ongoing monitoring, where models are assessed not only for performance metrics but also for their stability and resilience in the face of unexpected market events.

In summary, model validation and testing are not merely procedural steps to be navigated; they are fundamental to ensuring the reliability and effectiveness of quantitative strategies. Through a meticulous blend of theoretical validation, rigorous backtesting, real-time forward testing, and thorough statistical evaluation, practitioners can significantly enhance the robustness and credibility of their models. In doing so, they establish a solid foundation for sustainable success in the complex and dynamic landscape of financial markets.

Elevating Predictive Performance with Ensemble Methods in Finance

Ensemble methods have emerged as indispensable tools for boosting the performance of predictive models in the realm of quantitative finance. In the fiercely competitive landscape of financial markets, where accuracy is crucial, employing ensemble methods can provide a significant advantage.

The Essence of Ensembling

At the heart of ensembling lies a compelling principle: the collective judgment of a diverse group of experts often yields a more accurate outcome than that of any single expert. In quantitative finance, each "expert" represents a distinct predictive model that captures various facets of market behavior.

One of the foundational techniques of ensembling is bagging, short for bootstrap aggregating. This method involves training multiple instances of a model on different subsets of the training data and then averaging their predictions. This approach effectively reduces variance, smoothing out the idiosyncratic noise that a single model might capture. For example, when predicting stock prices, a bagging ensemble could consist of multiple variations of decision tree models, aggregating their predictions to emphasize consistent signals from the market rather than erratic noise.

Boosting for Superior Accuracy

Boosting is another prominent ensemble technique that works by sequentially training models to enhance prediction accuracy. Unlike bagging, which operates independently, boosting focuses on addressing the mistakes of previous models.

In financial contexts, boosting is particularly effective for tasks such as credit risk modeling. Here, recognizing subtle distinctions between creditworthy and high-risk borrowers is paramount. Through its iterative correction process, boosting incrementally refines the model's ability to classify borrowers accurately, thereby enhancing lending strategies and risk assessments.

The Power of Stacking

Stacking introduces a layered approach to ensembling, capitalizing on the distinct strengths of various model types. This technique involves training a meta-model that uses the predictions from base-level models as its input. The meta-model then learns to optimally integrate these predictions to elevate overall accuracy.

In a trading strategy scenario, where various inputs—such as price, volume, and macroeconomic indicators—are analyzed, stacking might involve models like logistic regression, support vector machines, and neural networks. Each of these models excels in capturing different relationships within the data. The stacked ensemble harnesses these varied insights, often using a linear regression model as the meta-model to create a comprehensive trading signal that guides decision-making.

Practical Implementation in Financial Strategies

The implementation of ensemble methods within financial strategies demands a meticulous approach to model selection and parameter tuning. Practitioners typically begin by assessing the individual performances of potential models through cross-validation to ensure that each model contributes unique insights essential for the ensemble's success.

Moreover, the inherently dynamic nature of financial markets necessitates continuous monitoring and recalibration of these ensemble models. Regular updates to algorithms and adjustments in the weighting of constituent models are imperative for ensuring that the ensemble remains responsive to changing market conditions. Achieving this necessitates a careful balance between analytical rigor and computational efficiency.

Navigating Challenges While Maximizing Benefits

While ensemble methods offer numerous advantages, they are not without challenges. The computational complexity required for integrating multiple models can be substantial, especially in high-frequency trading scenarios. Additionally, the intricacies involved in combining a host of models may obscure the ensemble's insights, complicating the interpretability of results.

To effectively address these challenges, financial practitioners must adopt a strategic approach that maximizes the potential of ensemble methods. Financial institutions are increasingly leveraging advanced technologies, such as cloud computing and distributed systems, to manage computational demands efficiently. Furthermore, developing simplified models or employing visualization tools can demystify processes, enhancing stakeholder communication and ensuring compliance with regulatory standards.

In summary, ensemble methods represent a powerful avenue for enhancing predictive performance in quantitative finance. As markets continue to evolve and the interplay between qualitative and quantitative data intensifies, the application of ensembling methods stands ready to foster innovation and success across the financial sector.

Tackling Overfitting with Regularization Techniques in Quantitative Finance

In the intricate world of quantitative finance, developing predictive models that not only perform well on historical data but also generalize effectively to unseen scenarios is of paramount importance. Yet, the highly variable nature of financial markets often lures modelers into the overfitting trap —where the model becomes overly complex, mimicking noise rather than genuine underlying patterns. The implementation of regularization techniques emerges as a robust strategy to counteract overfitting, ensuring models maintain predictive power while remaining resilient in dynamic environments.

Understanding Overfitting: A Common Pitfall

To grasp the concept of overfitting, imagine a model designed to forecast future stock prices based on historical data. When overfitting occurs, the model optimally identifies patterns specific to the training dataset but fails to extrapolate meaningfully to new, unseen data. This usually results from a model that is far too complex, responding too closely to the noise within the data rather than the true signals. Consequently, while the model may showcase impressive accuracy during training, it often falters in real-world applications, leading to significant predictive inaccuracies.

Regularization: The Art of Balance

Regularization is an indispensable approach that incorporates penalty terms to curtail model complexity, fostering an essential equilibrium between simplicity and performance. Among the most prominent regularization techniques in financial modeling are Lasso (L1 regularization) and Ridge (L2 regularization). These methods modify the model's cost function, integrating a penalty corresponding to the level of complexity.

Lasso Regression: Simplifying with Precision

Lasso regression plays a critical role in enhancing model simplicity by introducing an absolute value penalty that effectively brings certain coefficients to zero. This feature is especially beneficial for feature selection, allowing practitioners to retain only those variables that significantly impact predictions. In the context of finance, where models can entail a plethora of variables, Lasso aids in discerning the key factors driving asset prices, such as essential economic indicators.

``` python from sklearn.linear_model import Lasso import numpy as np

\#\# Simulating financial data
X = np.random.rand(100, 10)
y = np.random.rand(100)

\#\# Implementing Lasso regression with a specified alpha value
lasso_model = Lasso(alpha=0.1)
lasso_model.fit(X, y)

\#\# Displaying non-zero coefficients to identify influential features
print("Selected Coefficients:", lasso_model.coef_)
```

Ridge Regression: Stabilizing Predictions

Ridge regression operates with a squared penalty term that effectively constrains model parameters, minimizing the risk of extreme fluctuations indicative of overfitting. This technique proves invaluable in trading algorithms that depend on continuous signals, helping ensure that predictions remain robust and are not unduly sensitive to minor anomalies in the data.

``` python from sklearn.linear_model import Ridge

\#\# Implementing Ridge regression with a specified alpha value
ridge_model = Ridge(alpha=0.5)
ridge_model.fit(X, y)

\#\# Outputting coefficients to evaluate model behavior
print("Ridge Coefficients:", ridge_model.coef_)
```

Elastic Net: A Harmonious Blend of Lasso and Ridge

The Elastic Net method marries the penalties from both Lasso and Ridge, offering a more nuanced regularization framework. This technique is particularly advantageous in instances where predictors are highly correlated—a common scenario in financial datasets.

``` `python from sklearn.linear_model import ElasticNet

\#\# Implementing Elastic Net with parameters for L1 and L2 penalties
elastic_model = ElasticNet(alpha=0.1, l1_ratio=0.7)
elastic_model.fit(X, y)

\#\# Outputting coefficients to assess selected features
print("Elastic Net Coefficients:", elastic_model.coef_)
``` `
```

*Monitoring Complexity and Performance*

The effective application of regularization techniques requires meticulous calibration of hyperparameters—essentially determining the optimal amount of regularization to apply. Financial practitioners employ cross-validation, a method that evaluates a model's performance across various subsets of data, to fine-tune this balance between bias and variance.

Additionally, continuous validation against new data is vital to ensure ongoing model performance. This proactive approach enables practitioners to detect when a model begins to overfit or underfit, allowing for timely adjustments and recalibrations.

In summary, regularization techniques equip quantitative finance professionals with the tools needed to create predictive models capable of withstanding the volatility of global markets. As the pursuit of innovation accelerates in the financial sector, mastering the delicate interplay between complexity and generalization will empower practitioners to
```

excel as leaders. With adept use of regularization, the goal of achieving alpha transforms from a distant aspiration into a tangible reality.

Harnessing Natural Language Processing (NLP) for
Sentiment Analysis in Quantitative Finance

In the fast-paced world of quantitative finance, the ability to sift through vast amounts of unstructured textual data to uncover insightful patterns presents both a formidable challenge and a significant opportunity. With market dynamics increasingly shaped by diverse sources such as news articles, social media posts, and financial blogs, Natural Language Processing (NLP) emerges as a powerful ally for analysts seeking to quantify sentiment.

Understanding Sentiment Analysis

Sentiment analysis, often referred to as opinion mining, revolves around the systematic identification and categorization of sentiments expressed in text. Its primary objective is to assess the writer's attitudes toward specific subjects—be it a stock, company, or economic event. In the financial sphere, it's essential not only to capture the explicit sentiments conveyed through clear expressions but also to interpret the subtle undertones that can significantly influence market perceptions.

At the heart of sentiment analysis lies the use of lexicons— dictionaries of words assigned sentiment scores—or advanced machine learning models trained on annotated datasets. These models can effectively classify sentiments as positive, negative, or neutral. For financial analysts, the ultimate aim is to identify sentiment-driven indicators that can serve as a basis for timely trading actions, such as buying or selling securities in response to shifts in public sentiment.

Real-World Application: Analyzing News Impact

To illustrate the practical application of sentiment analysis, consider an automated system designed to gauge the sentiment of news articles concerning a particular company. This system can quickly evaluate whether the prevailing sentiment is predominantly positive, negative, or mixed, ultimately influencing investor decisions and stock prices.

```python
``` python import nltk from nltk.sentiment.vader import SentimentIntensityAnalyzer

\#\# Initializing the VADER sentiment intensity analyzer
nltk.download('vader_lexicon')
sia = SentimentIntensityAnalyzer()

\#\# Sample news headline
news_headline = "Company XYZ announces record earnings, boosting investor confidence"

\#\# Conducting sentiment analysis
sentiment = sia.polarity_scores(news_headline)
print("Sentiment Scores:", sentiment)
```

Harnessing Social Media Insights

Social media platforms, especially Twitter, are treasure troves of real-time sentiment data, permitting traders to gauge public sentiment almost instantaneously. For instance, a notable spike in negative sentiment towards a technology stock could prompt traders to adjust their positions ahead of any potential bearish news.

```python
``` python import tweepy

\#\# Sample logic to connect with Twitter API and analyze tweets
def analyze_tweet_sentiment(tweet_text):
sentiment = sia.polarity_scores(tweet_text)
return sentiment

\#\# Assuming the use of a list of tweet texts
```

```
tweets = ["Investors are losing faith in Company ABC",
"Revamping their strategy could pay off for Company ABC"]
```

\#\# Analyzing each tweet
for tweet in tweets:
sentiment = analyze_tweet_sentiment(tweet)
print(f"Tweet: tweet -> Sentiment: sentiment")

` ` `

Advancing with Machine Learning Models

While lexicon-based methods are beneficial, they may not capture the full depth of sentiment expressed in more complex financial narratives. Here, machine learning models come into play, enhancing sentiment analysis through improved contextual understanding. Advanced algorithms, such as Recurrent Neural Networks (RNNs) and state-of-the-art transformers—like BERT—enable the analysis of text in its entirety, recognizing intricate patterns and relationships that isolated terms might miss. These models can process full sentences, capturing meanings rooted in relative clauses, idiomatic expressions, and specialized financial jargon.

Training machine learning models requires comprehensive datasets with annotated text, allowing the models to learn from the rich tapestry of language found in news articles, earnings call transcripts, and financial reports. The result is a sophisticated AI tool capable of detecting sentiment anomalies with a speed and accuracy that outpaces traditional methods.

` ` `python from transformers import pipeline

\#\# Using a pre-trained transformer model for sentiment analysis
classifier = pipeline('sentiment-analysis')

\#\# Input text example
text = "The CEO's vision for the future has put investors at ease."

```
\#\# Analyzing sentiment using the transformer model
result = classifier(text)[0]
print(f"Label: result['label'], Confidence: result['score']:.2f")
` ` `
```

Striking a Balance Between Speed and Accuracy

Given the unpredictable nature of financial markets, it is crucial to integrate sentiment analysis with other quantitative metrics. While sentiment analysis serves as a vital leading indicator, aligning its findings with both fundamental and technical analyses can yield a more holistic trading framework. This synergy ensures that decisions are informed not just by transient public sentiment but also by solid, quantifiable data and strategic portfolio considerations. This technology serves as a lens into the perspectives shaping investor behavior, empowering traders and investors to respond proactively and strategically. As NLP techniques continue to evolve, the potential to extract actionable insights from unstructured data will further transform the landscape of trading and investment strategies. Those who leverage these advancements will not only remain adaptable in navigating the ever-changing market tides but will also lead the charge in the quest for sustainable alpha generation.

Harnessing Reinforcement Learning in Trading

In the rapidly evolving realm of quantitative finance, innovative artificial intelligence techniques are transforming traditional trading strategies. Among these, reinforcement learning (RL) has emerged as a particularly exciting approach. Unlike conventional models that depend on fixed datasets and rigid rules, RL introduces a dynamic framework where algorithms learn and adapt by interacting with their environment, thereby enhancing their decision-making processes. This shift not only opens up new horizons for trading strategies but also equips them to evolve in real-time alongside market changes.

Understanding Reinforcement Learning

At its essence, reinforcement learning draws inspiration from behavioral psychology, focusing on how agents learn to navigate their environments to achieve specific objectives. In the context of trading, an agent operates within the confines of a defined environment—such as a financial market—making decisions that lead to changes in the market state. The primary goal is to maximize cumulative rewards over time, which in trading can be measured through metrics like profit or risk-adjusted returns.

Every decision made by the agent—whether to buy, sell, or hold a position—carries consequences that the model assesses to refine its strategy. This feedback loop enables the RL model to adapt not only to historical data but to live market conditions and emerging trends, enhancing its responsiveness and efficacy.

Real-World Application: Optimizing Execution Algorithms

One of the most promising applications of reinforcement learning in trading is the optimization of execution algorithms. For instance, consider a trading agent tasked with executing large orders while minimizing market impact and potential price slippage. Traditional methods, such as volume-weighted average price (VWAP), adhere to preset rules that may not account for real-time market dynamics. In contrast, an RL agent can adapt its execution strategy based on live market conditions, including liquidity fluctuations and volatility levels.

To illustrate this concept, let's look at a simplified simulation of a trading environment designed for reinforcement learning:

```python
```python import numpy as np import gym from stable_baselines3 import PPO

\#\# Custom trading environment
```
```

```
class TradingEnv(gym.Env):
def __init__(self):
super(TradingEnv, self).__init__()
self.action_space = gym.spaces.Discrete(3) \# Buy, Sell, Hold
self.observation_space = gym.spaces.Box(low=0, high=1,
shape=(1,), dtype=np.float32)

def reset(self):
\#\# Initialize the environment
self.state = np.random.rand()
return self.state

def step(self, action):
\#\# Execute action and return new state and reward
next_state = np.random.rand()
reward = self._calculate_reward(action)
done = False
return next_state, reward, done,

def _calculate_reward(self, action):
\#\# Compute reward based on executed action and market
state
reward = np.random.rand() \# Placeholder reward logic
return reward

\#\# Training the reinforcement learning model
env = TradingEnv()
model = PPO("MlpPolicy", env, verbose=1)
model.learn(total_timesteps=10000)
` ` `
```

Advancing Through Deep Reinforcement Learning

Deep reinforcement learning (DRL) takes the foundations of traditional RL a step further by integrating advanced deep learning techniques, such as neural networks. This combination allows for the analysis of high-dimensional data, making it particularly suited for the complexities of financial markets that often exhibit vast state spaces and continuous action ranges.

For example, deep Q-networks (DQN) have been successfully employed to formulate trading strategies that can withstand various market conditions. In this setting, a neural network is trained to predict the optimal action-value function (Q-value), aiding the agent in selecting the most advantageous actions based on the current market state.

```python
import torch
import torch.nn as nn

## Define a simple Q-network for trading strategies
class QNetwork(nn.Module):
    def __init__(self, state_size, action_size):
        super(QNetwork, self).__init__()
        self.fc1 = nn.Linear(state_size, 128)
        self.fc2 = nn.Linear(128, 64)
        self.fc3 = nn.Linear(64, action_size)

    def forward(self, x):
        x = torch.relu(self.fc1(x))
        x = torch.relu(self.fc2(x))
        return self.fc3(x)

state_size = 10
action_size = 3
model = QNetwork(state_size, action_size)
```

Navigating the Challenges

Despite its potential, the deployment of reinforcement learning in trading introduces several challenges. The inherent volatility and randomness of financial markets can obscure meaningful patterns that algorithms need to identify. Moreover, balancing exploration—trying out new strategies —against exploitation—maximizing returns with known strategies—remains crucial to optimizing performance while avoiding significant losses.

Interpretability poses another hurdle. Complex neural networks commonly used in RL are often referred to as "black boxes," making it difficult to understand the rationale behind specific trading decisions. To mitigate this, integrating RL with interpretability tools like Shapley value explanations can provide insights into the model's decision-making process, fostering greater confidence in automated trading systems.

Reinforcement learning represents a significant advancement in the field of quantitative trading, offering the ability to navigate the complexities and ever-changing dynamics of modern financial markets. For those in the trading community, embracing RL not only enhances competitive parity but also establishes a transformative approach that is grounded in continuous learning and adaptation.

As the financial landscape becomes increasingly characterized by uncertainty and rapid change, the strategic integration of reinforcement learning is poised to redefine operational paradigms, empowering traders to thrive amid volatility and challenge.

Navigating the Ethical Implications of Machine Learning in Finance

As the financial sector transforms under the influence of machine learning technologies, the emphasis on ethical considerations has never been more paramount. In an environment where algorithms can sway global markets, the implications of their decisions are profoundly significant. While machine learning unlocks remarkable potential for innovation and efficiency, it also introduces considerable challenges that require thoughtful examination and responsible deployment.

The Complexity of Algorithms

From electronic trading to credit scoring and fraud detection, machine learning applications are becoming integral to finance, driven by the relentless pursuit of accuracy and speed. However, the algorithms that dictate these processes often mirror the biases of their creators and the data they assimilate. A primary ethical concern is algorithmic bias, a phenomenon where historical prejudices embedded in training data can perpetuate disparities. For example, credit scoring systems may inadvertently disadvantage individuals from underrepresented communities if trained on datasets that neglect or misrepresent these demographics.

One notable instance involved a credit card company whose algorithm consistently granted higher credit limits to male applicants compared to their female counterparts, despite similar financial profiles. This bias emerged from training data that reflected historic patterns rather than objective evaluations of creditworthiness. Mitigating this issue requires not only refining the quality and diversity of input data but also establishing a commitment to continuous auditing and adjustment of algorithms in response to shifting social and economic conditions.

The Imperative for Transparency and Accountability

The inherent complexity of machine learning models, especially those using deep learning techniques, can obscure the decision-making process, presenting significant ethical challenges related to transparency. In the finance sector, which thrives on trust and clarity, the prevalence of "black box" models can undermine confidence among consumers and regulatory bodies alike.

To address transparency concerns, there are promising initiatives like LIME (Local Interpretable Model-agnostic Explanations) and SHAP (Shapley Additive Explanations), which illuminate the rationale behind model outputs.

Safeguarding Privacy and Data Security

Machine learning systems rely heavily on vast and

varied datasets, many of which contain sensitive personal information. This reliance intensifies concerns regarding privacy and data security within the financial industry. Compliance with regulations such as the General Data Protection Regulation (GDPR) in Europe, which requires explicit consent for data use, is critical.

However, obtaining informed consent on the expansive scale necessary for machine learning can be challenging. This reality compels financial institutions to adopt robust data anonymization and encryption strategies to protect consumer data while still leveraging insights for predictive analytics. Striking the right balance between personalization and privacy is not only essential for compliance but also a core ethical imperative.

Ensuring Fairness and Equity

Machine learning holds remarkable potential to democratize finance by fostering inclusive credit assessments, optimizing investment strategies, and enhancing fraud detection. However, achieving true fairness requires a nuanced approach that transcends superficial metrics. It involves creating systems that are equitable across gender, racial, and socioeconomic lines.

For instance, alternative lending platforms employing machine learning to assess borrower risk must go beyond mere technical accuracy to ensure that their models do not inadvertently disadvantage specific groups. Vigilant ethical evaluation throughout the development cycle is vital in cultivating a more equitable financial landscape.

Evolving Regulatory Compliance

As machine learning rapidly reshapes financial practices, regulatory frameworks must adapt accordingly. Many existing regulations were developed with traditional finance in mind, inadvertently leaving gaps in the governance of emerging technologies. Policymakers face the pressing challenge of devising regulations that can effectively oversee this technological evolution without stifling innovation.

In response to these challenges, organizations like the Federal Reserve have begun to outline principles aimed at ensuring fairness, accountability, and transparency in financial algorithms. Updating and expanding these guidelines to consider the nuances of machine learning applications is crucial for aligning technological advancements with public interests and sound risk management.

Championing Ethical Stewardship

Financial institutions play a pivotal role in ensuring that the next generation of financial engineers and data scientists are equipped not only with technical skills but also with a robust sense of ethical responsibility. Embedding ethical training within educational curricula will empower professionals to recognize the broader implications of their work.

In summary, as financial markets increasingly intersect with machine learning, the urgent need to address ethical implications becomes clear. This vigilance will ensure that technology serves as a powerful catalyst for opportunity and trust, paving the way for a fair and thriving financial ecosystem that meets the needs of a diverse society.

CHAPTER 6: RISK MANAGEMENT IN QUANTITATIVE STRATEGIES

In the ever-evolving landscape of quantitative finance, the importance of risk management stands as a foundational principle. As financial instruments become more complex and market dynamics increasingly interwoven, effectively managing risk isn't just beneficial—it's essential. This discipline is not merely an adjunct to quantitative finance; it is its backbone, ensuring that the quest for returns coincides seamlessly with the imperative to preserve capital. This balance is not only vital for specific investment strategies but also crucial for sustaining a formidable presence in the financial markets over time.

Transforming Risk into Opportunity

Every quantitative strategy encounters risk; it is an inherent aspect of investing. However, the true craft of successful risk management lies in the ability to convert potential threats into calculated opportunities. Quantitative strategies leverage mathematical models and statistical tools, forming a sophisticated framework for identifying, assessing, and mitigating risk. One powerful tool in this arsenal is Value at Risk (VaR), which quantifies the potential loss a portfolio might experience under normal market conditions based on historical data.

Navigating Market Uncertainty

Effective risk management in quantitative finance also necessitates a keen awareness of the ever-changing nature of market conditions. While historical data can serve as a valuable guide, past performances often pale in comparison to unpredictable, high-impact events—be it the 2008 financial meltdown or the profound economic shifts prompted by the COVID-19 pandemic. Such instances highlight the limitations of conventional models and stress the need for robust risk management processes, including stress testing and scenario analysis. These practices are essential for anticipating potential tail risks that might not emerge from standard analytical methods.

Take, for instance, a hedge fund utilizing a statistical arbitrage strategy to exploit perceived discrepancies between correlated financial instruments. Although historical analyses may indicate a favorable risk profile, unexpected market shocks can disturb these relationships, leading to considerable losses. To counterbalance these risks, funds often implement stop-loss orders or diversify their strategy landscape, thereby reducing exposure to any one trading approach.

Mitigating Systemic Risks

In addition to strategy-specific risks, systemic risks present a formidable challenge to the stability of the entire financial framework. The collapse of Lehman Brothers serves as a poignant reminder that interconnectedness within the financial sector has the potential to trigger widespread repercussions. To combat systemic shocks, quantitative strategists increasingly incorporate macroeconomic indicators and global market trends into their risk models. This forward-looking approach allows them to forecast potential downturns and strategically manage capital allocation, thereby mitigating exposure to broader market vulnerabilities.

Harnessing the Power of Diversification

Diversification serves as a cornerstone of effective risk management, allowing investors to dilute unsystematic risk across a varied portfolio. For instance, a manager might combine equities with fixed-income securities, commodities, and international investments. This strategy ensures that volatility in one sector does not disproportionately affect the overall performance of the portfolio.

Cultivating a Risk Management Culture

Risk management transcends mere analytical measures; it represents a culture that must permeate every layer of an organization—from the trading desk to the executive suite. Establishing clear communication channels and a well-defined risk management framework empowers stakeholders at all levels to make informed decisions. Many institutions designate Chief Risk Officers (CROs) to oversee risk policies and ensure that all trading activities align with the firm's defined risk appetite. This leadership role is critical in fostering a proactive approach to risk exposure rather than a reactive one.

Tech Integration in Risk Management

In today's digital age, technology plays a pivotal role in reshaping the financial landscape, presenting both new opportunities and inherent vulnerabilities. Cutting-edge algorithms can sift through extensive datasets to reveal subtle indicators of risk. However, this sophistication also increases reliance on automated decision-making processes. As a result, the imperative for cybersecurity has never been more pronounced, prompting financial firms to invest heavily in safeguarding their technological infrastructures against cyber threats.

Moreover, the integration of machine learning techniques into risk management practices enhances the ability to monitor market conditions and performance metrics in real time. This dynamic adaptability allows institutions to respond swiftly to emerging risks. However, such reliance necessitates rigorous validation processes to ensure that theoretical models hold up under real-world scrutiny and adhere to ethical standards.

Navigating Ethical Considerations

Ethical considerations are vital in shaping robust risk management frameworks. Strategies that aggressively seek alpha at the cost of ethical integrity can trigger reputational damage and invite regulatory scrutiny, ultimately undermining stakeholder trust.

In summation, risk management is the cornerstone that grounds quantitative strategies in today's volatile market, ensuring that capital allocation and innovation are approached with caution and respect for prevailing market dynamics. The significance of risk management extends beyond the protection of individual investments; it plays a crucial role in upholding the stability of the financial system, embodying a commitment to responsible and sustainable economic growth.

Understanding Financial Risk: A Comprehensive Overview of Market, Credit, and Operational Risks

In the realm of quantitative finance, an in-depth comprehension of various financial risks is essential for shaping effective financial strategies. Among these risks, market, credit, and operational risks distinctly stand out as foundational elements that drive financial risk management. Each type has unique characteristics and influences portfolio performance, requiring tailored management approaches to minimize their potentially adverse impacts. Recognizing and understanding these risks is crucial for building robust risk management frameworks that protect against unforeseen losses while optimizing returns.

Market Risk: Navigating Volatility in Financial Markets

Market risk—often referred to as systematic risk—encompasses the potential for financial losses stemming from factors that influence overall market performance. Unlike unsystematic risk, which can be mitigated through portfolio diversification, market risk is intrinsic to the entire financial ecosystem. This risk is shaped by a myriad of macroeconomic factors, including fluctuations in interest rates, inflationary pressures, geopolitical developments, and technological disruptions.

Take, for instance, a portfolio heavily invested in technology stocks. If a new regulation suddenly emerges affecting the tech sector, the broader market could react negatively, significantly impacting the value of those assets. Similarly, an unexpected interest rate hike by central banks can ripple through financial markets, altering asset prices and investor sentiment across various sectors. To manage such vulnerabilities, quantitative strategies frequently employ hedging techniques, using instruments like options and futures to shield portfolios from the turbulence of market conditions.

Credit Risk: Assessing the Possibility of Default

Credit risk—commonly known as default risk—arises when a borrower is unable to meet their financial obligations, potentially resulting in losses for lenders. This risk is particularly relevant in lending practices and fixed-income investments, encompassing a range of financial instruments such as bonds and mortgages. Effectively assessing credit risk involves a rigorous evaluation of a borrower's creditworthiness and likelihood of default.

Consider a commercial bank in the process of vetting a loan application from a corporation. The bank would engage in comprehensive due diligence, scrutinizing the company's financial statements, credit history, and overall capacity to repay. Quantitative analysts often utilize predictive models, such as the Altman Z-score, to assess bankruptcy probabilities. Credit risk management strategies may include setting credit limits, diversifying portfolios, gaining exposure through securitization, and employing credit derivatives like credit default swaps (CDS) to mitigate risk.

Operational Risk: Safeguarding Against Internal Failures

Operational risk encompasses potential losses arising from internal failures, inadequacies in processes or systems, human errors, or external events. Unlike market or credit risk, operational risk is inherently tied to an organization's internal dynamics and operations. Common examples of operational risk include system failures, instances of fraud, legal liabilities, and external shocks such as natural disasters.

For instance, consider a financial institution experiencing an operational risk event when a critical trading system malfunctions during peak trading hours, resulting in missed trades and possible financial loss. Additionally, cases of employee misconduct, such as unauthorized trading, can inflict substantial reputational and financial damage. To mitigate operational risk, organizations often implement stringent internal controls, conduct regular audits, ensure compliance with regulatory standards, and maintain comprehensive disaster recovery plans.

Illustrative Example: A Tri-Fold Risk Assessment in Action

To provide clarity on these risks, let's examine a global investment firm managing a diverse asset portfolio:

- Market Risk Scenario: The firm holds significant investments in emerging market equities. When geopolitical tensions escalate in a key emerging nation, the equity market experiences a sharp decline, inciting widespread selling. To counter this regional market risk, the fund strategically employs futures contracts to hedge its exposure, effectively mitigating potential losses.

- Credit Risk Scenario: Among its investments, the firm allocates capital to corporate bonds. Upon discovering financial troubles within a prominent bond issuer, the firm swiftly utilizes a credit default swap to hedge against default risk, bolstering its portfolio's stability.

- Operational Risk Scenario: During a routine system upgrade, a technical glitch results in erroneous market orders. However, the firm's rigorous error-detection protocols swiftly identify and rectify the issue before it escalates into substantial losses, showcasing effective operational risk management.

Integrating a Comprehensive Risk Strategy

The interplay of market, credit, and operational risks underscores the necessity for a holistic approach to risk management.

It's imperative to view these risks not as discrete challenges, but rather as interconnected components of a unified risk management framework. A well-crafted strategy cultivates a risk-aware culture, embedding proactive risk management within every aspect of the decision-making process. With the constantly evolving financial landscape, these risk domains will continue to shape the strategies essential for success, highlighting the importance of adaptive and thorough risk management practices in today's complex financial environment.

Measuring Risk: VaR, CVaR, and Stress Testing
Value at Risk (VaR)

Value at Risk, or VaR, is perhaps the best-known metric for quantifying financial risk. It offers a tangible estimate of the potential loss in value of a portfolio over a defined time horizon, given a specified confidence level. In essence, VaR addresses a pivotal question: "What is the maximum expected loss for a portfolio over a designated time period, assuming normal market conditions?"

To calculate VaR, one starts with a portfolio characterized by its historical return distribution. Imagine a portfolio containing an asset whose daily returns conform to a normal distribution, which can be articulated through its mean and standard deviation. To find the VaR at a 95% confidence level, we utilize the corresponding z-score. For instance, with a portfolio valued at (1 million, a mean daily return of 0%, and a standard deviation of 2%, the calculation would proceed as follows:

[VaR95\% = Mean + (Z95\% Standard Deviation)]

Since (Z_95\% = -1.645) for a normal distribution, we can calculate:

[VaR_95\% = 0 + (-1.645 0.02 1,000,000) = -\)32,900]

This result indicates a 95% confidence level that the portfolio will experience a loss not exceeding (32,900 within a single day, under typical market conditions.

Conditional Value at Risk (CVaR)

While VaR provides a useful snapshot of potential loss, Conditional Value at Risk (CVaR), also known as Expected Shortfall, offers a more nuanced perspective by taking into account the magnitude of losses that occur beyond the VaR threshold. Unlike VaR, which focuses solely on the worst-case scenario that should not be surpassed, CVaR assesses the average loss in situations where losses exceed that threshold.

Let's revisit our earlier portfolio. If we hypothesize a series of possible losses ranging from)35,000 to (50,000 that could breach the)32,900 VaR, the calculation for CVaR would average these extreme losses:

[CVaR_95\% = Average of Losses = ((35,000 + 40,000 + 50,000) / 3) = \(41,666.67]

Thus, this analysis suggests that if losses surpass the)32,900 mark, the average loss could be around (41,666.67, offering a broader understanding of tail risk and potential vulnerability.

Stress Testing

While VaR and CVaR measure risk under expected market conditions, stress testing takes a different approach by subjecting portfolios to hypothetical extreme scenarios. These scenarios might encompass sudden financial crises, geopolitical upheavals, or sharp liquidity shortages, providing a more comprehensive view of how portfolios might perform under duress.

Consider a stress test designed to replicate the conditions of the 2008 financial crisis. This scenario could assume a drastic decline in equity prices, soaring bond yields, and severe liquidity constraints.

For example, a diversified portfolio might be projected to endure a 40% drop in equity value coupled with a 5% increase in bond yields. Such a simulation could expose critical vulnerabilities within the portfolio's structure. If results indicate a significant downturn, the stress test can illuminate exposure gaps, prompting necessary adjustments to enhance resilience against future crises.

Employing VaR, CVaR, and stress testing creates a comprehensive framework for measuring risk. As financial markets continuously evolve and the complexities of investing intensify, the strategic application of these techniques equips financial professionals to prepare for both anticipated and unforeseen events, ultimately safeguarding their financial goals in the pursuit of alpha. In this delicate interplay of risk comprehension, practitioners become better positioned to navigate the challenges and opportunities inherent in today's dynamic markets.

Navigating Risk-Reward Trade-offs in Alpha Generation

In the nuanced realm of quantitative finance, the quest for alpha—defined as the excess return above a benchmark or market average—demands a sophisticated understanding of the delicate interplay between risk and reward. Striking the right balance is essential not only for crafting strategies aimed at superior returns but also for minimizing exposure to potential downturns. This intricate balance is the backbone of advanced investment models aspiring to outperform the broader market while maintaining robust risk management practices.

Unpacking the Trade-off

At its core, the risk-reward trade-off underscores a timeless principle in finance: the potential for higher returns naturally accompanies greater risk. As finance professionals design strategies to capture alpha, it is imperative that they fully grasp their own risk tolerance and the uncertainties intrinsic to the financial landscape.

For example, a portfolio manager may utilize a range of quantitative models, each presenting a unique risk-reward profile. Momentum-based strategies may offer impressive returns in bullish environments but can exhibit significant volatility during downturns. In contrast, mean reversion strategies might generate steadier, albeit modest, returns. Each decision reflects a specific approach to risk and reward, requiring ongoing evaluation and recalibration.

A Structured Approach to Balancing Risk and Reward

Crafting an effective strategy involves several key steps:

1. Defining Risk Appetite: Clearly articulate the fund's risk tolerance. This involves quantifying the degree of risk that stakeholders are prepared to accept in exchange for potential alpha. For instance, an aggressive hedge fund may adopt a higher risk appetite compared to a conservative pension fund.

Engaging with stakeholders to understand their willingness and capacity for risk helps establish a foundational framework.

2. Diversification of Strategies: Implementing a diversified approach across various quantitative strategies can help mitigate overall portfolio risk. This diversified landscape acts as a buffer, ensuring the failure of a single strategy does not derail overall performance.

3. Evaluating Risk-Adjusted Metrics: Utilize performance metrics such as the Sharpe Ratio, which gauges risk-adjusted returns, to compare various strategies effectively. A high Sharpe Ratio indicates a favorable risk-reward balance, guiding informed decision-making. For example, consider two portfolios—A and B—yielding returns of 8% and 10%, respectively, with standard deviations of 5% and 12%. Calculating their Sharpe Ratios using a risk-free rate of 2% provides valuable insights:

4. Portfolio A: $((8\%-2\% / 5\%) = 1.2)$

5. Portfolio B: $((10\%-2\% / 12\%) = 0.67)$

This analysis reveals that Portfolio A delivers better risk-adjusted returns, influencing portfolio allocations favorably.

1. Scenario Analysis and Stress Testing: Beyond assessing individual strategies, conducting comprehensive scenario analyses and stress tests can illuminate potential performance under extreme market conditions. Such stress testing uncovers vulnerabilities within specific models, enabling proactive adjustments that safeguard against significant losses.

2. Dynamic Rebalancing: Maintaining the flexibility to adapt and rebalance portfolios in response to shifting

market dynamics is crucial. A initially high-risk strategy may need to be hedged or adjusted when market volatility spikes unexpectedly. This adaptive approach ensures alignment with established risk-reward benchmarks while keeping performance objectives in focus.

A Practical Case: Hedge Fund Strategy in Action

Consider a hedge fund that strategically employs both long-short equity and global macro strategies to exploit market inefficiencies. The long-short equity approach may present a higher beta, allowing the fund to capitalize on market movements in either direction, thus potentially delivering elevated returns but with elevated volatility. Meanwhile, the global macro strategy acts as a stabilizing force, strategically positioning the fund to take advantage of broader economic trends and currency fluctuations with relatively lower volatility. Routine evaluations of the synergy between expected alpha generation and the associated volatility ensure the fund remains aligned with its return objectives, while also managing risk prudently.

Mastering the intricacies of risk-reward trade-offs empowers finance professionals to design strategies that pursue alpha with both precision and foresight. Thoughtful management of these trade-offs not only enhances the potential for elevated returns but also fosters an investment environment resilient to market fluctuations. This understanding of the intricate relationship between risk and reward stands as a cornerstone of quantitative finance, emphasizing that the pursuit of alpha is not merely about ambitious targets, but about navigating the journey with wisdom and insight.

Elevating Your Investment Game: Diversification Strategies in Quantitative Finance

In the dynamic realm of quantitative finance, diversification stands as a cornerstone principle, integral not only for risk mitigation but also as a strategic catalyst for alpha generation.

Understanding the Power of Diversification

At its core, diversification rests on the understanding that different assets react distinctly to market fluctuations. When assets are highly correlated, they tend to rise and fall together, magnifying risk—especially in turbulent market climates. However, by blending uncorrelated or negatively correlated assets, investors can smooth out overall volatility, turning potential declines in one area into opportunities for gains in another.

In the world of quantitative finance, diversification transcends mere asset allocation; it encompasses a variety of models, strategies, and even investment timelines.

Strategic Approaches to Diversification

1. Cross-Asset Diversification: Expanding investments across diverse asset classes—such as equities, fixed income, commodities, and real estate—facilitates a broader exposure and lessens the portfolio's vulnerability to sector-specific downturns. For example, during bearish equity market trends, bonds may outperform, providing a shield against potential losses.

2. Geographic Diversification: Broadening horizons to include international markets introduces nuanced risks and opportunities. For instance, while U.S. and European markets might experience cyclical slowdowns, emerging markets could offer unique growth drivers spurred by different economic catalysts.

3. Strategy Diversification: Engaging multiple investment strategies enables investors to tap into a wide array of market opportunities. A quantitative portfolio may employ a blend of high-

frequency trading, statistical arbitrage, and global macro strategies, each with its own set of risk-return profiles. This multifaceted approach enhances the potential to optimize returns across fluctuating market conditions.

4. Time Horizon Diversification: Spreading investments across different timeframes can further bolster diversification efforts. Long-term strategies centered on fundamental value can secure alpha over extended durations, while short-term tactics capitalize on immediate price inefficiencies, creating a harmonized strategy that spans both the present and the future.

An Illustrative Example: Building a Multi-Strategy Portfolio

Envision a portfolio manager crafting a diversified investment masterpiece through carefully selected strategies, each contributing uniquely to the overall composition. Here's a potential structure:

- Momentum Strategy: This strategy targets stocks that exhibit upward price momentum, ready to harness the volatility with an eye toward potentially significant returns.
- Relative Value Strategy: Through pairs trading, the manager buys undervalued securities while simultaneously shorting overvalued counterparts, capitalizing on price inefficiencies and relative market dynamics.
- Volatility Arbitrage: By leveraging options, this strategy seeks to exploit discrepancies between market-implied and actual volatility, allowing for profit opportunities regardless of overall market direction.

Through this judicious allocation, the manager skillfully blends growth potential from equities, stability from bonds, diversification from commodities, and liquidity from cash-equivalent instruments to achieve a robust, well-rounded portfolio.

Evaluating the Effectiveness of Diversification

Quantitative finance practitioners assess the effectiveness of diversification using a variety of statistical measures, such as correlation coefficients and beta values for individual assets against the broader portfolio. A correlation matrix serves as a vital tool, illustrating how different assets interact with one another. Portfolio managers routinely adjust allocations based on these insights to ensure that diversification remains a powerful defense against concentration risk.

Additionally, analyzing portfolio variance provides insights into how individual asset variances contribute to overall portfolio risk.

Navigating Challenges and Unlocking Value

While diversification offers numerous benefits, it also poses challenges. Over-diversification—spreading investments too thinly—can erode potential returns and inflate transaction costs without significantly lowering overall risk. The key lies in striking a balance, ensuring that diversification serves its intended purpose of minimizing risk while enhancing returns.

However, by meticulously orchestrating diverse strategies, investors have the opportunity to construct a resilient investment framework that not only safeguards capital during downturns but also capitalizes on the myriad opportunities within global markets. This multifaceted approach empowers them to pursue alpha with vigor and adaptability.

In summary, diversification in quantitative finance is not simply about spreading investments widely; it's about artfully crafting an intelligent blend of asset classes, strategies, and timeframes to achieve sustainable, superior performance. The journey toward effective diversification is one of ongoing learning and adaptation—a continuous pursuit that strengthens the quest for alpha while navigating the complexities of financial markets.

Dynamic risk management techniques are crucial for successfully navigating the unpredictable and often volatile terrain of financial markets. These techniques distinguish themselves from static methods, which apply the same risk measures uniformly across different scenarios. Instead, dynamic risk management is characterized by its adaptability, allowing investors to modify strategies in response to constantly changing conditions. In this segment of our journey into quantitative finance, we will delve into the innovative approaches that are fundamental to effective risk management.

Understanding Dynamic Risk Management

At its essence, dynamic risk management is built on the principles of flexibility and responsiveness. It involves the ongoing adjustment of risk measures as new information becomes available and as market conditions shift. This adaptability can take various forms, such as recalibrating investment positions, fine-tuning hedging strategies, or employing novel models designed to identify and mitigate emerging threats. The primary objective is to retain portfolio stability while seizing opportunities that arise from fluctuating market dynamics.

Importantly, dynamic risk management is not merely a reactive endeavor. It necessitates proactive monitoring of key indicators such as volatility levels, liquidity conditions, and broader economic signals.

Strategic Techniques for Dynamic Risk Management

1. Volatility Targeting: One of the cornerstone strategies within dynamic risk management is volatility targeting. This method involves adjusting portfolio allocations according to prevailing market

volatility. For instance, during high-volatility periods, investors might reduce exposure to equities or other high-risk assets to mitigate potential losses. Conversely, in more stable environments, they could increase risk exposure to capitalize on favorable conditions.

Example: Consider a portfolio designed to maintain an annualized volatility of 10%. If market volatility surpasses this threshold, the strategy would involve boosting cash holdings or derivatives to lessen market exposure. On calmer days, however, the portfolio would shift towards more aggressive assets to enhance returns.

1. Adaptive Hedging Strategies: In ever-changing markets, hedging strategies must be equally flexible to counteract both expected and unforeseen market trends. This could mean utilizing options, futures contracts, or other derivatives that shield against adverse price movements while preserving the ability to adapt as conditions evolve.

Example: A firm could employ a collar strategy that involves purchasing put options to curtail downside risk while simultaneously selling call options to cover the cost, especially during periods of heightened volatility. As market conditions shift, the terms and configurations of these contracts would be updated to mirror the current risk environment.

1. Dynamic Stop-Loss Orders: The implementation of dynamic stop-loss orders can serve as a robust mechanism for limiting downside risk. These orders can be adjusted algorithmically based on market conditions, ensuring that investors can guard against significant losses without the need for constant manual monitoring.

Example: A trader could utilize a trailing stop-loss order that tracks a stock's price at a predetermined percentage during an uptrend. If market analytics indicate increased volatility, this order could adjust upward, helping to secure gains before a potential reversal occurs.

1. Scenario Analysis and Stress Testing: Consistent with a dynamic approach, scenario analysis and stress testing equip portfolios to tackle extreme market events by simulating different conditions that may impact asset prices and risk levels. This forward-thinking strategy allows for preemptive adjustments instead of reactive corrections.

Example: A portfolio manager might run simulations of scenarios like interest rate spikes or geopolitical crises.

Embracing Technological Innovations

Dynamic risk management is becoming increasingly linked with advancements in technology and quantitative finance. Innovations such as machine learning and artificial intelligence (AI) facilitate more precise risk assessments and prompt adjustments by continuously analyzing vast pools of data for patterns and anomalies.

Algorithmic models can autonomously recalibrate portfolio strategies based on real-time data feeds, enabling quicker reactions to emerging threats. For instance, AI algorithms may identify subtle shifts in market sentiment or detect significant buy-sell patterns, allowing for automated rebalancing to minimize risk exposure before human analysts can detect these changes.

Overcoming Challenges

Despite its clear advantages, dynamic risk management is not without its challenges. The complexity and financial burden of implementing such adaptive systems can be significant. Additionally, reliance on technology requires a thorough understanding of its limitations, including overfitting, which could lead to misinterpretation of signals from anomalous data points.

To address these concerns, financial firms must prioritize building a robust technological infrastructure while fostering a culture of continuous learning and skill development among their teams. Incorporating feedback loops and maintaining human oversight in decision-making processes can also help mitigate the risks associated with over-reliance on automated systems.

The Path Forward

Dynamic risk management represents a significant evolution in modern financial practices, establishing a nimble framework that seamlessly merges foresight with adaptability. As the financial landscape continues to change, so too must the strategies adopted to manage portfolio risk.

In conclusion, dynamic risk management is an essential element of contemporary quantitative finance strategies. Investors and portfolio managers who master this intricate dance of adaptability can not only bolster their defensive measures but also lay a strong foundation for discovering alpha in an ever-shifting market environment.

Implementing Robust Risk Limits in Trading Systems: A Key to Sustainable Success

In the dynamic landscape of trading, implementing risk limits stands as a fundamental pillar of any comprehensive risk management framework. These limits are not merely regulatory hurdles; they are essential for safeguarding portfolio integrity and ensuring profitability. This becomes especially crucial in volatile markets, where even minor fluctuations can lead to swift capital erosion.

Understanding the Importance of Risk Limits

At their core, risk limits serve as critical control mechanisms that dictate the maximum risk levels permissible within various components of a trading strategy. They create a structured environment in which traders can make informed decisions, free from the temptations of impulsive actions triggered by erratic market movements.

Moreover, beyond the confines of individual portfolios, risk limits play a vital role in stabilizing the broader financial system. This is particularly critical for institutional investors, where the scale of operations can exacerbate the consequences of poor risk management practices.

Types of Risk Limits

Example: A trading strategy may enforce a position limit of 5% of the total portfolio value for any one stock, ensuring that no single asset can disproportionately sway overall performance.

2. Value at Risk (VaR) Limits

Value at Risk is a widely recognized risk metric that estimates the potential loss of a portfolio over a specific time frame, with a defined confidence level. VaR limits determine the maximum acceptable risk, empowering traders to manage and curtail potential losses effectively.

Example: A hedge fund might establish a daily VaR limit of 1% of its portfolio value with a 95% confidence level. If the projected VaR exceeds this threshold, the trading system prompts a reassessment and possible reduction of high-risk positions.

3. Stop-Loss Limits

Stop-loss limits are automatic safeguards that trigger the closure of positions when losses reach a predetermined threshold, protecting capital from further declines. They bolster emotional discipline, enabling traders to adhere to rational decision-making even under market stress.

Example: A trader might set a stop-loss order that automatically sells a stock if its price drops by 10% from the entry point, effectively containing potential losses.

4. Market Risk Limits

Market risk limits dictate the overall exposure of a portfolio to specific market factors, including interest rates, currencies, and commodities.

Example: A trading desk could impose a market risk limit that restricts exposure to interest rate changes to a delta of 50 basis points, thus reducing vulnerability to rate fluctuations.

The Implementation Process: Steps to Success

Implementing risk limits within trading systems necessitates a methodical approach comprising several key steps:

1. Define Risk Appetite: Establishing the organization's risk tolerance serves as the foundation. This process involves defining how much risk the firm is willing to accept while pursuing its strategic objectives, influenced by regulatory requirements, stakeholder expectations, and current market conditions.

2. Set Specific Limits: Following the assessment of risk appetite, specific limits should be delineated across various dimensions—such as position size, market exposure, and risks associated with individual asset classes.

3. Integration with Trading Platforms: Risk limits must be seamlessly integrated into trading platforms to ensure compliance in real-time. This integration involves developing robust algorithms and automated systems capable of continually monitoring trading activities and enforcing these limits effectively.

4. Continuous Monitoring and Reporting: A comprehensive monitoring system is essential for tracking adherence to risk limits. This system should generate alerts or reports whenever limits are

breached or approached, enabling timely corrective action.

5. Review and Adjust: Risk limits should be regarded as dynamic parameters—regular reviews are necessary to account for evolving market conditions, shifts within the portfolio, and changes in strategic direction. Periodic audits can assess the effectiveness of current limits and prompt recalibration as needed.

Navigating Challenges and Considerations

While the implementation of risk limits is imperative, it does come with its set of challenges. Trading systems must navigate the delicate balance between protective measures and the potential for restricting profitability or strategic opportunity. Furthermore, these systems must be sophisticated enough to manage complex interactions between various risk factors and remain adaptable to market anomalies.

One common hurdle is determining appropriate levels for risk limits that accurately reflect both market conditions and investor expectations. Limits that are overly conservative can inhibit potential gains, while excessively lenient limits may expose portfolios to unnecessary risks. Effective communication between risk management professionals and traders is essential to strike this necessary balance.

Additionally, when developing automated systems for enforcing risk limits, firms must remain vigilant regarding issues such as latency and execution errors, which can result in unintended breaches or missed opportunities.

In conclusion, risk limits are indispensable for creating a robust trading environment that harmonizes risk management with performance aspirations. As financial markets grow increasingly complex and interconnected, the demand for sophisticated systems capable of efficiently enforcing these limits becomes ever more critical. A thoughtful approach to implementing risk limits not only protects against adverse market movements but also lays a solid groundwork for sustainable trading success, empowering firms to pursue alpha generation with confidence and precision.

Crisis Management and Contingency Planning in Quantitative Finance: A Comprehensive Guide

In the ever-evolving landscape of finance, the adage "Expect the unexpected" resonates deeply. Market volatility, unanticipated downturns, and global crises are not just theoretical possibilities; they are certainties that firms must be prepared to encounter. In this context, effective crisis management and contingency planning are not merely reactions to events as they unfold; they are strategic frameworks developed to sustain operational integrity and protect capital during turbulent times.

Understanding the Importance of Crisis Management

Crisis management in quantitative finance encompasses a proactive and structured approach to identifying, evaluating, and mitigating threats that could adversely affect trading operations. This process engages all facets of an organization, demanding prompt decision-making and thorough preparedness to navigate unforeseen challenges.

Learning from the Past: The 2008 Financial Crisis

The 2008 global financial crisis stands as a stark reminder of the repercussions of inadequate crisis management. Many firms found themselves ill-equipped to deal with the rapid decline in market conditions, resulting in devastating losses and, for some, insolvency. In contrast, those that not only survived but also thrived did so by rigorously applying crisis management principles, highlighting the necessity of thorough preemptive measures.

Essential Steps for Crafting an Effective Crisis Management Plan

The foundation of effective crisis management lies in the meticulous identification and analysis of potential risks. This involves assessing both internal challenges—such as technological failures or trading errors—and external factors, including economic downturns or geopolitical strife. A dynamic risk inventory must be maintained, evolving with changing market conditions.

Illustrative Example: A quantitative trading firm may recognize liquidity risk as a significant threat during an economic downturn, necessitating an evaluation of how reduced market activity could impact its trading execution capabilities.

2. Forming a Specialized Crisis Management Team

Establishing a dedicated crisis management team is pivotal for coordinating effective responses to crises. This team, typically composed of senior leadership, risk officers, legal counsel, and communication experts, collaborates to guide the firm through challenging situations with clarity and purpose.

3. Implementing Flexible Crisis Response Strategies

Developing well-defined response strategies is crucial for minimizing the fallout from crises. These strategies may include predetermined thresholds for unwinding positions, diversifying market exposures, or pivoting to conservative trading practices. Importantly, these strategies must be adaptable to the specific dynamics of each crisis.

Illustrative Example: In the event of a sudden currency devaluation impacting a trading firm's exposure to foreign exchange derivatives, a pre-emptive strategy might involve reducing position sizes or utilizing hedges to mitigate potential losses.

4. Establishing Clear Communication Protocols

Effective communication is vital during crises for managing the expectations of both internal and external stakeholders. Firms should develop structured communication protocols, appoint designated spokespeople, and implement alert systems to ensure consistent and timely messaging.

5. Conducting Regular Drills and Simulations

Routine crisis simulations are invaluable for preparing staff to respond adeptly under pressure.

Building Strong Contingency Plans

While crisis management centers on immediate responses, contingency planning focuses on long-term strategies designed to ensure business continuity in the aftermath of a crisis. A robust contingency plan should address operational recovery, financial stability, and strategic realignment to regain a competitive edge.

Operational continuity strategy ensures that critical functions remain intact amidst disruptions. This involves creating redundancies within systems, instituting data backup protocols, and establishing alternative trading platforms to safeguard seamless operations.

Illustrative Example: A forward-thinking trading firm might implement parallel infrastructure across geographically diverse locations to mitigate risks associated with localized disasters impacting primary trading activities.

2. Strategizing Financial Contingency Measures

Effective financial contingency planning entails securing liquidity lines, establishing credit facilities, and identifying potential capital infusion sources to navigate cash flow challenges during prolonged market disruptions.

Illustrative Example: A trading firm facing a sustained market downturn could rely on pre-negotiated credit lines to sustain operations and avoid the forced liquidation of valuable assets.

3. Embracing Strategic Realignment

In the aftermath of a crisis, firms often need to reassess their business models and risk management frameworks. This realignment may involve scaling back on high-risk ventures, diversifying asset classes, or exploring mergers and acquisitions to strengthen market positioning.

The Role of Flexibility and Adaptation

An enduring hallmark of successful crisis management and contingency planning is flexibility. The inherently dynamic nature of financial markets means that fixed plans can quickly become outdated. Organizations must cultivate agility, adapting their strategies and frameworks in response to an ever-changing environment. This adaptability often distinguishes firms that emerge resilient from those that struggle.

In conclusion, the bedrock of effective crisis management and contingency planning in quantitative finance lies in thorough preparation and adaptability. This resilience fosters investor confidence, protects capital, and ensures long-term success in an unpredictable financial landscape.

Through diligent planning and strategic foresight, quantitative finance firms equip themselves to navigate crises with confidence, reinforcing their commitment to integrity and excellence in the face of adversity.

Case Studies of Risk Management Failures in Quantitative Finance

In the intricate and ever-evolving realm of quantitative finance, effective risk management serves as a linchpin, determining the fine line between success and failure. Despite notable advancements in technology and analytical strategies, historical precedents reveal that lapses in risk oversight can result in catastrophic financial losses, heightened regulatory scrutiny, and, in some cases, the collapse of financial institutions.

The Collapse of Long-Term Capital Management (LTCM)

The case of Long-Term Capital Management (LTCM) stands as a quintessential example of risk management failure. Founded by a group of eminent Nobel laureates and seasoned Wall Street veterans, LTCM was celebrated for its groundbreaking quantitative models and strategic leverage. However, the firm's ambitious approach culminated in its dramatic collapse in 1998, posing severe threats to the stability of the global financial system.

Key Lessons from LTCM's Failure: - Overreliance on Models: LTCM's demise highlighted the perils of placing unbridled faith in quantitative models that inadequately accounted for extreme market shocks, such as the upheaval during the Russian financial crisis. Comprehensive stress-testing across a broader spectrum of scenarios could have illuminated critical vulnerabilities in their modeling approach. - Excessive Leverage: With leverage ratios occasionally exceeding 25:1, LTCM exemplified the risks associated with heavy borrowing. A more prudent risk management strategy would have imposed stringent limits on leverage, providing a buffer against adverse market fluctuations. - Lack of Diversification: Ironically, despite its advanced quantitative capabilities, LTCM's investment strategy concentrated risks rather than dispersing them, linking numerous trades in ways that amplified losses amid market shifts. A diversified approach could have mitigated these cascading effects.

JP Morgan's "London Whale" Incident

In 2012, JP Morgan Chase found itself embroiled in the infamous "London Whale" episode, where a trader's high-stakes credit derivatives positions led to losses exceeding)6 billion. This event not only marked a significant setback for the bank but also provoked a reevaluation of risk management practices across the industry.

Key Lessons from the London Whale Incident: - Inadequate Risk Oversight: The complexity and vastness of the trader's positions were inadequately monitored, permitting risky trades to accumulate unchecked. This underscores the pressing need for real-time risk assessment tools and vigilant oversight to promptly identify potential irregularities. - Failure in Communication and Reporting: A convoluted system of risk reports and controls faltered due to miscommunication and a culture of complacency. Streamlining reporting protocols, alongside promoting a culture of transparency, could have facilitated earlier detection and intervention. - Overconfidence in Trading Strategies: This incident illuminates the inherent dangers of placing excessive confidence in specific trading strategies and individual traders. Aligning risk-taking activity with the organization's broader risk tolerance is essential for cultivating a resilient risk management framework.

Amaranth Advisors' Natural Gas Folly

The downfall of Amaranth Advisors in 2006 serves as a cautionary tale of excessive speculation and insufficient safeguards in risk management, culminating in losses exceeding (6 billion due to concentrated trading in natural gas futures.

Key Lessons from Amaranth's Downfall: - Concentration of Risk in a Single Asset: Amaranth's significant exposure to natural gas futures exemplified the dangers tied to focusing investments heavily within a single asset class. A diversified portfolio approach, incorporating various instruments and geographies, is a cornerstone of effective risk management. - Poor Risk Mitigation Tactics: The fund's traders exhibited inadequate risk mitigation strategies, failing to establish robust hedges against potential downturns. The introduction of comprehensive hedging tactics could have diluted some of the extensive losses incurred. - Lack of Proper Governance Structure: The governance framework within Amaranth lacked the necessary rigor to challenge or rein in aggressive trading practices. This serves to highlight the importance of solid governance, reinforced by empowered risk committees capable of proactively addressing emerging risks.

Key Takeaways and Implications for the Future

These cautionary tales robustly illustrate that even the most advanced and resource-rich institutions can falter due to inadequate risk management practices. The critical lessons derived from these failures emphasize several important points: - The Human Element: Despite significant technological innovations, the effectiveness of risk management fundamentally relies on human judgment. Miscalculations can exacerbate exposure, underscoring the importance of continuous training and awareness initiatives that promote a strong risk culture. - Adaptive Systems: Dynamic risk management strategies are essential; they must be consistently updated in light of new data, evolving market conditions, and regulatory frameworks. Static risk frameworks are inherently vulnerable to obsolescence. - Cultural Alignment: Fostering a firm-wide culture that prioritizes risk awareness ensures that all members—including traders, risk managers, and board members—act in accordance with clearly defined risk tolerances.

In conclusion, these case studies remind us that robust risk management is not merely an ancillary function; it is a vital component that underpins financial integrity and the long-term viability of firms. Reflecting on these historical instances compels both financial institutions and professionals to learn from the past while innovating proactively in risk management methodologies and mindsets.

Future Trends in Risk Management Strategies

Enhanced Utilization of Artificial Intelligence
and Machine Learning

The integration of artificial intelligence (AI) and machine learning (ML) stands out as one of the most groundbreaking developments in risk management.

Real-World Applications: - Predictive Analytics: Financial institutions are increasingly employing machine learning models to predict market movements and potential security breaches. - Automated Risk Assessment: AI-driven systems are revolutionizing risk assessment by providing real-time analysis and responses to threats. For instance, credit evaluations are becoming more swift and precise, significantly expediting the underwriting process and enhancing overall efficiency.

Integration of Robust Cybersecurity Measures

In our increasingly digital world, cybersecurity is more crucial than ever within the realm of risk management. Future strategies will place a premium on protecting data integrity and privacy against sophisticated cyber threats.

Key Innovations: - Blockchain Technology: Emphasizing transparency and tamper-resistance, blockchain technology serves as a powerful tool for secure transactions and record-keeping. Financial institutions are actively exploring blockchain solutions to bolster their cybersecurity frameworks. - Zero-Trust Architectures: This innovative cybersecurity model operates on the premise that threats may originate from anywhere, both inside and outside the network.

Focus on Climate Risk Management

As Environmental, Social, and Governance (ESG) factors gain prominence, especially concerning climate change, it becomes imperative for firms to incorporate climate-related risks into their risk management frameworks. The financial implications of climate change — from asset values to investment portfolios — demand proactive and comprehensive strategies.

Strategic Approaches: - Scenario Analysis: Financial institutions are employing scenario analysis to explore the potential impacts of climate-related events on their financial stability. Stress-testing portfolios against scenarios such as rising sea levels or increased regulatory interventions related to carbon emissions helps firms prepare for an uncertain future. - Sustainable Investing Practices: There is an unmistakable trend toward sustainable investing, with more firms integrating ESG criteria into their risk management and investment strategies. This approach not only aligns with ethical business practices but also effectively manages long-term risks associated with environmental factors.

Aligning Regulatory Compliance with Risk Strategies

As regulatory frameworks continue to grow in complexity, organizations must cultivate nimble strategies that align risk management practices with compliance demands. Heightened regulations concerning data security, financial transparency, and consumer protection will necessitate robust systems that meet these evolving requirements.

Anticipated Developments: - RegTech Solutions: Financial institutions are turning to regulatory technology (RegTech) innovations to streamline compliance processes and ensure adherence to regulatory mandates. These technologies facilitate accurate and timely regulatory reporting, bolstering compliance efforts. - Proactive Governance Structures: Firms are increasingly establishing governance structures that seamlessly integrate risk, compliance, and audit functions with strategic objectives. This holistic approach ensures well-coordinated responses to regulatory changes and enhances internal risk assessments.

The Emergence of Behavioral Risk Analysis

Understanding human behavior in financial markets has emerged as a vital component of risk analysis.

Implications and Tools: - Behavioral Analytics Tools: Financial institutions are deploying behavioral analytics to recognize patterns in trading and investment behavior, assessing the emotional and psychological factors that drive market dynamics. These insights enable firms to anticipate and mitigate risks stemming from irrational market behaviors. - Cultural Risk Assessments: Acknowledging the influence of organizational culture on risk management, firms are increasingly conducting cultural risk assessments to identify vulnerabilities in management practices and corporate governance.

Concluding Thoughts on Future Risk Management Directions

The future of risk management in finance is intricately linked to the evolving interplay between technology, regulation, and human behavior. Institutions that proactively embrace these innovations and integrate them into their risk management frameworks will be well-positioned to navigate the complexities of modern financial environments. The convergence of AI, advanced cybersecurity measures, sustainable practices, regulatory compliance alignment, and behavioral insights heralds the creation of resilient strategies that safeguard financial health while promoting sustainable growth.

CHAPTER 7: ALGORITHMIC TRADING AND EXECUTION STRATEGIES

Algorithmic trading has fundamentally transformed the financial markets, ushering in a new era of precision, speed, and efficiency that traditional trading strategies often struggle to achieve. This evolution is not a temporary phase; instead, it marks a significant shift in how trades are executed and how investment strategies are crafted. As the integration of technology and finance deepens, grasping the essentials of algorithmic trading becomes crucial for anyone who aims to navigate the intricacies of contemporary investing.

Algorithmic trading involves the deployment of computer algorithms to automate trading processes. These sophisticated algorithms can process vast amounts of market data in real-time, empowering traders to make decisions driven by comprehensive statistical analysis rather than intuition or gut feeling. This method not only improves accuracy but also dramatically decreases transaction times, enabling the swift execution of trades that can capitalize on fleeting market opportunities.

A typical algorithmic trading system comprises three essential components: the trading strategy, the execution system, and the risk management framework. Each of these elements plays a vital role and relies on the others to function effectively. For example, take a straightforward momentum strategy which entails buying assets that are trending upwards and selling those that are declining. The algorithm must first discern the momentum signals based on price movements over a specified period, utilizing tools like moving averages or other technical indicators.

Let's consider a practical implementation using Python and the Pandas library to retrieve historical price data and compute a moving average:

```python
``` python import pandas as pd import numpy as np

\#\# Retrieve sample stock data
data = pd.read_csv('stock_prices.csv') \# Assume CSV contains 'Date' and 'Close' columns
data['Date'] = pd.to_datetime(data['Date'])
data.set_index('Date', inplace=True)

\#\# Calculate 50-day moving average
data['50_MA'] = data['Close'].rolling(window=50).mean()

\#\# Generate buy/sell signals
data['Signal'] = np.where(data['Close'] > data['50_MA'], 1, 0) \# 1 indicates a buy signal
data['Position'] = data['Signal'].diff()

` ` `
```

This approach automates the creation of trading signals while permitting traders to backtest their strategies against historical data, allowing for refinement prior to the allocation of real capital.

The execution systems work hand in hand with the trading strategies to ensure trades are executed at optimal prices.
```

High-frequency trading (HFT) firms, for instance, employ advanced execution algorithms that utilize strategies such as Volume Weighted Average Price (VWAP) or Time Weighted Average Price (TWAP). These techniques are designed to minimize market impact by distributing large trades over multiple executions throughout the trading day.

To further illustrate, consider a VWAP implementation: If you aim to purchase 10,000 shares of a stock while avoiding significant price movement, a VWAP algorithm would break this large order into smaller parts, executing them at regular intervals throughout the trading day. This strategy ensures that your average purchase price aligns closely with the stock's average price within that timeframe.

Moreover, robust risk management is a fundamental aspect of any algorithmic trading system. It plays a critical role in identifying and mitigating potential losses through various strategies. For example, incorporating stop-loss orders serves to protect capital by automatically liquidating an asset once it reaches a specified loss threshold. Here's how an algorithm might facilitate this process:

```python
def implement_stop_loss(current_price, stop_loss_percentage): stop_loss_price = current_price * (1 - stop_loss_percentage / 100) return stop_loss_price

\#\# Example: Current price of stock is \)100, and stop-loss is set at 5%
stop_loss_price = implement_stop_loss(100, 5)
print("Stop-loss price set at: \(", stop_loss_price)

```

While the benefits of algorithmic trading are numerous—such as enhanced execution speed, reduced transaction costs, and the capability to backtest strategies—there are also significant challenges to consider. Dependence on technology can pose risks, including system failures, network outages, or flawed algorithms that may lead to substantial financial setbacks. Additionally, market dynamics can shift unpredictably, rendering models grounded in historical data less effective in real-time trading scenarios.

Furthermore, the competitive nature of algorithmic trading can result in the overcrowding of popular strategies, diminishing potential returns. An arbitrage opportunity, for instance, may vanish within minutes as numerous traders capitalize on it, making it increasingly difficult to execute profitable trades.

Regulatory concerns are equally paramount. The heightened scrutiny from regulatory agencies, such as the SEC in the United States and various European entities, has created a complex web of compliance requirements that algorithmic traders must navigate. Understanding the legal ramifications of trading practices—especially within high-frequency environments—becomes essential for maintaining compliance and avoiding substantial penalties.

In conclusion, exploring the realm of algorithmic trading reveals a sophisticated interplay among strategy, execution, and risk management. As market participants increasingly leverage automated solutions, those who can harness the power of algorithms with both responsibility and effectiveness stand to gain a distinct competitive advantage. The journey into algorithmic trading extends beyond mere speed and technology; it encompasses the development of resilient, adaptable strategies capable of thriving in a rapidly changing financial landscape. Each trader's approach may vary, but the shared goal of excellence within algorithmic trading remains a common aspiration across the professional spectrum.

Algorithmic trading represents a dynamic and evolving landscape, rich with diverse strategies tailored to meet varying market conditions and trader goals. Among the most significant approaches are market-making and arbitrage algorithms, both of which play pivotal roles in understanding automated trading mechanisms. While both strategies prioritize optimizing trade execution and risk management, they are fundamentally distinct in their objectives, methodologies, and the tools they utilize.

Market Making Algorithms

At its core, market making is a liquidity-providing strategy that involves simultaneously submitting buy and sell orders. Market makers profit from the bid-ask spread—the difference between the price at which they are willing to buy (the bid) and the price at which they are prepared to sell (the ask).

The effectiveness of a market-making algorithm largely depends on its ability to predict short-term price fluctuations and respond nimbly to varying market conditions. For instance, a sophisticated algorithm may utilize a dynamic pricing mechanism that adjusts its quotes based on parameters such as trading volume, market volatility, and temporal factors.

To illustrate this concept, let's look at a simple Python implementation of a market-making algorithm that adjusts bid and ask prices based on recent price trends:

```python
```python import random

def market_maker(current_price, spread, volatility):
\#\# Simulating price fluctuations influenced by market dynamics
price_fluctuation = current_price + random.normalvariate(0, volatility)
bid_price = price_fluctuation - spread / 2
ask_price = price_fluctuation + spread / 2
return bid_price, ask_price

\#\# Example scenario with a market price of \)100, a spread of \(0.10, and volatility of \)0.02
```
```

```
bid, ask = market_maker(100, 0.10, 0.02)
print("Bid Price: \(", bid)
print("Ask Price: \)", ask)

` ` `
```

In this script, the market_maker function computes new bid and ask prices by introducing normally-distributed fluctuations, simulating a market maker's adaptive response to price changes while maintaining a consistent spread. This ability to adjust in real time is essential for ensuring competitiveness and liquidity in the marketplace.

While market-making strategies can be profitable, they are not without risks—especially in volatile environments. A robust risk management framework is vital for mitigating potential losses. Employing mechanisms such as stop-loss orders or position limits can help safeguard against excessive exposure, ensuring that a trader's positions remain within acceptable thresholds.

Arbitrage Algorithms

In stark contrast, arbitrage strategies are designed to capitalize on price discrepancies for the same asset across different markets or among related assets. The fundamental premise behind arbitrage is exploiting opportunities for risk-free profits arising from pricing inefficiencies. For example, if a stock trades at a lower price on one exchange compared to another, an arbitrageur can buy the stock where it is cheaper and sell it where it commands a higher price.

One well-known variant of arbitrage is statistical arbitrage, which identifies pricing inefficiencies between correlated securities using complex quantitative models. Such strategies heavily rely on mathematical and statistical techniques to predict potential price movements.

To exemplify a basic arbitrage opportunity through Python, consider the following code, which identifies and quantifies a price discrepancy:

```python
``` python import pandas as pd

\#\# Sample data representing prices on two exchanges
data =
'Exchange_A': [100.5, 101.2, 100.8, 101.0],
'Exchange_B': [101.5, 101.0, 100.7, 101.3]

df = pd.DataFrame(data)

\#\# Identifying potential arbitrage opportunities
df['Arbitrage_Opportunity']      =      df['Exchange_A']      <
df['Exchange_B']

\#\# Calculating potential profits from identified arbitrage
df['Profit'] = df['Exchange_B'] - df['Exchange_A']
df['Profit'] = df['Profit'].where(df['Arbitrage_Opportunity'], 0)

print(df)
```
```

In this example, the algorithm flags an arbitrage opportunity whenever the price on Exchange A is lower than that on Exchange B, calculating the potential profit from executing that trade. This approach enables traders to gauge potential gains before making decisions.

However, while the allure of arbitrage trading can be substantial, several challenges exist. Market inefficiencies tend to be fleeting; by the time a trader acts on a visible price discrepancy, that opportunity may have evaporated. Furthermore, transaction costs—especially in high-frequency trading scenarios where every millisecond counts—can significantly diminish potential profits.

Comparative Framework

When contrasting market making and arbitrage, the primary distinction is their core objectives. Market makers focus on providing liquidity and profiting from the bid-ask spread, while arbitrageurs aim to exploit ephemeral pricing discrepancies for immediate profit. Both strategies demand sophisticated algorithms, quick decision-making, and rigorous risk management practices.

Integrating these strategies into a trading portfolio can diversify approaches and enhance overall returns. Traders must stay attuned to their trading environments, consistently refining algorithms to capitalize on the opportunities that arise within fluctuating market dynamics.

Optimizing Trading Performance: A Deep Dive into VWAP and TWAP Execution Strategies

Execution strategies play a crucial role in enhancing the performance of trading algorithms, enabling traders to minimize market impact while executing substantial orders. Among the most prevalent methodologies in this area are Volume Weighted Average Price (VWAP) and Time Weighted Average Price (TWAP). Although both strategies aim to optimize trade execution by thoughtfully determining the timing and size of orders, their methodologies and contexts for use differ markedly.

Volume Weighted Average Price (VWAP)

VWAP is a sophisticated execution strategy that aspires to match or exceed the average price of an asset traded over a defined time period, weighted by volume. This approach allows traders to execute a series of buy or sell orders in accordance with the trading volume, thus reducing market impact and avoiding major price fluctuations.

Key Features of VWAP

1. Volume Sensitivity: VWAP incorporates the volume of the asset traded at various price levels throughout the trading day. This dynamic ensures that larger portions of the order are executed when the stock experiences heightened trading activity, leading to

more favorable average prices.

2. Benchmarking Tool: For institutional investors, VWAP serves as a vital benchmark.

3. Day-Long Execution: Designed for trades executed within a single trading day, VWAP allows traders to actively participate in the market, all while considering prevailing volume trends to optimize their execution.

To illustrate the VWAP calculation, consider this simple Python implementation:

```python
```python import pandas as pd

\#\# Sample intraday trade data
data =
'Price': [100, 101, 102, 100, 99, 101],
'Volume': [10, 20, 15, 25, 30, 20]

df = pd.DataFrame(data)

\#\# Calculate VWAP
df['Cumulative_Volume'] = df['Volume'].cumsum()
df['Cumulative_Value'] = (df['Price'] * df['Volume']).cumsum()
vwap          =          df['Cumulative_Value'].iloc[-1]          /          df['Cumulative_Volume'].iloc[-1]

print("VWAP:", vwap)

```
```

In the code snippet above, we compute the VWAP by first determining the cumulative value of trades (price multiplied by volume) and then dividing it by the cumulative trading volume. This methodology is essential for assessing trade efficiency and performance.

Risks and Considerations

Despite its strengths, VWAP does have limitations. In illiquid markets, relying on VWAP can sometimes lead to suboptimal pricing, as the average may not accurately reflect fair market value. Additionally, during periods of significant market volatility or unforeseen events, the reliability of VWAP may be compromised. Thus, traders should always consider market context when deploying this execution strategy.

Time Weighted Average Price (TWAP)

Conversely, TWAP is an execution strategy that seeks to execute orders evenly over a specified time frame, independent of trading volume. This method divides the total order into smaller, equally spaced transactions throughout the trading period, making it particularly beneficial in markets less influenced by volume dynamics.

Key Features of TWAP

1. Temporal Focus: TWAP inherently treats each time interval as equal, excelling in scenarios where minimal market exposure is crucial. It allows traders to spread trades over time rather than being swayed by inherently variable trading volume.

2. Simplicity in Execution: This approach is straightforward and can be easily implemented across various trading systems. Traders simply specify the total order size and execution duration, and the algorithm takes care of the incremental trade sizes.

3. Suitability for Illiquid Assets: TWAP shines in illiquid markets, where large orders might lead to significant price fluctuations.

A sample implementation of a TWAP algorithm in Python is as follows:

```python
import numpy as np

def twap(total_order_size, total_time, intervals):
    \#\# Calculate the size of each interval
```

```
size_per_interval = total_order_size / intervals
time_intervals = np.linspace(0, total_time, intervals + 1)

\#\# Create execution schedules
execution_plan = []
for interval in range(1, len(time_intervals)):
execution_plan.append((time_intervals[interval],
size_per_interval))

return execution_plan

\#\# Example scenario: executing an order of 100 shares over 5
intervals
order_plan = twap(100, 60, 5)
for execute_time, order_size in order_plan:
print(f"Execute    order_size    shares    at    execute_time:.2f
seconds")
```
` ` `

In this example, the twap function calculates an execution plan outlining when to place orders throughout a specified period. This strategy allows traders to minimize the impact of their trades on market prices.

Risks and Considerations

While TWAP offers valuable advantages, it is not without challenges. One significant limitation is its inability to adapt to changing market conditions. In highly volatile environments, the rigid nature of TWAP can lead to less-than-optimal execution prices. Additionally, in fast-moving markets, the fixed timing of trades could result in missed opportunities or unfavorable pricing.

Comparative Framework

When evaluating VWAP and TWAP, the fundamental distinction lies in their respective execution philosophies. VWAP is sensitive to market conditions and volume, customizing trades based on volume-weighted prices, while

TWAP prioritizes consistent execution over time irrespective of volume fluctuations. Each strategy possesses unique strengths, making it vital for traders to assess their specific trading objectives and market environments when selecting an execution strategy. Mastering these execution methodologies not only mitigates adverse market effects but also contributes significantly to the overall success of trading endeavors.

Maximizing Execution Efficiency in Trading: The Critical Role of Latency and Technology

In the fast-evolving landscape of financial markets, the efficiency of execution often hinges on the crucial factors of latency and technology. As trading becomes increasingly competitive, where mere microsecond differences can mean the difference between profit and loss, a deep understanding of these dynamics becomes essential for both quantitative strategists and traders. Latency—the delay between order initiation and execution—can dramatically impact trading outcomes, particularly in high-frequency trading scenarios.

Understanding Latency: Categories and Implications

Latency is not a one-size-fits-all concept; it can be categorized into several distinct types:

1. Network Latency: This refers to the time it takes for data to travel from a trader's systems to the exchange. Effective network latency management is pivotal, as even the smallest delays can hinder a trader's ability to capitalize on fleeting market opportunities.

2. Processing Latency: This involves the time a trading algorithm needs to perform the necessary calculations to generate an order. In competitive trading environments, the speed of computation can be a game-changer.

3. Exchange Latency: Once an order reaches an

exchange, there's an additional delay before it is processed and executed. This layer of latency can significantly impact the execution of orders, especially when markets move rapidly.

For traders relying on microsecond decisions, even a 10-millisecond reduction in latency can translate to significant tactical advantages—allowing for the timely capture of price discrepancies or trends ahead of competitors. Thus, mitigating latency is not just a technical enhancement; it's a fundamental strategic imperative.

Building a Robust Technological Infrastructure

To combat latency, traders are increasingly investing in state-of-the-art technology. High-frequency trading firms, in particular, leverage colocated servers—computers stationed in the same data centers as exchanges—thereby minimizing the physical distance signals must travel and drastically reducing network latency.

Consider the innovative use of Field Programmable Gate Arrays (FPGAs). These customizable hardware components allow firms to execute trading algorithms far more rapidly than traditional CPUs.

Here is a simplified illustration of how latency considerations might be integrated into a basic trading algorithm using Python: ```python import time import random

```python
def execute_order(price, volume):
    network_delay = random.uniform(0.001, 0.01) \# Simulated 1 to 10 milliseconds
    time.sleep(network_delay)

    processing_time = 0.002 \# 2 milliseconds
    time.sleep(processing_time)

    print(f"Executed order: volume shares at \(price:.2f")

\#\# Simulate order execution
```

```
start_time = time.time()
execute_order(100.50, 10)
end_time = time.time()
print(f"Total latency: (end_time - start_time) * 1000:.2f ms")
```

` ` ` This example illustrates the intricate relationship between latency and order execution timing.

The Critical Role of Data Feed Technologies

Access to high-quality, low-latency data feeds is equally vital for successful trading. Implementing direct market access (DMA) ensures traders receive the latest market data for making informed decisions. High-speed data feeds from exchanges, transmitted through application programming interfaces (APIs), can substantially reduce information latency.

For instance, integrating a WebSocket connection enables continuous subscriptions to real-time market data streams, delivering updates instantaneously—thus facilitating faster reaction times to price changes.

Here's how one might implement a WebSocket connection for real-time market updates: ` ` `python import websocket import json

```
def on_message(ws, message):
data = json.loads(message)
print(f"Received data: Price: data['price']")
```

\#\# Establish WebSocket connection
ws = websocket.WebSocketApp("wss://api.exchange.com/market-data",
on_message=on_message)

ws.run_forever()

` ` ` Utilizing this Python snippet to connect to a WebSocket allows traders to access real-time market data, enhancing their ability to respond swiftly to market movements and execute strategies effectively.

Balancing Trade-Offs in Pursuit of Low Latency

While reducing latency is a primary focus, traders must also navigate the trade-offs associated with it. Lower latency often necessitates substantial financial investments in advanced hardware and technology infrastructure. Furthermore, strategies designed for low latency can result in increased transaction costs due to higher trading frequencies. It is essential for traders to weigh the benefits of faster execution against the potential escalation in trading expenses that may accompany high-frequency functionality.

In conclusion, the interplay between latency and advanced technological infrastructure in execution strategies cannot be overstated. This understanding empowers quantitative strategists to continually refine their execution methodologies, leading to improved alpha generation. In the modern trading environment, success hinges not only on having the best strategy but also on executing it with remarkable speed and precision.

Core Performance Metrics

When it comes to assessing the effectiveness of trading algorithms, a set of fundamental performance metrics stands out. Each of these metrics sheds light on different aspects of an algorithm's performance, encompassing everything from profitability to risk exposure. Here are several metrics that are particularly important:

The Sharpe Ratio is a cornerstone metric for evaluating risk-adjusted returns. It measures the excess return earned per unit of volatility, providing a clear picture of how effectively an investment compensates for risk. A higher Sharpe Ratio indicates superior risk-adjusted performance, making it a fundamental tool for traders.

[Sharpe Ratio = (Return - Risk-Free Rate / Standard Deviation of Return)]

To illustrate, consider two distinct trading algorithms:

- Algorithm A produces an average return of 15% with a standard deviation of 10%, against a risk-free rate of 2%. The calculation of its Sharpe Ratio is as follows:

[Sharpe Ratio (A) = (15\% - 2\% / 10\%) = 1.3]

- Algorithm B, in contrast, offers a return of 12% with only a 5% standard deviation. Its Sharpe Ratio becomes:

[Sharpe Ratio (B) = (12\% - 2\% / 5\%) = 2.0]

Although Algorithm A has a higher return, Algorithm B demonstrates a far superior risk-adjusted performance. This scenario underscores the necessity of considering risk alongside returns when evaluating algorithmic trading strategies.

2. Maximum Drawdown

Maximum Drawdown (MDD) measures the most significant decline from a portfolio's peak value to its trough. This metric is crucial as it quantifies potential losses, helping traders appreciate the worst-case scenarios that their investments could face. A lower MDD value signifies better risk management practices.

[MDD = (Peak Portfolio Value - Trough Portfolio Value / Peak Portfolio Value)]

For instance, if a portfolio's value peaks at)100,000 and drops to (70,000 before any recovery, the maximum drawdown would be:

[MDD = (100,000 - 70,000 / 100,000) = 0.30 or 30\%]

Understanding MDD equips traders with insights into their psychological risk tolerance and aids them in making astute adjustments to their strategies.

3. Alpha and Beta

Alpha and Beta are essential metrics that evaluate an algorithm's performance relative to a chosen benchmark. Alpha quantifies the value added by the algorithm beyond market movements, with a higher alpha indicating outperformance. Conversely, Beta assesses the algorithm's sensitivity to market fluctuations, with values greater than 1 indicating increased volatility compared to the benchmark.

[Alpha = R_a - (R_f + (R_m - R_f))]

Where: - (R_a) = Actual return of the trading algorithm - (R_f) = Risk-free return - (R_m) = Market return - ( ) = Beta of the trading algorithm

For example, if a trading algorithm achieves a return of 10%, with a market return of 8%, a risk-free rate of 2%, and a Beta of 1.5, the calculation of alpha would be:

[Alpha = 10\% - (2\% + 1.5 (8\% - 2\%)) = 10\% - 10\% = 0\%]

Here, the algorithm matches the market performance after adjusting for risk, suggesting a potential need for refinement in its strategy.

Composite Metrics for Holistic Evaluation

While individual metrics are instrumental, a holistic view emerges when multiple metrics are combined, providing a more comprehensive assessment of an algorithm's performance.

The Calmar Ratio combines return and risk, measuring the annualized return in relation to the maximum drawdown.

[Calmar Ratio = (Annualized Return / Maximum Drawdown)]

For instance, if a strategy produces an annualized return of 20% with a maximum drawdown of 15%, the Calmar Ratio would be:

HAYDEN VAN DER POST

[Calmar Ratio = (20\% / 15\%) = 1.33]

A ratio above 1 signifies healthy performance, particularly in terms of risk management.

2. Information Ratio

The Information Ratio assesses the consistency of an algorithm's performance against a benchmark, emphasizing the returns generated in excess of the benchmark relative to the tracking error.

[Information Ratio = (Average Excess Return / Tracking Error)]

For example, if an algorithm has an average excess return of 5% over a benchmark and a tracking error of 8%, its Information Ratio would be:

[Information Ratio = (5\% / 8\%) = 0.625]

A ratio exceeding 1 typically indicates strong performance, showcasing the algorithm's ability to consistently outperform its benchmark.

To effectively gauge the impact of trading algorithms, a thorough understanding and application of these performance metrics are indispensable. Each metric reveals unique insights into performance dynamics, empowering traders to refine their strategies and mitigate risks. When utilized collectively, these metrics create a powerful analytical arsenal that informs ongoing strategy adjustments, fosters continuous improvement, and enhances the potential for achieving alpha generation.

Armed with these insights, traders can more adeptly navigate the complexities of performance evaluation, leading to informed decisions that align strategically with their objectives. In the fiercely competitive landscape of quantitative finance, clarity in performance measurement can be the decisive factor between thriving and merely surviving.

In the dynamic world of quantitative finance, a deep understanding of market microstructure stands as a cornerstone for crafting effective trading strategies and enhancing alpha generation. Market microstructure delves into the intricacies of how market mechanisms, trading processes, and participant behaviors converge to shape the landscape in which assets are exchanged.

Key Components of Market Microstructure

The field of market microstructure is rich with essential components, each playing a vital role in influencing trading decisions and overall market performance.

The choice of order type can have a profound impact on market dynamics. Traders can select from various orders—including market orders, limit orders, and stop-loss orders—each serving different strategic purposes.

For instance, when a trader submits a market order, it executes instantly at the prevailing market price. Conversely, a limit order allows the trader to specify the maximum price for buying or the minimum for selling, fostering a different interaction with market liquidity. The decision between these order types can significantly affect price stability and slippage.

Consider a scenario where a trader places a sizable market order; the immediate demand may push prices higher than expected, resulting in less favorable execution. Conversely, a well-designed quantitative execution algorithm may lean toward limit orders, strategically minimizing slippage and thereby enhancing the average fill price.

2. Liquidity and Price Impact

Liquidity fundamentally defines how smoothly assets can be traded without exerting undue influence on their prices. High liquidity typically allows for quick transactions at stable prices, whereas low liquidity can trigger pronounced price volatility during larger trades.

Take, for example, a stock exhibiting a robust daily trading volume of 500,000 shares versus a more illiquid stock trading only 50,000 shares per day. If a trader seeks to acquire 10,000 shares of the highly liquid stock, they are likely to do so with negligible price impact. In stark contrast, purchasing the same quantity of the thinly traded stock may inflate its price, eroding potential returns.

Quantitative trading models often account for liquidity by analyzing metrics such as bid-ask spreads and trading volumes.

3. Information Asymmetry and Market Participants

The landscape of market microstructure also encompasses the critical concept of information asymmetry, where disparities in information among market participants can create opportunities for informed traders. These traders, equipped with unique insights or superior analytical tools, can capitalize on market inefficiencies to boost their performance.

For instance, in the fast-paced realm of technology stocks, traders with access to high-frequency data and sophisticated analytics may identify patterns before they are reflected in prices. A well-crafted quantitative trading strategy might harness news sentiment analysis, processing vast amounts of data to anticipate price movements driven by informational advantages.

4. Price Discovery Mechanism

Price discovery is the intricate process through which market participants collectively determine the price of an asset based on supply and demand dynamics. Theoretical frameworks within market microstructure suggest that the interplay between buyers and sellers, shaped by their motivations and available information, is pivotal in this process.

Imagine a scenario where a company reports exceptional earnings, prompting a wave of buying interest. As demand surges, the stock price is likely to rise, reflecting buyers' willingness to pay more before the information is fully absorbed by the market. Algorithms that can swiftly integrate real-time data can seize these fleeting opportunities, executing trades to optimize entry points ahead of broader market adjustments.

Algorithmic Applications

A profound grasp of market microstructure not only informs trading strategies but also enhances the sophistication of algorithmic design. Quantitative traders leverage insights drawn from microstructure analyses to create algorithms that:

- Develop optimal execution strategies aimed at minimizing transaction costs and mitigating market impact.
- Strategically place orders by considering expected liquidity and analyzing the order book depth.
- Employ advanced machine learning models to adapt trading strategies in real-time as market conditions fluctuate, using historical performance data to inform decisions.

For instance, an algorithm could analyze past trading volumes and price movements to identify ideal entry and exit timing under comparable liquidity scenarios. This predictive capability empowers the algorithm to initiate proactive strategies rather than merely reacting after price movements occur.

The synergy between market microstructure and quantitative trading strategies highlights the necessity of a dual approach: mastering theoretical frameworks alongside their practical implementations. As market environments continually shift, traders must perpetually refine their models, integrating insights from market microstructure theory to optimize execution quality and overall profitability.

In the competitive landscape of finance, an edge is gained not solely through the quantitative sophistication of models but through a nuanced understanding of the market environment in which they operate.

In the fast-paced world of algorithmic trading, the importance of understanding regulatory implications cannot be overstated. These regulations are not just a set of bureaucratic obstacles; they are essential components that define the operational landscape for traders and firms. Through a robust regulatory framework, the industry aims to safeguard market integrity, transparency, and fairness. Failing to adhere to these rules can lead to significant consequences, including substantial fines, loss of trading licenses, and irreparable damage to reputations. As trading technology advances and increasingly intertwines with regulatory standards, it becomes imperative for quantitative traders to approach this complex environment with both diligence and sophistication.

Understanding the Regulatory Landscape for Algorithmic Trading

Around the globe, regulatory bodies have established various frameworks aimed at governing algorithmic trading practices. These regulations address critical issues such as market manipulation, systemic risk, and protections for retail investors. In the United States, for example, the Securities and Exchange Commission (SEC) and the Commodity Futures Trading Commission (CFTC) play crucial roles in overseeing trading activities across various exchanges, ensuring compliance at all levels.

Firms engaged in algorithmic trading are often required to register with the appropriate regulatory authorities and to meet specific reporting obligations. Take, for instance, broker-dealers: they must not only disclose the intricacies of their algorithmic strategies but also demonstrate how these strategies align with their risk management frameworks and address any potential failures. Such mandated disclosures allow regulators to gain valuable insights into trading behaviors, enabling them to oversee activities effectively and intervene should issues arise.

Key Regulations Shaping Algorithmic Trading

Several regulations illustrate the profound impact of legal frameworks on the operations of quantitative traders.

2. MiFID II: A European Benchmark

The Markets in Financial Instruments Directive II (MiFID II), implemented by the European Union, marks a significant regulatory evolution affecting algorithmic trading. This comprehensive legislation includes provisions focused on enhancing transparency and imposing stricter guidelines on algorithmic trading systems.

A pivotal requirement under Article 17 of MiFID II is for firms employing algorithmic trading to ensure their systems are resilient, perform reliably during market stress, and undergo regular testing. Transparency is also a crucial focus; firms are tasked with disclosing the operational details of their algorithms to bolster market integrity. Compliance necessitates thorough backtesting of all trading strategies, thereby ensuring that potential disruptions are preemptively identified and mitigated. For instance, a trading firm using a high-frequency trading algorithm must adhere to stringent performance and risk standards established by MiFID II, safeguarding against adverse reactions from both clients and regulators in the event of erratic trading patterns.

3. Reg NMS: Ensuring Market Fairness in the U.S.

In the United States, Regulation National Market System (Reg NMS) is fundamental to the framework guiding algorithmic traders. Designed to promote market transparency and efficiency, this regulation lays out a foundation for fair market access. It requires brokers to execute orders following designated pricing rules, mandating adherence to the National

Best Bid and Offer (NBBO) standards.

For example, algorithmic traders must ensure their systems are programmed to refrain from executing trades at prices inferior to the NBBO when routing orders across various exchanges. Non-compliance can result in regulatory scrutiny and potential penalties.

The Crucial Role of Risk Management Protocols

Effective risk management is intrinsically linked to regulatory compliance. Quantitative strategies must not only align with regulations but also incorporate robust controls to identify and mitigate risks related to automated trading. High-frequency trading firms often implement advanced pre-trade risk controls to avert substantial losses stemming from algorithmic errors or unintended trading behaviors.

4. Illustrating Risk Control Mechanisms

Consider a quantitative trader who designs an algorithm to exploit arbitrage opportunities across multiple exchanges. To fulfill regulatory obligations, the firm might establish a cap on the exposure each transaction can incur in relation to the firm's overall capital. Furthermore, implementing real-time monitoring of all executed trades allows for the swift cancellation of any trades that appear suspicious or anomalous, thereby preempting regulatory alarms.

The Evolving Nature of Regulation in Algorithmic Trading

The regulatory landscape governing algorithmic trading is continuously evolving. In recent years, regulators have reacted not only to identified risks but also to the changing dynamics of the market—especially in the wake of incidents that highlighted the far-reaching consequences of unregulated trading activity. A significant example is the Flash Crash of 2010, which underscored the potential for rapid and erratic price movements to cause widespread market dislocation —prompting regulatory reviews and subsequent policy adjustments.

5. Future Directions in Algorithmic Trading Regulations

As algorithmic trading becomes increasingly integrated into financial markets, traders should remain vigilant regarding upcoming regulatory trends. Potential focal points for future regulations may include:

- Interconnectivity Risks: There may be greater scrutiny on how interconnected trading systems across various markets could amplify systemic risk. Regulatory bodies may require enhanced disclosures regarding algorithms that interact with multiple exchanges.

- Ethical AI Applications: As artificial intelligence continues to shape trading paradigms, regulators are likely to establish guidelines that govern the ethical deployment of AI algorithms, particularly those exhibiting self-learning capabilities.

A comprehensive understanding of regulatory implications equips quantitative traders with essential tools to excel in a complex compliance environment. Approaching regulations not as mere obstacles but as vital frameworks for responsible trading empowers firms to adeptly navigate the intricate challenges of algorithmic trading. Staying informed about regulatory developments and adjusting strategies accordingly will be critical for ongoing success in the dynamic landscape of quantitative finance.

Backtesting execution strategies is an essential practice in the realm of algorithmic trading, acting as a crucial link that connects theoretical concepts to actual market behavior. It enables traders to simulate how their strategies would have performed against historical data, shedding light on their potential effectiveness and associated risks. This rigorous process not only allows for the refinement of strategies but also fosters greater confidence before committing real capital to market trades.

Understanding the Fundamentals of
Backtesting Execution Strategies

To embark on an effective backtesting journey, it's imperative to start with a precise definition of the strategy's parameters. This includes determining entry and exit points, defining the trade duration, and establishing criteria for executing trades. For instance, consider a basic momentum-based trading strategy that seeks to leverage price fluctuations. A trader might define their entry criteria as the stock price crossing above its 50-day moving average, while concurrently implementing a stop-loss level to mitigate potential risks.

Central to backtesting is the collection of robust historical stock price data, encompassing essential information such as opening, high, low, and closing prices over a defined period. Astute traders understand that market conditions—like volatility and liquidity—can greatly influence execution quality. Therefore, an effective backtest must comprehensively consider not only the trading signals but also how the market might respond to those signals.

A Step-by-Step Approach to Backtesting

1. Data Collection: Gather historical data pertinent to the assets and trading strategy in question. This data can be sourced from trusted financial platforms like Bloomberg and Reuters or obtained from open-source datasets.

2. Define Execution Variables: Identify critical parameters, including order types (e.g., market or limit orders), execution strategies (such as co-located servers or smart order routing), and associated costs like slippage and commissions.

3. Develop a Backtesting Engine: Utilize programming

languages, such as Python or R, to automate the backtesting process. Here's an illustrative Python snippet to demonstrate how to structure a backtest for a simple moving average crossover strategy:

```python
python import pandas as pd import numpy as np

\#\# Load historical data
data = pd.read_csv('historical_stock_data.csv')
data['Date'] = pd.to_datetime(data['Date'])
data.set_index('Date', inplace=True)

\#\# Calculate moving averages
data['SMA50'] = data['Close'].rolling(window=50).mean()
data['SMA200'] = data['Close'].rolling(window=200).mean()

\#\# Generate buy/sell signals
data['Signal'] = 0
data['Signal'][50:]    =    np.where(data['SMA50'][50:]    >
data['SMA200'][50:], 1, 0)
data['Position'] = data['Signal'].diff()

\#\# Calculate portfolio value
initial_capital = 100000
shares = 100
data['Portfolio']           =           (data['Close']          *
data['Position'].shift()).cumsum() * shares + initial_capital
```

1. Simulate Trades: Execute trades according to the defined signals, ensuring that each trade is processed at the closing price of each signal bar while incorporating transaction costs into the simulation.

2. Evaluate Performance Metrics: Assess the strategy using relevant performance metrics, including:

3. Sharpe Ratio: This measures the risk-adjusted performance of the strategy.

4. Maximum Drawdown: This indicates the largest peak-to-trough decline observed during the backtesting period.

5. Win/Loss Ratio: It reflects the proportion of profitable trades relative to losing ones.

6. Conduct Sensitivity Analysis: Adjust key assumptions to explore their effects on performance. This could involve altering transaction costs, modifying time frames, or simulating various market conditions.

Recognizing Limitations and Challenges

While backtesting offers valuable insights, it is not without its limitations. Historical performance does not guarantee future success; therefore, traders must proceed with caution. A common pitfall is overfitting—where a strategy is overly tailored to past data, potentially leading to subpar performance in real-world trading. Additionally, it's vital that backtests account for transaction costs and slippage, as neglecting these factors can result in an overly optimistic portrayal of a strategy's effectiveness.

Case Study: A Detailed Evaluation of an Execution Strategy

Let's delve into a comprehensive backtest of a straightforward execution strategy aimed at minimizing slippage. Imagine a trader using an algorithm that places trades based on prevailing market conditions while simultaneously issuing limit orders just above the current market price to minimize slippage.

1. Execution Setup: Achieving minimal slippage starts with defining the maximum acceptable deviation from the anticipated price, which could be calculated as a percentage of the stock's average daily trading range.

2. Running the Backtest: As the backtest unfolds, each triggered limit order is assessed against historical execution prices. It is crucial to document instances where the specified price could not be achieved due to market movements to evaluate the overall effectiveness of limit orders compared to market orders.

3. Analyzing Results: After simulating trades over five years' worth of historical data, a trader may uncover that while their strategy achieved a 70% fill rate at the desired limit price, slippage adversely affected overall profitability, ultimately compressing the effective Sharpe Ratio. These findings necessitate a reevaluation of the strategy, prompting adjustments to the limit price or an exploration of alternative execution strategies, such as VWAP (Volume Weighted Average Price) orders, which may enhance fill rates under specific market conditions.

Backtesting execution strategies is not merely a one-time endeavor; it is a continuous cycle of refinement and adaptation. Savvy traders recognize the importance of backtesting as a persistent practice, allowing them to iteratively improve their strategies in response to ever-evolving market dynamics.

Cross-Asset and Multi-Market Trading Considerations

Understanding Interconnected Markets

At the core of successful cross-asset trading lies the dynamic interplay between various financial instruments — such as equities, fixed income, commodities, and currencies. A deep understanding of how these assets influence one another is essential for creating effective strategies. For instance, shifts in interest rates can trigger cascading effects across markets, dampening bond prices and, indirectly, impacting equities reliant on favorable borrowing conditions. A strategically designed trading plan acknowledges these interrelationships and positions itself to exploit them effectively.

Consider a scenario in which increasing interest rates in a significant economy fuel expectations of a strengthening currency. A well-crafted cross-asset strategy might involve shorting bonds anticipated to decline in value while simultaneously initiating long positions in the currency futures of that nation. The resulting interconnected positions can function not only as a hedge but also as a stabilizing force for returns amidst fluctuating market conditions.

Diversifying Across Geographies

Multi-market trading enhances the analysis by extending its focus beyond asset classes to encompass geographical diversification. Global markets frequently respond to macroeconomic events in distinct manners, influenced by differing economic frameworks and regulatory landscapes. A proficient strategist must evaluate these global nuances and weave them into their models to capture profitable opportunities.

For example, a geopolitical occurrence affecting European equities may elicit a different reaction in Asian markets based on their specific exposure to the event. Crafting successful multi-market strategies demands exhaustive data collection and analysis, enabling thinkers to comprehend local market behaviors, assess liquidity conditions, and gauge execution costs.

Harnessing Technology for Execution

In today's trading environment, technology serves as the backbone of effective cross-asset and multi-market trading. Cutting-edge tools allow traders to process vast datasets, uncover meaningful patterns, and execute transactions at unprecedented speed. Advanced algorithms, fueled by machine learning, can analyze correlations across different asset classes and recognize price disparities, thus delivering invaluable insights into market mechanics.

Take statistical arbitrage as an illustrative example. This strategy leverages historical relationships among asset prices to identify trading opportunities. With rapid computational capabilities, traders can swiftly pinpoint and capitalize on anomalies. Imagine if gold and silver, traditionally correlated, temporarily diverge in price; an algorithm could autonomously initiate trades to seize potential profits as these assets realign with their historical relationships.

Navigating Risks and Implementing Mitigations

Although cross-asset trading holds the potential for attractive returns, it is accompanied by inherent risks that must not be overlooked. A comprehensive understanding of factors such as currency volatility, varying regulatory environments, and liquidity challenges is crucial for effective risk management. For instance, a sudden political upheaval might lead to unexpected currency declines, which can dramatically impact the profitability of cross-border trading strategies.

To counterbalance these risks, it's essential to adopt a robust risk management framework that incorporates nuanced hedging instruments and flexible adjustment strategies. Employing portfolio stress testing against both historical data and hypothetical scenarios can provide critical insights into how different market shocks might impact trading strategies, thereby allowing proactive recalibrations.

Real-World Applications

A prominent example of successful cross-asset strategies can be observed in leading hedge funds that adopt a multi-strategy approach. These funds expertly balance various trading methods—such as global macro positions, relative value trades, and volatility arbitrage—across a wide array of asset classes.

To thrive in the arena of cross-asset and multi-market trading, quantitative traders must continuously adapt to the evolving landscape of market interconnections and technological innovations. A sophisticated yet flexible trading approach is essential, incorporating data-driven models, vigilant risk management, and an ongoing assessment of market conditions. As the global financial ecosystem continues to evolve, mastering the art of navigating these interconnected platforms not only unlocks pathways to alpha generation but also signals the next frontier of innovative trading strategies.

The Future of Trading Technology: An In-Depth Exploration

As financial markets increasingly embrace the digital revolution, the evolution of trading technology is being driven at an unprecedented pace. These advancements are reshaping the trading landscape with novel tools and methodologies that empower quantitative strategists, enhancing operational efficiencies and opening doors to innovative alpha-generating strategies. The future of trading technology is a tapestry woven from breakthroughs in artificial intelligence (AI), blockchain, quantum computing, and other transformative innovations—all poised to redefine the very mechanics of financial trading.

Artificial Intelligence: Transforming the Trading Landscape

Artificial intelligence is set to play a pivotal role in shaping the future of trading. The sophistication of AI-powered algorithms allows traders to analyze colossal datasets at lightning speed and with remarkable precision, uncovering patterns that were once hidden from sight. For instance, deep learning models enable the processing of unstructured data types—like news articles or social media sentiment— effectively informing trading decisions.

A particularly exciting application of AI in the trading domain is the use of reinforcement learning in portfolio management. This interactive technique mimics human learning processes, iteratively refining strategies through a cycle of trial and adjustment. Imagine a reinforcement learning algorithm that autonomously rebalances a portfolio in response to fluctuating market dynamics.

Blockchain: Enhancing Security and Efficiency

The rise of blockchain technology heralds a transformative era for trading practices, marked by improved transaction efficiency and heightened security. Known for its transparency and integrity, blockchain secures individual transactions through an immutable ledger, which ultimately builds trust and traceability among market participants.

One particularly exciting avenue is the use of smart contracts —self-executing agreements where the terms are encoded within the blockchain. Picture a future where cross-border trades settle instantly upon fulfilling predefined conditions, effectively eliminating the delays that often plague traditional settlement processes. This innovation stands to significantly mitigate counterparty risk while enhancing market liquidity, thereby fostering a more resilient and inclusive trading ecosystem.

Quantum Computing: A New Frontier

While still in its infancy, quantum computing promises to upend conventional computational limits, offering quantum speed boosts for processing intricate algorithms. Though practical applications in trading remain on the horizon, the potential impact is immense. The capability to solve complex linear equations at such accelerated rates could pave the way for developing avant-garde quantitative strategies that meld speed with computational power.

Consider this: tasks that may currently require hours or even days of computation could be completed in mere seconds with quantum technology. The ramifications for traders are groundbreaking—improved precision in modeling risk scenarios and the ability to respond rapidly to shifting market conditions could redefine competitive advantages in the marketplace.

Decentralized Finance: A Paradigm Shift

Decentralized finance (DeFi) is poised to revolutionize the traditional finance paradigms by eliminating intermediaries through blockchain-powered digital platforms.

In this evolving landscape, we can envision the emergence of synthetic assets—financial instruments whose value derives from underlying assets like stocks or commodities, somewhat akin to options and futures. These assets can be traded on decentralized exchanges, offering new avenues for hedging and speculation, unrestricted by the limitations often imposed by centralized brokers.

Harnessing Edge Computing for Low Latency

In the high-stakes world of trading, where milliseconds can mean the difference between profit and loss, minimizing latency is paramount. Enter edge computing—an innovative approach that brings data processing closer to the source, significantly reducing the time spent waiting for data to travel between central servers and trading platforms.

Imagine an algorithmic trading system equipped to conduct real-time data analysis right on the trading floor, leveraging edge computing to execute trades almost instantaneously. This capability for rapid action will become increasingly critical as markets evolve into highly automated and competitive arenas.

The future of trading technology presents a landscape ripe with opportunity, characterized by challenges that will require traders to adapt continually. Embracing these advancements mandates a commitment to enhancing skill sets and a proactive approach to understanding the latest technological progress while holding fast to foundational trading principles.

As the fabric of financial markets intertwines more deeply with technological innovation, quantitative strategists stand on the brink of extraordinary advancements. Mastery over these upcoming developments will not only sharpen a trader's competitive edge but also point the way toward groundbreaking strategies in an exciting new era of finance.

CHAPTER 8: BEHAVIORAL FINANCE AND MARKET INEFFICIENCIES

Behavioral finance lays bare the intricacies of phenomena that classic financial theories can't quite explain, such as unexpected asset price movements and market anomalies. Conventional finance rests on the premise of the efficient market hypothesis (EMH), suggesting that asset prices reflect all available information. Behavioral finance, contrastingly, contests this view by illustrating that human irrationality and cognitive biases often lead to discernible patterns and market inefficiencies, paving the way for informed trading strategies.

Cognitive Biases: The Invisible Forces at Play

Cognitive biases—systematic deviations from rational thought—play a crucial role in decision-making processes within financial markets. Behavioral finance identifies a range of biases that consistently influence investor behavior:

1. Overconfidence Bias: Many investors tend to overestimate their knowledge and predictive abilities. This overconfidence can lead to reckless trading decisions, as individuals miscalculate risks

based on an inflated sense of self-assuredness. For instance, a trader might engage in frequent speculative transactions, certain they can accurately forecast price movements, only to face substantial losses as they confront unpredictable market shifts.

2. Anchoring: This bias occurs when individuals cling too closely to an initial piece of information while making decisions. For example, an investor might become fixated on a stock's historical price, using that figure as a benchmark—even when conditions change drastically. This reliance can lead to misguided choices amid volatile market fluctuations.

3. Loss Aversion: A well-documented phenomenon, loss aversion reflects a tendency for individuals to prioritize avoiding losses over achieving gains. This bias can manifest as a refusal to sell losing investments, driven by the hope that prices will rebound, rather than taking the pragmatic step of cutting losses at the right moment.

The Emotional Underpinnings of Market Movements

Emotions significantly impact financial decision-making, often amplifying cognitive biases. Consider the phenomenon of fear of missing out (FOMO), which can prompt investors to buy at peak prices, driven by anxiety over potential gains slipping away. Conversely, panic can incite hasty selling during market downturns. Collectively, these emotional responses create market sentiment that can lead to feedback loops, causing price fluctuations that exceed fundamental valuations, ultimately resulting in market bubbles or crashes.

Take the dot-com bubble of the late 1990s as a prime example. Fueled by rampant enthusiasm about the internet revolution, investors drove stock prices to unprecedented heights, largely ignoring basic valuation principles. The ensuing crash underscored the profound influence of sentiment on market dynamics.

Harnessing Behavioral Insights for Quantitative Strategies

For quantitative strategists, an understanding of behavioral patterns provides a wealth of opportunities to create models that exploit human misjudgments.

Moreover, the infusion of sentiment analysis into quantitative models has gained considerable traction. Utilizing natural language processing (NLP) tools, analysts can assess market sentiment through news articles, earnings calls, and social media, yielding real-time indicators of collective investor mood.

The Imperative of Behavioral Awareness in Investing

Integrating behavioral finance into trading strategies not only equips investors with a competitive advantage but also promotes a more holistic perspective on market analysis. As the digital landscape expands and psychological insights mature, recognizing and adapting to human behavior becomes essential for those aspiring to deepen their understanding of market mechanisms.

Ultimately, behavioral finance reveals the limitations of traditional financial models while enriching the field of quantitative strategies. Embracing these insights is a vital step towards creating more sophisticated and resilient models in which the exploration of human emotion becomes a powerful tool rather than an obstacle to informed decision-making. This synergy aligns seamlessly with the overarching goal of outperforming market benchmarks while maintaining a balanced approach to risk and reward.

In the complex choreography of financial markets, where traders constantly strive to forecast price movements and capitalize on them, the subtle yet powerful influence of cognitive biases plays a critical role. These biases, deeply rooted in human psychology, shape how traders perceive, interpret, and respond to financial signals and market developments.

Overconfidence Bias

One of the most prevalent cognitive biases in trading is overconfidence bias. This bias results in an exaggerated belief in one's ability to predict market outcomes, often driving traders to engage in excessive trading and underappraise risks. Picture a trader who, buoyed by a streak of recent successes, becomes convinced that they possess a unique insight into market dynamics. They may impulsively pursue high-risk trades, dismissing potential pitfalls. Such overconfidence was starkly illustrated in the lead-up to the 2008 financial crisis, characterized by a widespread underestimation of risk as many investors believed the housing market would continue its upward trajectory indefinitely.

Anchoring

Anchoring bias occurs when traders fixate on initial pieces of information, often distorting their evaluations of assets and overlooking emerging opportunities. For instance, a trader might anchor to a stock's historical peak price, stubbornly believing it will rebound despite significant changes in the company's fundamentals. This fixation can hinder timely adjustments to their investment strategies, particularly during periods of volatility when swift recalibrations are essential. The anchoring effect can be particularly damaging during economic upheavals, such as the abrupt market corrections seen during major global crises.

Confirmation Bias

Confirmation bias manifests as a tendency to seek out information that reinforces existing beliefs while dismissing contradictory evidence. This selective perception can lead traders to surround themselves with data that supports their market outlooks, creating a skewed understanding of reality. For example, a bullish trader focused exclusively on positive corporate earnings within the technology sector may ignore broader economic signals, such as faltering consumer spending in related industries. This lack of objectivity can substantially compromise their investment decisions.

Loss Aversion

Loss aversion describes the inclination to prioritize avoiding losses over securing gains of equal value. Within trading contexts, this bias often leads to holding onto losing positions far longer than logic would suggest, driven by a fear of realizing losses. As a result, traders may find themselves trapped in underperforming assets, missing out on more promising opportunities elsewhere. A poignant example is observed during the dot-com bubble's implosion, where many traders clung desperately to tumbling tech stocks, hoping for a miraculous recovery—often to their great detriment.

Recency Bias

Recency bias involves an overemphasis on recent trends when predicting future outcomes. Traders influenced by this bias may become overly enthusiastic following a series of positive market movements or unduly pessimistic after minor downturns. Decision-making based on short-term patterns rather than long-term economic fundamentals can lead to misguided strategies. This behavior was notably evident during the swift market recovery following the initial COVID-19 sell-off in March 2020, when many investors mistakenly interpreted a brief rebound as the dawn of a new bull market, overlooking the serious underlying economic uncertainties.

Herd Behavior

Herd behavior stems from the natural human tendency to conform to group actions, often leading to the phenomenon of a 'bandwagon effect' in trading. When traders observe a significant number of their peers opting for specific stocks or asset classes, they may feel compelled to follow, driven by the fear of missing out. This collective behavior can exponentially escalate market bubbles, as demonstrated by the GameStop trading frenzy in early 2021. Motivated by social media-driven momentum, both individual and institutional investors experienced significant volatility and financial repercussions as they chased rapidly inflating prices.

Implications for Quantitative Strategies

Being aware of these biases allows quantitative strategists to craft models that capitalize on behavioral patterns inherent in the markets. For example, contrarian strategies can advantageously take positions opposite to the crowd during times of extreme sentiment, while adaptive models can identify overbought or oversold market conditions caused by recency and anchoring biases, providing strategic entry and exit points. This fusion of knowledge equips them to counteract the noise and emotional turbulence that often obscure sound financial judgment. Cultivating a disciplined mindset is essential for consistently generating alpha in the face of the complexities posed by ever-evolving market conditions.

Acknowledging and understanding cognitive biases not only offers a tactical advantage in developing quantitative strategies but also fosters a more structured and effective trading approach.

The Dynamic Role of Sentiment in Financial Markets

In the intricate tapestry of financial markets, sentiment emerges as a potent yet elusive force—one that can sway investor behavior with the same magnitude as company earnings or pivotal economic indicators. Trader sentiment, often expressed through fluctuating levels of optimism or pessimism, significantly influences market movements.

Understanding the Sentiment-Market Connection

At its core, sentiment embodies the collective emotions and

attitudes of investors towards specific assets or broader market conditions. This psychological layer diverges from traditional rational analysis, which prioritizes concrete data points. Sentiment captures the varied emotional factors that drive market behavior—often leading individuals to make choices that defy logical expectation. This emotional backdrop can intensify prevailing trends, trigger market reversals, and contribute to increased volatility.

Consider the case of a burgeoning tech startup: when positive sentiment is fueled by upbeat media coverage and an enthusiastic social media presence, it can spark a buying frenzy that drives stock prices far beyond their intrinsic values. Conversely, during periods of economic uncertainty— such as the early days of the COVID-19 pandemic—fear-driven sentiment can prompt sudden sell-offs, as widespread panic cascades through the market.

Navigating Sentiment Indicators

To gauge the prevailing mood in the market, quantitative strategists often turn to sentiment indicators as vital tools for analysis. These indicators, drawn from a variety of sources, offer valuable insights into the emotional landscape governing market behavior.

- Sentiment Surveys: Instruments like the AAII Investor Sentiment Survey provide quantitative measures of bullish and bearish sentiments among investors.

- Options Market Metrics: The put/call ratio serves as a barometer of sentiment in the options market, illustrating the balance between bearish and bullish bets. A high put/call ratio may indicate excessive pessimism, signaling a contrarian buying opportunity.

- Social Media Analytics: The advent of natural

language processing (NLP) facilitates the analysis of sentiment across vast platforms of digital communication.

Interpreting these indicators requires a sophisticated understanding of sentiment dynamics. For instance, an elevated put/call ratio may suggest an overly negative outlook, creating potential buying opportunities for those willing to challenge the consensus.

Behavioral Patterns Stemming from Sentiment

Market movements driven by sentiment often reflect distinct behavioral patterns. One prominent example is herding behavior, in which investors imitate one another's actions, thereby amplifying price movements. This phenomenon can lead to the creation of speculative bubbles, reminiscent of the dot-com era when exuberant sentiment overshadowed fundamental evaluations.

Moreover, the cyclical nature of exuberance and pessimism can deepen market volatility. During euphoric periods, investors might disregard potential red flags, resulting in unsustainable asset price increases. Conversely, during pessimistic phases, even favorable developments can be eclipsed by dominant negative sentiment, stifling market recoveries.

The Integration of Sentiment into Quantitative Models

By incorporating sentiment analysis into quantitative frameworks, traders can enhance their predictive capabilities and refine their strategic positions. Advanced machine learning algorithms can analyze historical sentiment alongside price movements to identify patterns and provide forecasts.

For instance, a sentiment-driven momentum strategy may leverage real-time sentiment scores to corroborate bullish signals, thereby allowing traders to mitigate their exposure in unfavorable conditions. This approach has proven particularly effective in volatile sectors like cryptocurrency, where sentiment often acts as a principal price mover. Models adept at detecting shifts in sentiment have afforded traders substantial advantages, enabling them to navigate landscapes shaped by heightened speculation.

Identifying Market Anomalies Through Sentiment

Quantitative strategies that integrate sentiment analysis are uniquely positioned to uncover market anomalies. Periods of extreme sentiment can lead to temporary divergences from market efficiency, unveiling opportunities for arbitrage.

Embracing the role of sentiment in market fluctuations empowers traders to transcend the limitations of conventional financial analysis. This blend of psychological insight with quantitative rigor not only enhances trading resilience but also fosters a more profound understanding of the human factors driving financial markets.

In an ever-evolving market landscape influenced by emotional currents, the ability to interpret and harness sentiment provides a strategic advantage.

Exploring Market Inefficiencies: Uncovering Opportunities in Financial Markets

Market inefficiencies refer to the instances when asset prices deviate from their true intrinsic values. These deviations occur due to various factors, including irrational investor behavior, transaction costs, and barriers to information flow. Identifying these inefficiencies is essential for developing robust quantitative strategies aimed at outperforming the market.

Historical Perspectives on Market Inefficiencies

Historically, market inefficiencies have played a critical role in shaping financial narratives, often leading to dramatic gains or catastrophic losses. Consider the infamous Tulip Mania of

17th-century Holland or the dot-com bubble that gripped the early 2000s. In both cases, exultant sentiment and rampant speculation drove asset prices far beyond their fundamental values, creating fertile ground for market inefficiencies.

Examining these historical events reveals valuable lessons about the cycles of irrational market behavior and the patterns that signal emerging inefficiencies.

Key Tools for Identifying Market Inefficiencies

In the quest to uncover market inefficiencies, quantitative analysts employ a myriad of techniques and tools. Familiarity with these methodologies enables strategists to pinpoint where and when anomalies occur.

- Statistical Arbitrage: This approach utilizes advanced statistical models to identify pricing discrepancies between related securities. For instance, pairs trading takes advantage of the price relationship between two correlated stocks. When the price diverges significantly from historical norms, traders can anticipate a return to the mean, executing trades that capitalize on this inefficiency.

- Event Studies: By analyzing how markets react to corporate events—such as earnings announcements or product launches—traders can unveil inefficiencies arising from mispriced assets. This methodology scrutinizes immediate market reactions against long-term performances, revealing potential overreactions or underreactions to events.

- Technical Analysis: Utilizing chart-based techniques such as moving averages and the relative strength index (RSI), traders can identify trends and reversals that indicate inefficiencies. Unlike fundamental analysis, which relies on company metrics, technical analysis focuses on price movements, yielding insights into market sentiments that contribute to inefficiencies.

Real-World Cases of Market Inefficiency

One compelling illustration is the January Effect, a phenomenon where stock prices tend to rise in January following declines in December. This seasonal pattern often results from investors selling off underperforming stocks for tax benefits at year-end and subsequently reinvesting in the new year. Quantitative strategists can leverage historical data to create models that exploit this consistent pattern, positioning themselves to benefit from expected price upticks.

Another notable example is the small-cap anomaly, where smaller companies consistently outperform their larger counterparts.

The Influence of Information Asymmetry

Market inefficiencies often emerge from information asymmetry—situations where one group of participants possesses superior access to information compared to others. High-frequency trading firms, for instance, harness sophisticated algorithms to acquire and act on information mere milliseconds ahead of their competitors, allowing them to profit from fleeting inefficiencies before they correct themselves.

However, it's not just the speed of information access that matters. Qualitative factors—including expert insights and proprietary research—also play crucial roles in gaining an informational edge, empowering traders to anticipate market shifts ahead of broader trends.

Navigating the Challenges of Exploiting Inefficiencies

While market inefficiencies offer tantalizing opportunities, they also present significant challenges. Transaction costs, the rapid dissemination of information, and the unpredictable nature of market sentiment can diminish potential profits.

Moreover, inefficiencies can be transient, necessitating agile responses and ongoing model refinements to maintain effectiveness.

Equally important is understanding the regulatory landscape. Engaging in unethical practices or exploiting privileged information not only raises moral concerns but also legal ramifications. A rigorous adherence to ethical standards is paramount in developing successful trading strategies.

Advancing Detection with Machine Learning

Machine learning emerges as a powerful ally in the pursuit of identifying and exploiting market inefficiencies with precision and speed. Sophisticated algorithms can sift through vast datasets, uncovering hidden correlations and subtle patterns that human analysts might overlook.

For instance, reinforcement learning models can simulate trading environments where strategies interact with synthetic markets, making adjustments based on feedback from past actions. This adaptive approach enhances the ability to respond to inefficiencies, optimizing trading strategies for increased accuracy and returns.

The pursuit of identifying and capitalizing on market inefficiencies remains an engaging and complex aspect of quantitative finance. Traders and analysts who excel in this discipline can gain a crucial competitive edge, positioning themselves to seize unique opportunities for enhanced returns.

Success in this arena requires a harmonious blend of historical insight, advanced analytical tools, and strategic foresight. As market conditions continuously evolve, every inefficiency corrected paves the way for the discovery of new ones. To thrive, practitioners must remain vigilant, innovative, and ethically grounded, balancing analytical rigor with the dynamic realities of global financial markets.

Quantitative Approaches to Behavioral Finance

Behavioral finance delves into the intricate ways psychological influences and cognitive biases shape the financial decisions made by individuals and the broader market. This divergence presents a rich playground for quantitative strategies designed to exploit predictable patterns rooted in human emotion and cognition. Integrating behavioral finance with quantitative methods requires a sophisticated blend of statistical precision and deep psychological insight.

Bridging Behavioral Insights with Quantitative Models

In order to harmonize the principles of behavioral finance with quantitative analysis, strategists develop models that quantify the impact of psychological factors on asset pricing. The key challenge lies in transforming qualitative theories into rigorous, quantifiable strategies that can withstand scrutiny across various market conditions.

Prevalent Biases and Quantitative Exploitation

The foundation of effective quantitative modeling in behavioral finance is laid upon several cognitive biases that significantly shape market behavior:

- Overconfidence Bias: Many investors exhibit overconfidence in their ability to predict market movements, often leading to excessive trading and mispricing of assets. Quantitative models can analyze trading patterns to identify instances of overconfidence, utilizing statistical thresholds to gauge when this bias skews prices. Strategies that counter overconfident trends can harness these mispricings, enabling investors to capture alpha.

- Anchoring: Investors often anchor their judgments to initial pieces of information, such as the initial price of an asset, which can skew future assessments. Quantitative models that compare historical pricing patterns against recent market data can help forecast potential corrections triggered by dependency on outdated information.

- Loss Aversion: The tendency to prioritize avoiding losses over achieving gains can lead to irrational decision-making and herd behavior.

Quantifying Sentiment Indicators

Investor sentiment provides a critical lens through which to view market dynamics, acting as a barometer of collective perceptions among market participants. Quantitative analysts translate sentiment data into numeric formats, employing advanced sentiment analysis techniques on a myriad of sources such as news articles, blogs, and social media.

For instance, a noticeable dip in positive sentiment during favorable earnings announcements may highlight an inefficiency that investors can exploit. Backtesting historical sentiment trends alongside market performance allows quantitative models to refine strategies aimed at predicting shifts in market sentiment.

Market Sentiment and Price Anomalies

Research has shown that price anomalies often arise from underlying sentiment shifts, creating opportunities for savvy investors. For example, momentum strategies thrive on market underreaction to good news and overreaction to bad news, positioning investors to maintain long positions in assets with favorable sentiment while shorting those facing negative sentiment backlash. Such strategies rely on observed delays in market reactions to information, creating openings for timely trades that capture price corrections.

Implementing Behavioral Strategies with Technology

The rapid advancements in computational technology and machine learning techniques have propelled the capabilities of quantitative models, allowing for the automated detection of behavioral patterns. Leveraging vast datasets, researchers can test various behavioral hypotheses and refine parameters to cultivate robust predictive models.

Innovative approaches, such as the employment of artificial neural networks, are especially promising. These models are capable of identifying intricate, non-linear relationships between behavioral indicators and price movements.

Case Studies: Real-World Applications

One compelling example of successfully integrating sentiment analysis into investment strategies involved predicting post-recession stock market recoveries.

Another notable case employed Google search volume indices as a gauge of investor anxiety. Strategies that tracked spikes in search activity around financial distress terms demonstrated a strong capacity for predicting heightened market volatility, allowing for timely asset reallocations to mitigate potential losses.

The intersection of behavioral finance and quantitative analysis offers a profound framework for uncovering and exploiting market inefficiencies. As technology progresses and data becomes increasingly accessible, these integrated methodologies will enhance predictive accuracy and deepen our understanding of the psychological dynamics at play in financial markets.

In a landscape where conventional financial logic often fails to account for behavioral factors, adeptly blending quantitative rigor with psychological insight will undoubtedly be crucial for sustainable alpha generation.

Illuminating Behavioral Anomalies in Finance

Behavioral anomalies manifest as subtle but critical deviations from the rational behavior that conventional financial models often assume. These irregularities, deeply rooted in psychological nuances, present intriguing opportunities for astute investors willing to explore their origins and implications. Through these illuminating case studies, we can observe the intricate interplay between investor psychology and market dynamics, offering essential lessons for practitioners striving to refine their investment strategies.

The Dot-Com Bubble: An Exploration of Irrational Exuberance

In the late 1990s, the technology sector experienced meteoric growth, largely propelled by speculative fervor rather than the fundamental values typically associated with sound investments. Fueled by visions of revolutionary technological advancements and the promise of remarkable returns, investors succumbed to a pervasive wave of irrational exuberance—a term made famous by then-Federal Reserve Chairman Alan Greenspan. This exuberance was exemplified by the excessive capital inflow into countless Internet startups, many of which boasted little more than a bold idea without a sustainable business model.

Quantitative analysts meticulously dissected this era, revealing alarming discrepancies between the Nasdaq index and traditional valuation frameworks. They noted that the price-to-earnings ratios of technology stocks reached staggering heights, well above long-term averages. By short-selling overpriced tech stocks prior to the bubble's catastrophic burst, these savvy investors demonstrated how understanding behavioral anomalies can yield substantial financial gains.

The Global Financial Crisis: A Lesson in Loss Aversion

The 2008 financial crisis starkly illuminated the devastating effects of loss aversion—a cognitive bias that leads investors to fear losses more intensely than they value equivalent gains. The propulsion of the housing market, strikingly buoyant in the years leading up to the crisis, was not merely a byproduct of financial innovation but also a breeding ground for cognitive dissonance among investors. Homebuyers, seduced by the illusion of perpetual appreciation and emboldened by lenient lending practices, ignored significant underlying risks.

As mortgage-backed securities began to unravel, the ensuing mass exit of investors highlighted the visceral grip of behavioral biases on market activity. Induced panic resulted in a frantic sell-off that precipitated a severe liquidity crisis. Within this tumult, quantitative models that had been honed through historical stress-testing proved invaluable. Investors employing these models navigated the storm with greater resilience by diversifying their portfolios into safe-haven assets like gold and government bonds, effectively shielding themselves from the brunt of significant losses.

The COVID-19 Pandemic: When Emotion Meets Market Volatility

The onset of the COVID-19 pandemic in early 2020 ushered in unprecedented market volatility as global investors grappled with the resulting economic uncertainty. Behavioral finance theories suggested that this volatility would be driven largely by emotional responses, particularly fear, as individuals scrambled for clarity amidst chaos.

Researchers utilizing machine learning models to analyze social media sentiment discovered a striking correlation between fear-driven discourse and movements in market volatility indices. Investors who harnessed these insights crafted volatility-responsive strategies that adapted to the erratic landscape, favoring equities with low beta or retreating into defensive sectors like utilities and healthcare. In doing so, they positioned themselves to benefit from the relative stability offered during such tumultuous times.

Case Study: The GameStop Phenomenon and the Reddit Revolution

In January 2021, the financial world witnessed a captivating intersection of social media influence and retail investor behavior, epitomized by the GameStop short squeeze. Sparked by retail traders congregating on platforms like Reddit's WallStreetBets, this phenomenon highlighted a remarkable behavioral anomaly where traditional valuation metrics were disregarded in favor of fervent collective speculation.

Scrutinizing the extraordinary trading volume and rapid price surges during this period revealed the sheer potency of emergent group behavior—the likes of which diverged sharply from conventional market dynamics driven by institutional actors.

Unveiling Broader Implications

These compelling case studies serve to emphasize the enduring and profound impact of behavioral anomalies on financial markets. They illustrate that quantitative methodologies, skillfully blended with insights from psychology, can form a robust framework for navigating the inherent unpredictability of human behaviors in market dynamics. Whether tapping into vast streams of online sentiment or leveraging historical irregularities, quantitative strategies remain dynamic and continue to evolve in response to the complex relationship between emotion and economic shifts. As global markets grow increasingly interconnected and sentiment-driven, these case studies underscore the imperative for vigilance, creativity, and innovation in maintaining a competitive edge in the ever-shifting landscape of quantitative finance.

The integration of behavioral insights into quantitative financial models is an exciting frontier that has the potential to uncover hidden market dynamics and enhance decision-making processes.

At the heart of this integration is a critical understanding that markets are not strictly rational entities. Human emotions, cognitive biases, and the shortcuts individuals take in their decision-making process profoundly impact market behaviors. When considered in aggregate, these factors can give rise to observable patterns that astute analysts can exploit through carefully designed quantitative models.

To effectively weave behavioral insights into quantitative frameworks, it is essential first to identify the specific biases and irregularities prevalent in market situations. Take, for instance, the availability bias, wherein investors place excessive importance on the most recent information, often leading to overreactions to current events.

Imagine creating a trading algorithm with the capability of predicting market movements by employing news sentiment analysis. While traditional models might depend solely on historical pricing data, a model informed by behavioral economics could analyze the wording employed in financial news articles and social media conversations to gauge shifts in sentiment. Leveraging sophisticated techniques from natural language processing (NLP), these models not only capture emotional tones but also predict behavioral responses, thereby uncovering potential market movements ahead of time.

An illustrative example is a sentiment-driven trading decision system. If you are developing a model focused on forecasting stock prices, you could assign sentiment scores to news articles related to a particular company. This allows for the detection of correlations between variations in sentiment scores and corresponding fluctuations in stock prices. For instance, a sudden spike in negative sentiment could herald an impending sell-off, enabling investors to make strategic adjustments to their positions proactively.

To ensure that this integration is practical and methodical, it's essential to design your model with the following considerations in mind:

1. Utilize Reliable Data Sources: Curate data from multiple avenues, including financial news outlets, corporate earnings calls, and social media platforms. It's crucial to assess each source for trustworthiness

and potential biases to maintain the integrity of the model.

2. Leverage Sentiment Analysis Engines: Either develop or adopt cutting-edge NLP tools that convert textual data into quantifiable sentiment scores. Tools like NLTK for Python or proprietary sentiment analysis software can provide valuable insights effectively.

3. Adapt to Time Sensitivity: Acknowledge the rapid shifts in market sentiment. Your model should be designed to capture and respond to these changes swiftly, ideally in near real-time.

4. Incorporate Behavioral Metrics: Integrate metrics such as volatility indexes, which already embody broader market sentiment. Combining these with direct sentiment analysis can increase the model's predictive accuracy significantly.

5. Employ Robust Backtesting: Implement rigorous backtesting to evaluate how the incorporation of sentiment influences prediction quality. This process allows you to fine-tune model parameters based on empirical results to enhance efficacy in real-world applications.

While the integration of behavioral insights can be transformative, it is essential to remain vigilant about the dangers of overfitting—where a model becomes excessively tailored to historical sentiment data, leading to poor predictive performance in the future. To mitigate this risk, regularly updating models with the latest data and conducting out-of-sample testing are vital practices.

Ultimately, merging behavioral insights with quantitative models represents a powerful confluence of psychology and analytics, enriching our understanding of financial markets. As this field continues to develop, practitioners need to find a delicate balance between behavioral theory and empirical evidence to preserve and amplify the actionable value of their strategies.

Risk management in behavioral finance transcends conventional quantitative approaches by weaving in the psychological factors that significantly influence decision-making.

Behavioral finance highlights our tendency to stray from rational decision-making, primarily due to deeply ingrained cognitive biases. These biases—such as overconfidence, loss aversion, and herd behavior—have profound implications for market behavior and the assessment of risk.

Take, for instance, loss aversion: a phenomenon where investors feel the pain of losses more acutely than the pleasure derived from equivalent gains. This bias can lead to counterproductive behaviors, such as clinging to losing investments far longer than advisable or prematurely selling profitable ones. To navigate this bias effectively, a risk management strategy rooted in behavioral finance could include predetermined stop-loss orders and systematic rebalancing routines that help enforce disciplined decision-making.

Overconfidence presents another significant challenge, often causing traders to underestimate risks and overestimate their ability to forecast market movements. This misguided self-assurance can lead to overexposure—taking larger positions than warranted by an individual's risk tolerance. To combat this tendency, robust risk management strategies might establish strict position limits and employ scenario analyses that illustrate the potential repercussions of over-leveraged positions across various market conditions.

Integrating behavioral insights into risk management can manifest through several key strategies:

1. Scenario Planning and Stress Testing: Design scenarios that take behavioral biases into account, particularly in volatile markets. This involves simulating situations of panic-induced selling or episodes of irrational optimism, allowing managers to prepare for market fluctuations driven by these emotional factors.

2. Feedback Mechanisms: Create systems for immediate recognition and correction of behavioral biases. For example, maintaining trading journals can assist investors in identifying detrimental patterns in their trading habits, fostering self-awareness and facilitating positive adjustments.

3. Behaviorally-Informed Risk Metrics: Traditional risk measurements like Value at Risk (VaR) and Conditional Value at Risk (CVaR) can be enriched by incorporating behavioral insights. Adjusting these metrics to account for shifts in risk tolerance, particularly during phases of overconfidence or loss aversion, provides a more accurate representation of potential vulnerabilities.

4. Training and Education: Invest in educating traders and risk managers regarding common cognitive biases and their manifestation in investment decisions. Programs targeting decision-making under uncertainty can significantly diminish susceptibility to emotional and cognitive distortions.

5. Automated Decision Rules: Develop automated protocols to mitigate emotional influences during high-stress trading periods. Algorithmic trading systems can enforce predefined trading limits or trigger actions based on objective criteria, effectively circumventing human biases that can cloud judgment.

When effectively implemented, these strategies can enhance traditional risk models, fostering a resilient framework that thrives amid unpredictable and emotionally charged market environments. Adopting behavioral finance perspectives allows for a more holistic approach that recognizes the complex, intangible human elements often overlooked in conventional risk assessments.

Nevertheless, prudence is essential to avoid overly complex models or improper attribution of causation. Not all market fluctuations stem from behavioral phenomena, and misinterpretation could inadvertently complicate risk frameworks. Continuous refinement through empirical testing, ongoing learning, and fostering a culture that embraces behavioral insights remain critical to ensuring that risk models remain balanced and pragmatic.

In summary, integrating behavioral finance into risk management enriches our understanding of market dynamics and investor behavior. This comprehensive approach paves the way for more effective risk mitigation strategies, enabling better protection of portfolios against both quantitative volatility and psychological pitfalls. Through this multifaceted lens, financial risk management evolves into a dynamic discipline that accounts not just for numerical calculations, but also for the human reactions that drive market processes.

In the intricate world of financial markets, where emotions often soar alongside the stakes, sentiment indicators emerge as invaluable tools for unraveling the psychological forces at play. These indicators track the mood, opinions, and attitudes of market participants, providing a glimpse into the collective psyche that drives market movements. When combined with traditional quantitative analyses, sentiment indicators can offer investors a distinctive predictive advantage, enabling them to anticipate shifts and adapt their strategies proactively.

The essence of sentiment indicators lies in understanding that emotions play a pivotal role in investment decisions. They often give rise to patterns that are not only identifiable but also exploitable. Unlike conventional market data, which relies on historical performance and fundamental analysis, sentiment delves into more abstract dimensions such as hope, fear, and uncertainty.

Social media sentiment analysis plays a crucial role in this context. Platforms like Twitter, Reddit, and various financial blogs generate vast amounts of textual data that can be analyzed to gauge prevailing market sentiments. Utilizing natural language processing techniques, investors can sift through this data to uncover trends. For example, a significant uptick in positive sentiment towards a particular asset may indicate bullish behavior even before traditional metrics register any change. The infamous GameStop trading frenzy serves as a textbook case illustrating how collective sentiment, sourced from online discussions, can dramatically impact stock prices. This event not only opened doors for strategic gains but also underscored the importance of diligent risk assessment.

To harness the power of sentiment indicators effectively, consider the following approaches:

1. Sentiment Indexes: Develop indexes that aggregate sentiment data from diverse sources, transforming qualitative insights into quantifiable metrics. Take, for instance, the Consumer Confidence Index (CCI), which reflects consumer sentiment about economic conditions and serves as a reliable indicator for broader market trends. Financial analysts can also create proprietary indexes to track daily sentiment fluctuations, offering real-time insights into market attitudes.

2. Machine Learning Models: Leverage advanced machine learning algorithms to refine the sentiment

extraction process. For example, analyzing sentiment from corporate earnings call transcripts can yield predictive insights regarding subsequent stock price reactions.

3. Integration with Technical Analysis: Complement sentiment signals with conventional technical analysis tools. When a positive sentiment trajectory coincides with bullish technical indicators—such as moving averages or breakout patterns—this alignment can bolster predictive confidence, guiding investors on when to enter or exit positions.

4. Event-Driven Strategies: Craft trading strategies driven by significant market events or announcements that impact sentiment.

For instance, imagine an algorithm designed to capitalize on sentiment surrounding quarterly earnings reports. This model might analyze sentiment not just from press releases or CEO comments but also track real-time sentiment shifts on social media platforms.

Despite their potential, utilizing sentiment indicators does present certain challenges. It is crucial to recognize that sentiment data can be noisy and subject to swift changes, often more so than traditional market data. Relying on sentiment-driven trades based on fleeting emotions without empirical backing can lead to misguided conclusions if applied too broadly.

Additionally, ethical considerations come into play when implementing sentiment analysis. The risk of inflating predictions through manipulative sentiment—whether via social bots or orchestrated misinformation campaigns—must be navigated with care to uphold analytical integrity.

In conclusion, the true power of sentiment indicators lies in their ability to illuminate the psychological landscape that underpins financial decision-making. When integrated thoughtfully with other analytical methods, sentiment analysis transcends conventional metrics, offering nuanced insights into market dynamics.

Behavioral finance stands at the intriguing crossroads of psychology and economics, providing invaluable insights that can be instrumental in generating alpha—a term used to describe excess returns on an investment relative to the market index. This field of study delves into the cognitive biases and emotional responses that often influence investors' decisions, leading to market behaviors that deviate from the efficient market hypothesis.

A fundamental aspect of behavioral finance is the recognition that financial markets do not always operate under the assumptions of perfect efficiency. Conventional finance theories suggest that investors behave rationally, basing their decisions solely on logic and available data. However, extensive research in behavioral economics reveals a different reality: individuals often succumb to biases such as overconfidence, loss aversion, and herd mentality.

Consider, for instance, the momentum effect—a well-documented market anomaly where securities that have previously performed well tend to continue their upward trajectory in the short term. This phenomenon can be attributed to behavioral biases, particularly herding, where investors collectively gravitate toward popular stocks, driving their prices even higher than their intrinsic values. Strategists who create quantitative models incorporating momentum indicators can effectively identify securities likely to ride this wave of positive sentiment before the inevitable mean reversion occurs.

Another essential concept in behavioral finance is anchoring— the phenomenon where individuals heavily rely on the initial piece of information, or "anchor," when making decisions.

This bias can result in investors clinging to historical price levels, even as new, relevant information warrants a reevaluation of an asset's value.

Additionally, the disposition effect illustrates a common behavioral bias wherein investors are inclined to sell winning investments too early, while holding onto losing ones, hoping they will recover. Contrarian investing—a strategy that intentionally goes against prevailing market trends—often draws from this inclination, allowing investors to benefit from the natural human instinct to flee from declining prices while chasing after soaring ones.

Integrating these behavioral insights into quantitative models involves a harmonious blend of psychological understanding and analytical rigor. One effective approach is the implementation of machine learning algorithms to detect anomalies driven by sentiment. For example, clustering techniques can be used to group stocks displaying similar sentiment trends influenced by behavioral biases.

Moreover, backtesting these strategies against historical datasets enriched with sentiment indicators and psychological triggers is vital for establishing their predictive efficacy. This empirical validation ensures that the developed strategies are not merely theoretically sound but also robust and responsive in real-world trading environments.

A striking example of behavioral finance in action can be noted during the 2008 financial crisis. During this tumultuous period, biases such as overconfidence led many financial institutions to underestimate systemic risks, while herd behavior contributed to widespread market panic as firms rushed to liquidate assets. Strategies that were attuned to the nuances of these behavioral signals prior to the crisis were better positioned to navigate the volatility, effectively mitigating losses and, in some instances, profiting by identifying overvalued assets to short.

While the marriage of behavioral finance and quantitative strategies is filled with potential, it is essential to proceed with caution. The inherently subjective nature of psychological assessments can complicate model precision. To address this challenge, it is crucial to develop comprehensive frameworks that blend both quantitative data and qualitative behavioral insights, ensuring a balanced and thorough approach.

In conclusion, behavioral finance offers a profound understanding of market dynamics, particularly through the lens of human psychology. Coupling these insights with cutting-edge advancements in data analytics and machine learning equips investors with powerful tools for enhancing their ability to generate alpha in an increasingly intricate financial landscape.

CHAPTER 9: PORTFOLIO CONSTRUCTION AND OPTIMIZATION

The concept of portfolio theory was first introduced by Harry Markowitz in his groundbreaking work on Modern Portfolio Theory (MPT). This revolutionary approach redefined how risk is perceived and managed in investment practices. At its essence, Markowitz's theory suggests that by thoughtfully combining different assets within a portfolio, an investor can achieve a lower overall risk profile than the individual risks associated with each asset alone, thanks to the principle of diversification. This paradigm shift encouraged investors to prioritize the collective risk of their portfolio rather than fixating solely on the volatility of individual investments.

To illustrate this theory in action, consider an investor weighing two distinct stocks: one, a technology firm renowned for its rapid growth but also marked by considerable volatility; the other, a utility company known for its stability and more modest, yet consistent, returns. On their own, the tech stock presents a higher risk profile due to its erratic price movements, whereas the utility stock offers a sense of security. However, when these assets are combined, their differing risk-return characteristics create a complementary effect. In periods of economic expansion, the tech stock may experience significant appreciation, while during downturns, the utility stock's reliable performance helps to cushion overall portfolio volatility. This reciprocal relationship underscores Markowitz's crucial insight: the correlation between asset returns greatly influences the dynamics of portfolio risk.

One of the practical applications stemming from portfolio theory is the calculation of expected return and risk for a given portfolio. The expected return ((E(R_p))) is determined by the weighted average of each individual asset's anticipated return:

$$[E(R\_p) = w\_1E(R\_1) + w\_2E(R\_2) + + w\_nE(R\_n)]$$

Here, (w_i) represents the proportion of the asset within the portfolio, while (E(R_i)) denotes the expected return of asset (i).

Conversely, determining portfolio risk involves a more intricate approach incorporating the variances and covariances of returns to account for the interactions among different assets:

$$[\sigma\_p^2 = \sum\_i=1^n\sum\_j=1^n w\_i w\_j \sigma\_i \sigma\_j \rho\_ij]$$

In this formula, (\sigma_i) and (\sigma_j) symbolize the standard deviations of assets (i) and (j), respectively, and (\rho_ij) signifies the correlation coefficient indicating how the returns of these assets move in relation to one another.

Portfolio theory further leads us to the concept of the efficient frontier—an essential element of MPT. Graphically represented, the efficient frontier delineates a collection of optimal portfolios that offer the highest expected return for any given level of risk. Portfolios that lie on this curve are considered efficient, meaning they maximize return for their risk profile, while those located beneath the frontier fall short of fully leveraging the potential of diversification.

With advancements in computational methods and risk assessment techniques, contemporary investors increasingly employ sophisticated algorithms to identify optimal positions along the efficient frontier. These tools allow for dynamic adjustments to asset allocations in response to changing market conditions, highlighting the critical role that quantitative strategies play in refining portfolio optimization.

The Capital Market Line (CML) complements these concepts by illustrating the relationship between risk-free assets and optimal risky portfolios. The slope of the CML represents the market risk premium, encapsulating the trade-off between risk and return. Investors can adjust their portfolios along the CML through techniques such as leveraging or borrowing, thus tailoring their investment approach to align with their unique risk tolerance and return expectations.

Moreover, portfolio theory must also account for external influences such as market anomalies and behavioral factors that can impact asset returns. Traditional models often presumed rational investor behavior and frictionless trading; however, insights from behavioral finance have enriched this understanding by acknowledging the unpredictable nature of human psychology and its influence on market dynamics.

For example, a strategic portfolio could leverage behavioral biases, such as overreaction or underreaction in stock prices, to better position itself for future corrections. Practical applications might involve applying behavioral insights to refine asset selection or to modify exposure in anticipation of shifts driven by investor sentiment.

The principles of portfolio theory not only form the foundation for advanced investment strategies but also invite a deeper exploration of the subtle interplay between theory and practice in optimal portfolio construction and dynamic asset allocation. Each added layer of complexity opens the door to enhanced opportunities for investors, enabling them to pursue superior risk-adjusted returns in an ever-shifting financial environment.

In the intricate landscape of modern finance, the concept of the efficient frontier stands out as a cornerstone of portfolio theory. This powerful graphical representation not only delineates the range of potential risk-return combinations available to investors but also serves as a vital compass for those aiming to optimize their investment portfolios.

At the heart of the efficient frontier lies the principle of diversification, a revolutionary idea first introduced by economist Harry Markowitz. Each point on this frontier signifies a portfolio that achieves the highest expected return for a given level of risk, while simultaneously detailing the optimal configuration that minimizes risk for a specified level of return. In this context, risk is measured by the standard deviation of a portfolio's returns, which acts as a key indicator of its volatility.

To illustrate this concept, let's imagine an investor working with three distinct asset classes: a high-volatility technology index, a stable government bond index, and an intermediate commercial property index. Each asset comes with its own unique risk-return profile. When these combinations are plotted on a risk-return graph, they converge to form a curve: the efficient frontier. This curve delineates the boundary between optimal and inferior portfolios, guiding investors toward the most effective asset mixes.

Consider the following expected returns and standard deviations for these three asset classes:

1. Technology Index: Expected return of 12%, standard deviation of 20%
2. Government Bonds: Expected return of 4%, standard deviation of 5%
3. Commercial Property: Expected return of 8%, standard deviation of 10%

For example, if an investor allocates 50% of their portfolio to the Technology Index, 30% to Government Bonds, and 20% to Commercial Property, they can calculate the overall expected return of the portfolio:

$[E(R\_p) = 0.5 \ 12\% + 0.3 \ 4\% + 0.2 \ 8\% = 8.8\%]$

Assuming no correlation between the assets for simplicity, the portfolio's standard deviation $((\sigma\_p))$ can be approximated as:

$[\sigma\_p = sqrt((0.5 \ 20\%)^2 + (0.3 \ 5\%)^2 + (0.2 \ 10\%)^2) = 11.6\%]$

This particular allocation showcases a point on the efficient frontier, effectively balancing potential returns with their associated risks.

Integral to the concept of the efficient frontier is the risk-return trade-off that investors face. Higher potential returns often come hand-in-hand with increased risk, encapsulated by the shape of the efficient frontier. This relationship underscores the importance of selecting portfolios that lie on the frontier; portfolios below it indicate opportunities for improvement—where either the same return can be achieved at a lower risk or a higher return can be attained without increasing risk.

This trade-off emphasizes the need for investors to pursue risk-adjusted returns—returns that account for the level of risk taken. Tools such as the Sharpe Ratio allow investors to assess the efficiency of their portfolios by calculating the return per unit of risk. A higher Sharpe Ratio signifies a more favorable risk-return scenario, steering investors toward more rewarding investment strategies.

A key element of this discourse is the Capital Market Line (CML), which intersects the efficient frontier. Beginning at the risk-free rate, the CML extends outward, tangentially touching the frontier to denote the optimal mix of risk-free assets, such as treasury bonds, and risky investments. At this intersection, the maximum Sharpe Ratio is achieved, guiding investors toward constructing a well-integrated portfolio that balances both risk and return.

Investors may engage with the CML in various ways, utilizing leverage to enhance expected returns by increasing their exposure to risk through borrowing, or conversely, adopting a more cautious strategy by favoring risk-free investments. Each of these approaches shifts the portfolio's position along the CML, allowing for a customized investment strategy that reflects individual risk tolerance.

Ultimately, a deeper understanding of the efficient frontier and the associated risk-return trade-off transcends simple allocation techniques, transforming portfolio management into a strategic process informed by quantitative analysis and investor psychology.

In the intricate world of portfolio management, asset allocation stands as a cornerstone, representing both the art and science of balancing risk and return to fulfill an investor's specific objectives. At its heart, asset allocation involves strategically distributing investments among diverse asset classes—such as equities, bonds, real estate, and commodities —to optimize the delicate trade-off between risk and reward.

A foundational aspect of effective asset allocation is its strong emphasis on diversification as a strategy for risk mitigation. The well-known adage of not putting all your eggs in one basket is particularly relevant in this context.

Take, for instance, the traditional 60/40 portfolio strategy. This classic model allocates 60% of the total portfolio to equities and 40% to bonds. Historically, equities have been associated with higher long-term returns, albeit accompanied by greater volatility, while bonds provide more stable income with lower risk. This combination seeks to harness the growth potential of equities while offering a cushion against downturns through the relative stability of bonds.

Here's how the numbers break down:

1. Equity Allocation (60%): Assuming an expected return of 10% for equities, this portion would contribute 6% to the portfolio's total expected return.
2. Bond Allocation (40%): With a bond yield of 4%, this segment contributes 1.6% to the overall expected return.

Thus, the total expected return for the 60/40 portfolio can be calculated as follows:

$$[E(R\_p) = (0.6 \ 10\backslash\%) + (0.4 \ 4\backslash\%) = 7.6\backslash\%]$$

While this straightforward allocation has successfully served many investors by providing a balanced risk-return profile, the modern market landscape demands more sophisticated strategies that address complexities such as globalization, technological advances, and shifting fiscal policies.

Enter dynamic asset allocation, a more contemporary approach that adjusts the asset mix in reaction to changing market conditions, economic indicators, and variations in the investor's risk tolerance or investment horizon. Unlike static strategies, such as the 60/40 model, dynamic allocation allows for greater flexibility and responsiveness, although it typically entails a more advanced analytical framework and diligent monitoring.

For example, quantitative models may signal an increase in equity allocation during the early phases of a bull market to capitalize on growth opportunities, while simultaneously reducing stock exposure as markets reach peaks or exhibit signs of decline. In the realm of fixed income, asset allocations might shift in response to fluctuating interest rate environments, allowing investors to capitalize on favorable yield curves or credit spreads.

Another increasingly popular strategy is the core-satellite

approach, which combines a core of stable, traditional assets, such as broad market index funds, with satellite investments that are more volatile and higher-risk, such as sector-specific or international funds. This strategy enables investors to maintain a reliable foundation of performance while strategically targeting specific market dynamics to seize additional return opportunities.

Moreover, incorporating alternative assets—like commodities, real estate, hedge funds, or private equity—adds another dimension to asset allocation strategies. These non-traditional asset classes often show low correlation with traditional markets, enhancing diversification benefits and potentially serving as hedges against inflation or economic downturns. However, integrating these assets requires careful consideration regarding liquidity, valuation methods, and prevailing market conditions.

Ultimately, strategic asset allocation is as much an art as it is a science. It necessitates a thorough understanding of financial instruments, market dynamics, and individual investor preferences while maintaining the adaptability to respond to new information and personal circumstances. Effectively designing a robust investment portfolio hinges on a disciplined approach that marries analytical rigor with intuitive foresight, tailoring strategies for both resilience and opportunistic growth.

Developing effective asset allocation strategies involves more than just market analysis; it requires a deep comprehension of an investor's unique financial situation.

In the complex landscape of portfolio management, the quest for optimization plays a crucial role in shaping investment strategies into finely-tuned mechanisms of financial success. Techniques such as the Markowitz Efficient Frontier and the Black-Litterman model are highly regarded for their ability to refine asset allocation, ultimately aiming to secure the highest possible returns for a given level of risk.

The Markowitz Efficient Frontier: A Revolutionary Approach

Introduced by Harry Markowitz, the Efficient Frontier fundamentally transformed portfolio management with its innovative methodology that quantifies the delicate balance between risk and return. The result is illustrated in what is known as the "efficient frontier," a graphical representation that showcases the optimal combination of assets designed to maximize rewards while controlling for risk.

To better understand this concept, consider the scenario of an investor evaluating three distinct assets: A, B, and C. Each asset comes with its own expected returns and associated risks. Calculate Expected Returns and Risks: Suppose Asset A offers an expected return of 8% with a standard deviation of 5%, Asset B provides a return of 10% with a standard deviation of 6%, and Asset C yields a return of 12% with a standard deviation of 9%.

1. Assess Covariances: The relationships among these assets yield Cov(A,B) = 0.003, Cov(A,C) = 0.002, and Cov(B,C) = 0.004.

2. Optimize Portfolio: Utilizing these inputs, a variety of portfolio combinations are generated, pinpointing those that reside on the efficient frontier, each promising the maximum expected return for increased portfolio risk.

The resulting curve serves as a vital guide for investors, steering them toward optimal portfolios and empowering them to strategically navigate the trade-off between risk and potential returns. A key strength of this approach is its focus on diversification, promoting the spreading of risk across a spectrum of assets to lessen the impact of any single investment's underperformance.

Nevertheless, the Markowitz model is not without its

challenges. The accuracy of its inputs is critical; inaccuracies in projections for future returns or covariances can introduce significant vulnerabilities. In recognition of these limitations, the financial sector has increasingly sought models that leverage broader market insights for a more robust analysis.

Black-Litterman Model: A Synergistic Perspective

Enter the Black-Litterman model, an innovative approach designed to rectify potential misestimations in expected returns by incorporating both historical data and investor perspectives. Developed by Fischer Black and Robert Litterman, this model provides a nuanced framework that melds market-derived equilibrium returns with individual investor insights into the asset allocation process. Unlike models that rely solely on historical performance, Black-Litterman uses market consensus as a foundation, allowing investors to tailor asset weights according to their unique expectations.

To illustrate this model, consider the following application:

1. Market Equilibrium Returns: Begin by determining baseline returns that reflect market consensus, typically derived from a global benchmark index.

2. Incorporate Investor Views: Imagine an investor posits that Asset B is poised for significant outperformance, predicting a return that exceeds the market average. Instead of relying solely on statistical data, the investor weaves this insight into the portfolio strategy, adjusting the proportions of assets B and C accordingly.

3. Adjust Covariances: With a fresh perspective on correlations and variances that account for both market equilibrium and individual views, the portfolio is reconstructed to reflect these revised expectations. This hybrid approach is particularly

well-suited for dynamic markets where assumptions about future performance can be uncertain, creating a strategy that is not only resilient but also adaptable in a landscape marked by constant change.

Navigating Optimization Techniques

Effectively executing these optimization techniques necessitates meticulous attention to detail to mitigate potential risks. It requires precise data analysis, patience, and a discerning eye for interpreting market conditions along with investor biases. Additionally, the capacity to dynamically adjust inputs as fresh information emerges is vital for maintaining the relevance and accuracy of the models in practice.

Ultimately, whether leveraging the disciplined diversification of the Markowitz model or the integrated approach of Black-Litterman, the art of portfolio optimization remains a sophisticated endeavor. This balance of mathematical precision with human intuition allows investors to safeguard against risks while capitalizing on growth opportunities. The journey of portfolio optimization transcends mere formulaic application; it embodies the pursuit of an ideal—a harmonious blend of quantitative analysis and strategic foresight—enabling investors to navigate the volatile currents of the financial markets with confidence and skill.

Enhancing Portfolio Durability Through Alternative Assets

In an ever-changing financial landscape, investors and portfolio managers are on a relentless quest to bolster the resilience and performance of their portfolios. The inherent volatility of traditional investment vehicles compels a shift toward innovative strategies. One such strategy—incorporating alternative assets—offers compelling diversification benefits and the potential for enhanced returns. As we embark on this exploration, it is crucial to unpack the subtleties of these assets, evaluate their strategic importance, and develop practical integration techniques that resonate with today's financial realities.

Understanding Alternative Assets

Alternative assets encompass a broad spectrum, including real estate, commodities, hedge funds, private equity, and more. What sets these investments apart from conventional ones, such as stocks and bonds, is their distinctive risk-return profiles and generally low correlation to traditional markets. This unique blend can mitigate portfolio risk while also unlocking avenues for higher returns. For investors and portfolio strategists aiming to outperform the market, mastering how these dynamics align with overarching portfolio goals is essential.

Real Estate: A Tangible Asset with Lasting Value

Real estate remains a foundational choice within the realm of alternative investments. Its tangible nature doesn't just attract investors; it offers reliable income streams through rental yields and acts as a robust hedge against inflation. Property values often rise in tandem with broader economic conditions, helping to safeguard the portfolio even during tumultuous times. For instance, an institutional portfolio might allocate around 10% to commercial real estate via diversified real estate investment trusts (REITs). This strategic positioning can yield consistent income and potential capital appreciation, particularly in environments where interest rates remain low, thus providing a buffer against volatility in stock markets.

Commodities: Riding Economic Waves

Commodities—ranging from precious metals like gold to essential resources such as oil and grains—serve as a crucial diversifier during various economic cycles. Typically, their performance improves during economic expansions. Commodities like gold, often viewed as a safe haven asset, become particularly attractive during market downturns, serving as a protective measure. A sophisticated portfolio could integrate a commodity index fund, which aggregates various goods to smooth out the inherent volatility of individual commodities. Such an approach maintains the hedging advantages of commodities while reducing the risks associated with severe price fluctuations.

The Rise of Cryptocurrencies

In recent years, cryptocurrencies have emerged as an exciting, albeit volatile, asset class. Bitcoin, Ethereum, and other digital currencies offer a high-risk, high-reward profile that is hard to ignore. Savvy investors may consider allocating a modest portion of their portfolio—say, between 2% to 5% —to cryptocurrencies. This requires a careful balancing act, weighing the potential for significant gains against the risks posed by volatility and regulatory uncertainties. Successful integration of cryptocurrencies necessitates a comprehensive understanding of blockchain technology, the evolving regulatory landscape, and overall market sentiment, enabling investors to tap into the growth potential of this digital frontier.

Private Equity: Capturing Value in Undervalued Markets

Investing in private equity involves taking direct stakes in non-public companies, which can present significant opportunities for growth through active management and strategic restructuring. While these investments are typically illiquid, this very characteristic can offer an illiquidity premium, rewarding investors who have the patience to commit their capital for extended periods. Incorporating private equity effectively entails collaborating with established funds or experienced managers who specialize in particular sectors, aligning investor interests with areas demonstrating strong growth potential.

Hedge Funds: Strategies for Mitigating Risk and Amplifying Returns

Hedge funds employ a range of strategies, from long/short

equity to global macro and event-driven approaches, with the goal of achieving positive returns while managing risk. Utilizing leverage and various financial instruments, hedge funds can deliver uncorrelated returns that enhance portfolio resilience. It's vital, however, for investors to thoroughly understand the specific strategies employed by each fund to ensure alignment with overall portfolio objectives and to avoid unnecessary overlap with existing traditional assets.

Thoughtful Allocation and Rigorous Risk Management

Determining the appropriate size of alternative asset allocations is a delicate balancing act that involves comparing potential returns with the associated risks. Portfolio managers must create a cohesive framework that respects the principles of diversification while remaining attuned to each investor's unique risk tolerance and investment horizon. Continuous due diligence and performance evaluations are critical elements of this process.

For example, a well-structured portfolio might allocate 10% to real estate, 5% to commodities, 3% to cryptocurrencies, 7% to private equity, and 5% to hedge funds. Such an allocation aims to distribute risk effectively while leveraging the distinctive advantages offered by different alternative assets. Quantitative methodologies, including mean-variance optimization enhanced by specific models for alternative investments, can greatly assist in creating balanced and diverse portfolios.

The investment landscape is continuously evolving, and the incorporation of alternative assets into portfolios represents a robust avenue for diversifying risk and optimizing returns. This integration demands a thorough understanding of the individual characteristics of each asset class, as well as a keen awareness of current market conditions and investor objectives.

Dynamic Portfolio Adjustment Methodologies

Dynamic portfolio adjustment serves as a pivotal strategy for investors and portfolio managers aiming to navigate the complexities and fluctuations of today's financial markets. At its core, dynamic portfolio management emphasizes the intentional and systematic rebalancing of a portfolio to not only align with established investment objectives but also to seize emerging opportunities. This practice strives to maintain an optimal equilibrium between risk and return while enabling investors to adapt flexibly to ever-changing market dynamics.

The Rationale for Dynamic Adjustments

Financial markets are inherently dynamic, influenced by a multitude of factors ranging from economic indicators and political movements to technological advancements. Traditional buy-and-hold strategies often fall short in capitalizing on the short-lived nature of these market phenomena. Dynamic portfolio adjustment methodologies rise to this challenge by adopting a flexible, forward-looking approach that actively engages with market conditions.

Tactical Asset Allocation (TAA)

At the forefront of dynamic adjustment strategies is Tactical Asset Allocation (TAA). This approach involves making short-term, strategic shifts in the allocation of assets based on the analysis of prevailing market conditions or significant economic indicators. For instance, if an investor anticipates a rise in interest rates, they may reduce their exposure to long-duration bonds while reallocating resources toward equities likely to benefit from an economic upturn. This strategic maneuver aims to exploit transient market inefficiencies while remaining anchored to overarching long-term investment goals.

Adaptive Rebalancing Techniques

Adaptive rebalancing embraces a nuanced methodology

by realigning the portfolio's asset weights in response to significant deviations from target allocations. Unlike static rebalancing, which occurs at predetermined intervals, adaptive techniques activate when specific thresholds are breached. For example, should a portfolio originally balanced at 60% equities and 40% bonds see its equity allocation surge beyond 65% due to a bull market, adaptive rebalancing dictates selling the excess equities to reinvest in bonds or other underrepresented asset classes. This blend of discipline and adaptability ensures that the portfolio remains in sync with its risk profile.

Incorporating Momentum Strategies

Momentum strategies are increasingly relevant in the realm of dynamic portfolio management. This approach focuses on identifying and investing in assets that have demonstrated strong past performance, operating under the assumption that such trends are likely to continue. For instance, during a period driven by rapid technological advancement, a dynamic portfolio manager may allocate additional funds to the technology sector, capitalizing on its growth potential.

Scenario Analysis and Stress Testing

Scenario analysis emerges as an indispensable tool in dynamic portfolio adjustment, allowing managers to evaluate the potential impact of various economic situations—such as recessions or shifts in interest rates—on portfolio performance. When coupled with stress testing, which simulates extreme market conditions, scenario analysis illuminates areas of vulnerability within the portfolio. Armed with these insights, managers can proactively adjust allocations to mitigate identified risks. For instance, if analysis indicates susceptibility to a sharp rise in energy prices, increasing exposure to alternative energy stocks can effectively serve as a buffer against potential negative impacts.

Dynamic Hedging

Dynamic hedging entails the continuous management of derivative positions to offset potential movements in asset prices, thereby preserving portfolio value. For example, a fund might deploy dynamic options strategies to safeguard against potential downturns while maintaining opportunities for upside. If a grim economic forecast heightens the risk of equity declines, portfolio managers may implement protective put options on key index holdings, ensuring that losses are limited while remaining poised for recoveries when conditions improve.

Algorithmic Adjustment Tools

With the rapid advancements in technology and data analysis capabilities, algorithmic tools have become invaluable in facilitating dynamic portfolio management. These tools automate the adjustment process based on predetermined criteria, harnessing machine learning to enhance both the timing and precision of reallocations. For example, a machine learning model might analyze historical market data patterns to predict asset class performance, dynamically adjusting portfolio weightings to optimize risk-adjusted returns.

Continuous Monitoring and Real-Time Feedback

The success of dynamic portfolio adjustments hinges on continuous monitoring and real-time feedback. Implementing robust systems that track market movements and evaluate portfolio performance in real-time empowers managers to reposition swiftly when necessary. Modern technology platforms offer alerts that notify managers when asset weights diverge from targets or when market conditions necessitate a reevaluation of strategic positions, ensuring informed decision-making is both timely and effective.

Dynamic portfolio adjustment methodologies present a wealth of opportunities for adapting to a rapidly evolving market landscape while effectively managing risk and optimizing returns. This proactive approach not only fortifies portfolio resilience but also aligns with investor objectives, positioning portfolios to take advantage of the dynamic financial ecosystem. Through a disciplined and methodical application of these strategies, dynamic adjustments can enhance performance, safeguarding investment strategies against the uncertainties that lie ahead.

Performance Evaluation and Attribution Analysis

In the dynamic landscape of investment management, the ability to assess portfolio performance accurately is vital for understanding success and shaping future strategies. Performance evaluation encompasses more than just the calculation of returns; it involves a deep exploration of the myriad factors that drive those returns. When paired with attribution analysis, this process allows managers to dissect the sources of performance, distinguish skill from serendipity, and refine their investment strategies to foster future success.

Foundations of Performance Evaluation

At its essence, performance evaluation involves scrutinizing a portfolio or fund's returns in relation to a benchmark. This benchmark may be a relevant index, a composite of similar funds, or bespoke benchmarks tailored to the specific goals of the investment strategy.

Adjusting for risk is another pivotal element of performance evaluation. Simple measures like total return overlook the nuanced reality of the varying risk levels taken to achieve those results. Here, risk-adjusted performance metrics come into play—key tools such as the Sharpe Ratio and Sortino Ratio. The Sharpe Ratio evaluates performance by examining return per unit of total risk (standard deviation), while the Sortino Ratio hones in on downside risk, offering a more refined view that aligns with investor sensitivity to losses.

Attribution Analysis: Unveiling the Drivers of Performance

While performance evaluation quantifies success, attribution analysis provides the critical task of elucidating it. This nuanced analysis breaks down portfolio returns into contributory components linked to specific decisions, such as asset allocation, security selection, and timing strategies. The focus is on dissecting overall performance to discern contributions from both systematic market movements and active management decisions.

Example: Sector Allocation Attribution

Consider a portfolio diversified across technology, healthcare, and energy sectors. To determine whether outperformance relative to a benchmark was driven by strategic sector allocation or judicious security selection within those sectors, the manager can isolate the contributions accrued from over- or under-weighting each sector. This granular approach enables the manager to pinpoint the sources of return derived from strategic decisions.

1. Sector Allocation Effect: This metric assesses the performance impact stemming from deviations in sector weights compared to the benchmark. If a significant allocation to tech—where performance soared—outpaced the benchmark, the allocation decision would clearly enhance performance.

2. Security Selection Effect: This aspect examines the value added through specific security choices within those sectors. For instance, if a manager successfully identifies top-performing tech stocks within a broader sector surge, this adept selection further elevates portfolio returns.

Factor-Based Attribution

Factor-based attribution dives deeper into the economic and risk factors driving portfolio performance. This methodology dissects returns into exposures to well-documented risk factors such as market, size, value, momentum, and quality—

all of which are core principles of factor investing.

For instance, consider a multi-factor equity portfolio that outperforms due to significant exposure to the momentum factor. Through attribution analysis, the contributions from this tilt are revealed, empowering the manager to assess whether maintaining such exposure aligns with their desired risk-return profile.

Advanced Tools and Techniques

In today's data-driven environment, technology has become an essential companion in performance evaluation and attribution analysis. Advanced analytical platforms enable a meticulous examination of factor exposures, often employing machine learning algorithms to unearth subtle, non-linear relationships between asset performance and known factors. These insights allow managers to deftly refine their investment strategies.

Example: Machine Learning in Attribution Analysis

Imagine a portfolio utilizing machine learning to probe the complex interactions between macroeconomic indicators and asset prices. The insights gleaned empower managers to dynamically adjust portfolios, capitalizing on emerging opportunities while staying vigilant against potential risks.

Implementing Performance Evaluation and Attribution

To effectively leverage performance evaluation and attribution analysis, a structured approach is essential. Start by clearly defining appropriate benchmarks and risk-adjusted metrics for assessing performance. Establish a systematic process for conducting attribution analysis, specifying the various factors and effects that warrant regular examination.

Continuous learning is integral to maximizing the benefits of these analytical tools for enhanced investment decisions. Through consistent review of evaluation and attribution reports, managers can refine their strategies, adapt over time, and communicate their value to stakeholders effectively. This practice melds quantitative insights with informed judgment, crafting a robust investment strategy tailored to the ever-evolving market landscape.

Performance evaluation and attribution analysis are indispensable for any investor or portfolio manager striving for excellence. They not only provide a clear measure of an investment strategy's success but also illuminate the underlying drivers of returns.

In this relentless pursuit of excellence, a comprehensive understanding of the multifaceted nature of performance will guide informed decision-making. This ensures portfolios meet their objectives efficiently and intelligently. Embracing these advanced methodologies paves the way for a deeper comprehension of market dynamics, equipping investors with the tools needed to navigate the intricate world of finance.

The Role of Constraints in Portfolio Construction

In the intricate world of portfolio management, constraints serve as vital navigational beacons, shaping the investment process by delineating the boundaries within which portfolio managers operate. These constraints are far more than mere limitations; they play an essential role in risk management, regulatory compliance, and client expectations. For portfolio managers committed to enhancing returns while maintaining a robust risk profile, a deep understanding of these constraints and their strategic application is paramount.

The Foundations of Portfolio Constraints

At the core of effective portfolio management lies the delicate balance between risk and return. Constraints serve as a guiding framework, ensuring that the pursuit of higher returns does not inadvertently heighten exposure to undesirable risks or divert from established investment objectives. Constraints can be categorized into two primary types: hard constraints and soft constraints.

Hard Constraints are non-negotiable rules that cannot be bypassed. These stringent guidelines often arise from regulatory requirements, internal risk management policies, or explicit investor mandates. Examples of hard constraints include maximum allocations to certain asset classes, restrictions on investments in specific countries, or outright bans on sectors deemed unethical by certain investment criteria.

Soft Constraints, in contrast, consist of flexible guidelines rather than rigid barriers. These constraints allow portfolio managers to leverage their discretion based on market conditions and emerging opportunities. Examples include aspirational goals such as achieving a specific ESG (Environmental, Social, and Governance) score or maintaining a balanced sectoral distribution.

Practical Applications of Constraints

Rather than functioning solely as restrictions, constraints can be strategically employed to enhance the resilience of a portfolio. Below are illustrative applications of constraints in portfolio construction.

Example 1: Sector and Geographic Constraints

Consider the case of a global equity portfolio that mandates a maximum 20% allocation to any single sector. This stipulation protects against over-concentration risks while compelling the manager to seek high-quality investments across various sectors.

Similarly, geographic constraints might limit exposure to emerging markets, reflecting a cautious approach due to heightened volatility or geopolitical uncertainties. In this context, a portfolio manager might cap emerging market investments at 15% of total assets, carefully balancing the allure of potential high returns with the associated risks.

Example 2: ESG Constraints

In an era marked by increasing emphasis on socially responsible investing, ESG criteria have gained significant traction. A portfolio may incorporate constraints that exclude investments in fossil fuel companies or prioritize firms with commendable ESG scores. Such constraints not only resonate with clients' ethical values but can also help mitigate exposure to regulatory risks and changing consumer behaviors.

In this framework, managers can utilize data-driven analysis to screen potential investments, ensuring they meet the specified ESG standards. Tools such as Sustainalytics or MSCI ESG ratings enable portfolio managers to evaluate companies against these prudent benchmarks.

Optimizing with Constraints

The incorporation of constraints into portfolio management necessitates sophisticated optimization techniques to achieve the ideal risk-return trade-off. Traditional models, like Markowitz's mean-variance framework, can be adapted to include these constraints effectively.

Example: Constrained Optimization

Imagine a portfolio manager leveraging an optimization routine to maximize the Sharpe Ratio while adhering to constraints on asset weights. Utilizing quadratic programming, the manager explores various asset combinations to identify the optimal return for each unit of risk taken, all while ensuring that asset weights remain within designated limits.

In such scenarios, advanced software systems like MATLAB or specialized platforms such as Bloomberg's PORT function prove indispensable. These tools facilitate precise modeling and execution of strategies laden with constraints, giving managers the insight and control required for optimal decision-making.

Navigating Real-World Challenges

While constraints provide essential structure, they can also introduce challenges. Excessively rigid constraints may hinder a manager's capacity to seize investment opportunities or adapt to shifting market conditions. Therefore, striking a balance between maintaining necessary constraints and allowing for flexibility is crucial to effective portfolio management.

Furthermore, constraints should be continuously assessed and refined in response to evolving market dynamics or shifts in client objectives. This proactive approach supports a nimble and adaptive investment strategy, crucial for sustained long-term success.

In the realm of portfolio construction, constraints serve as both crucial parameters and strategic instruments for achieving investment goals. They offer a necessary framework for risk management and compliance, while also presenting opportunities for competitive advantage when applied thoughtfully. Savvy portfolio managers must navigate these constraints skillfully, using them to inform and enrich their decision-making processes rather than inhibit them. In the complex choreography of portfolio construction, constraints transform from mere limitations into powerful opportunities for refining and enhancing investment strategies.

Crafting a Multi-Strategy Portfolio: An In-Depth Approach to Investment Diversity

At the crossroads of precision and adaptability lies the multi-strategy portfolio—a sophisticated investment framework that intertwines various strategies to harness their collective strengths. This approach not only enhances diversification but also aims to mitigate risks and improve returns beyond what single-strategy portfolios can achieve. However, the successful execution of a multi-strategy portfolio demands a deep comprehension of each underlying approach, as well as their dynamic interactions within the portfolio.

Harmonizing Diverse Strategies for Robust Returns

Multi-strategy portfolios thrive on the rich tapestry of financial markets by integrating an array of strategies—including global macro, event-driven, long/short equity, and relative value. Each brings its own distinct attributes and potential advantages, equipping the portfolio to navigate various market environments with resilience.

Illustrating the Synergy: Global Macro and Long/Short Equity

Consider the interplay between global macro and long/short equity strategies. A global macro approach leverages overarching economic trends to forecast market movements across diverse asset classes. Meanwhile, a long/short equity strategy allows managers to capitalize on individual stock performance by taking long positions in undervalued stocks and short positions in overvalued ones. This symbiotic relationship aids in balancing overall risk and enhancing the portfolio's performance across different market climates.

Designing and Managing the Multi-Strategy Portfolio

The construction of a multi-strategy portfolio is a meticulous endeavor that requires careful selection and integration of diverse strategies based on their inherent characteristics, correlations, and potential synergies. Managers must thoroughly assess the risk-return profiles of each strategy to ensure they collectively contribute to a more stable and appealing portfolio.

Strategic Allocation and Dynamic Rebalancing

Strategic allocation forms the backbone of a robust multi-strategy portfolio, demanding a careful and calculated distribution of capital across the chosen strategies. This decision-making process is informed by both quantitative analyses—such as historical performance data and risk assessments—and qualitative insights derived from market insights and trends.

Furthermore, employing a dynamic rebalancing approach is crucial for keeping the portfolio aligned with its target allocations. For example, a diligent portfolio manager might allocate 40% of capital to market neutral strategies aimed at mitigating systematic risk while dedicating 30% to relative value trades designed to seize specific arbitrage opportunities. The remaining 30% could be earmarked for opportunistic strategies, targeting short-term market dislocations.

Every allocation decision is influenced by a rigorous evaluation of strategy performance and inter-strategy synergies, harnessing advanced historical data analytics and predictive modeling techniques to optimize results.

Real-World Application: A Case Study from the Hedge Fund Sector

To illustrate the practical implementation of a multi-strategy approach, let's explore a hedge fund that successfully combined credit arbitrage, volatility trading, and quantitative macro strategies. This dynamic alignment not only yielded consistent returns but also provided stability during tumultuous market phases.

In times of heightened market volatility, the hedge fund's volatility trading strategy effectively navigated price fluctuations, providing essential counterbalance to the widening credit spreads that often accompany turbulent markets. Concurrently, the quantitative macro component adjusted its exposure based on evolving macroeconomic indicators, ensuring that the fund maintained a steady performance regardless of the prevailing market direction.

This case underscores the critical importance of strategic allocation and the need for adaptability, as the hedge fund continually monitored and rebalanced its approach using real-time data inputs, thus preserving its competitive edge.

Navigating Risk in Multi-Strategy Portfolios

The complexity of risk management within multi-strategy

portfolios is a multifaceted challenge. The inherent diversity of the strategies, each possessing its own risk factors, necessitates the establishment of a sophisticated risk management framework that thoroughly assesses the intricate web of risk exposures and the interplay among strategies.

Employing Scenario Analysis and Stress Testing

To navigate potential market disruptions, portfolio managers often utilize scenario analysis and stress testing. Techniques such as Monte Carlo simulations and factor modeling are invaluable tools for predicting extreme outcomes, allowing managers to scrutinize the portfolio's resilience across various stress scenarios.

For instance, amidst rising geopolitical tensions, detailed scenario analysis may reveal heightened exposure to geopolitical risks embedded within the global macro component. This insight could prompt proactive adjustments to shift allocations toward strategies that are less sensitive to such risks, preserving the overall integrity and stability of the portfolio.

In summary, developing a multi-strategy portfolio represents a sophisticated investment methodology that harmonizes diversification, strategic foresight, and robust risk management practices.

Maximizing the benefits of this sophisticated investment approach requires ongoing diligence and adaptability from managers, who must continuously reassess their strategies in response to evolving market conditions.

Navigating New Horizons: Future Trends in Portfolio Management

As the financial landscape undergoes rapid evolution, portfolio management stands at the intriguing intersection of innovation and tradition. Emerging trends are set to revolutionize asset management, driven by technological advancements, shifts in investor preferences, and ongoing changes in economic conditions. For today's portfolio managers, grasping these trends is not just important—it's essential for thriving in this dynamic environment.

Embracing Technology: The Dominance of AI and Machine Learning

The influence of technology on finance is profound, particularly with the emergence of artificial intelligence (AI) and machine learning (ML) revolutionizing portfolio management practices. These technologies enhance analytical capabilities, empowering managers to process vast amounts of data quickly and accurately, ultimately informing their decision-making processes.

AI-Powered Portfolio Optimization

Take AI-driven portfolio optimization, for instance. This approach leverages sophisticated algorithms that learn from historical performance data to forecast future market trends and asset behavior. As market conditions evolve, these insights allow for timely adjustments to portfolios, ensuring that performance remains aligned with investor goals.

Moreover, AI tools play a critical role in risk management by simulating an array of market scenarios that help assess potential impacts. This predictive capability equips managers with the foresight needed to adjust strategies proactively, enhancing their resilience against market volatility.

The Shift Towards Sustainable and ESG Investing

An increasingly prominent trend in portfolio management is the prioritization of sustainable investing and adherence to Environmental, Social, and Governance (ESG) criteria. Today's investors are transcending the traditional focus on financial returns, opting instead for investment strategies that reflect ethical values and sustainability considerations.

Incorporating ESG Factors into Strategy

As portfolio managers incorporate ESG criteria into their investment frameworks, they do so not just for ethical reasons, but because companies that prioritize sustainability tend to perform better over the long haul. Research suggests that firms with robust governance and proactive environmental practices are adept at managing risks and are well-positioned for sustainable growth.

Integrating ESG factors necessitates sophisticated data analysis tools. For example, portfolio managers might develop scoring systems that evaluate a company's environmental impact and social responsibility when selecting stocks for investment. This alignment of sustainability with financial performance is poised to drive innovation in investment solutions that resonate with investors' values while also achieving strong returns.

Personalization in Investing: A Tailored Approach

The digital age heralds a new era in personalized investing, where individual preferences and financial goals play a pivotal role in portfolio construction. Supported by advancements in fintech, this trend offers unparalleled customization opportunities.

The Rise of Robo-Advisors and Fintech Solutions

Robo-advisors exemplify this shift, leveraging algorithms to provide tailored investment guidance based on individual risk tolerance and financial aspirations. This democratization of investment management opens the door for a wider audience to access sophisticated strategies that were once the exclusive domain of high-net-worth individuals.

Additionally, fintech tools facilitate the integration of behavioral finance insights, helping mitigate emotional biases and ensuring that investors remain committed to their personalized strategies. With intuitive user interfaces and real-time feedback, these platforms guide investors toward achieving their financial objectives.

Expanding Investment Horizons: New Asset Classes on the Rise

As portfolio managers seek new avenues for growth, the exploration of alternative asset classes represents a significant trend.

Venturing into Cryptocurrencies and Digital Assets

Cryptocurrencies and digital assets have emerged as viable components of diversified portfolios. Despite their inherent volatility, these assets offer potential for substantial returns and diversification, especially as the regulatory landscape stabilizes. Forward-thinking managers are recognizing the strategic value of digital assets, not merely as speculative investments, but as hedging tools against traditional market fluctuations.

The advent of tokenization is further revolutionizing investments by enhancing liquidity in previously illiquid markets, such as real estate and art.

The Enduring Value of Human Insight

Amidst a backdrop of rapid technological advancements and an expanding asset universe, the human element of portfolio management remains irreplaceable. As we move into the future, the emphasis will increasingly be on cognitive diversity, critical thinking, and adaptability—traits that machines cannot yet replicate.

The Complementarity of Technology and Human Judgement

While technology excels at processing data and identifying patterns, the intuition and experience of skilled portfolio managers play a crucial role in navigating unpredictable market conditions. Humans bring a nuanced understanding and foresight to decision-making, ensuring that portfolios not only adhere to data-driven insights but also align with broader investment objectives.

Managers who adeptly integrate technical abilities with human insights will be better equipped to tackle complexities that defy algorithmic analysis, thus reinforcing their value as trusted stewards of wealth in an increasingly automated financial world.

The landscape of portfolio management is on the cusp of significant transformation, fueled by advancements in technology, a commitment to sustainability, increasing personalization, and the timeless value of human creativity. Managers who adeptly weave these emerging trends into their investment strategies will be well-positioned to navigate challenges and seize opportunities.

CHAPTER 10: CASE STUDIES AND REAL-WORLD APPLICATIONS

Founded by visionary investor Ray Dalio, Bridgewater Associates stands as a paragon of success in the realm of quantitative hedge funds. Its investment philosophy is anchored in a commitment to transparency and a rigorous, systematic approach that draws heavily on macroeconomic principles. At the heart of Bridgewater's operations is its flagship strategy, Pure Alpha, which masterfully combines diversified asset allocation with the analysis of vast data sets to identify and exploit patterns across global markets.

A cornerstone of Bridgewater's success is its radical transparency policy. This initiative cultivates a collaborative atmosphere where team members are encouraged to challenge assumptions and rigorously test investment models, ensuring that decisions are rooted in strong empirical insights. Furthermore, the integration of cutting-edge technologies—including machine learning and extensive historical data analysis—enhances decision-making processes, allowing the firm to develop forecasts and allocate assets with precision.

Renaissance Technologies: The Apex of Statistical Trading

Renowned for its remarkable performance and enigmatic

operations, Renaissance Technologies exemplifies the power of advanced quantitative analysis in delivering extraordinary financial results. Its Medallion Fund, which remains closed to outside investors, has produced exceptional annual returns by capitalizing on short-term market inefficiencies and employing statistical arbitrage.

The driving force behind Renaissance's success is a stellar team comprising mathematicians, physicists, and computer scientists. This diversified expertise enables the firm to construct intricate quantitative models that leverage non-intuitive market signals, predicting price movements with uncanny accuracy. Central to this success is Renaissance's proprietary database, which underpins the development of sophisticated models tailored for high-frequency trading.

Two Sigma: Pioneering Advanced Analytics

Two Sigma exemplifies the fusion of quantitative finance with advanced technological capabilities, establishing a benchmark for innovation within the hedge fund industry.

Employing a diversified array of investment strategies across equities, fixed income, and commodities, Two Sigma fosters an environment that encourages intellectual curiosity and technological innovation. Among its notable features is a cloud-based platform designed to enhance computational efficiency and facilitate rapid adjustments to trading strategies in response to shifting market conditions.

AQR Capital Management: Bridging Academic Rigor with Practical Insight

AQR Capital Management has carved a niche for itself by seamlessly blending academic research with practical finance, earning accolades for its pioneering, research-driven investment strategies. Co-founded by Clifford Asness, AQR implements a multifactor investment approach that integrates insights from behavioral finance with quantitative models focused on value, momentum, and defensive attributes.

The firm's ongoing commitment to research and development is pivotal to its success. Furthermore, AQR's dedication to transparency empowers investors to grasp the underlying mechanisms and assumptions guiding its strategies, thus cultivating trust and long-term relationships.

Common Threads of Success

While the approaches of these hedge funds may vary, several underlying themes contribute to their successes. Their reliance on sophisticated quantitative models is complemented by robust risk management protocols, safeguarding against adverse market fluctuations and preserving their growth trajectories.

Equally significant is their commitment to fostering a collaborative culture where innovation and technological expertise thrive. These organizations capitalize on interdisciplinary teams, embracing a range of perspectives that lead to innovative solutions for intricate market challenges.

Finally, a disciplined commitment to research and continuous improvement distinguishes these funds.

In conclusion, the narrative of successful quantitative hedge funds transcends the mere pursuit of alpha; it illustrates the intricate balance between technology, data, and human insight. Each fund showcases a unique aspect of the transformative power of quantitative strategies in enhancing financial outcomes, offering invaluable lessons for aspiring portfolio managers and investment firms eager to push the boundaries of possibility within the dynamic world of finance.

In the complex and ever-evolving landscape of financial markets, quantitative strategies have solidified their position as essential tools for discerning intricate trends and producing enhanced returns. These strategies, guided by sophisticated mathematical models and advanced algorithms, empower investors to identify inefficiencies and reveal latent opportunities within market dynamics. In this exploration, we will delve into several notable quantitative strategies, each contributing uniquely to the financial landscape while shedding light on their underlying mechanics and practical applications.

Momentum Trading: Harnessing the Power of Trends

At the heart of many successful quantitative methodologies lies momentum trading. This strategy is founded on the well-established observation that assets that have performed well in the past often continue to do so in the near future.

One common method of executing momentum trading involves the use of technical indicators such as the Relative Strength Index (RSI) or moving average crossovers. These tools help identify shifts in trend, providing traders with critical signals for entering or exiting positions. For example, a typical momentum strategy might involve purchasing stocks that are hitting recent highs while simultaneously selling stocks that are nearing recent lows, operating under the premise that trends tend to persist.

Momentum strategies are not exclusive to equities; their versatility extends across a wide array of asset classes, including commodities, currencies, and fixed income securities. This adaptability showcases the robustness of momentum trading, making it a favored choice among quantitative investors eager to tap into the collective psychology that ebbs and flows through markets.

Mean Reversion: Capitalizing on the Correction Cycle

In contrast to momentum strategies, mean reversion relies on the premise that asset prices will ultimately gravitate back toward their historical averages. This approach suggests that fluctuations in price—whether the result of excessive optimism or undue pessimism—offer prime opportunities for traders to profit as prices adjust back toward their mean.

Statistical arbitrage is a prominent technique within mean reversion strategies, where traders engage in simultaneous long and short positions to exploit pricing discrepancies amidst correlated securities. The anticipation is that the price differential will narrow as the assets revert to their historical norms, leading to profitable outcomes.

A practical example of mean reversion can be illustrated through pairs trading, which involves monitoring two historically correlated stocks—like Coke and Pepsi. If their price ratio deviates from its historic average, a trader might short the higher-priced stock while purchasing the lower-priced counterpart, betting on the eventual return to equilibrium.

Factor Investing: Navigating Macro and Microeconomic Influences

Factor investing represents a comprehensive quantitative approach that involves constructing investment portfolios based on specific attributes or "factors" known to drive securities' performance. Commonly examined factors encompass value, growth, size, quality, and market volatility.

One of the most significant applications of factor investing is the Fama-French three-factor model, which expands on traditional asset pricing theories by incorporating size and value factors to explain stock returns more comprehensively. This model serves as a foundational framework for constructing portfolios tailored to leverage specific economic drivers.

In practice, asset managers implementing factor investing may prefer securities that exhibit strong value indicators, such as low price-to-earnings ratios, while deliberately underweighting growth stocks. This deliberate positioning aims to create a portfolio tilted toward potentially higher risk-adjusted returns, with managers dynamically adjusting factor exposures in response to changing market conditions.

Statistical Arbitrage: Exploiting Market Inefficiencies

Statistical arbitrage (stat arb) is a sophisticated quantitative strategy that capitalizes on short-term market mispricings through the application of high-frequency trading and advanced algorithms. This approach utilizes statistical relationships between securities, employing techniques such as mean reversion and regression analysis to execute swift, data-informed trades.

At the heart of statistical arbitrage is the use of computational prowess to analyze extensive data sets rapidly, allowing traders to spot fleeting price deviations across correlated assets. For instance, machine learning algorithms can be deployed to recognize patterns and predict minor stock price shifts in real-time, facilitating timely trading decisions.

Machine Learning and AI: Pioneering the Future of Trading

The rise of machine learning and artificial intelligence has revolutionized quantitative strategies by enhancing their predictive capacities and enabling the real-time analysis of vast, unstructured data sources like social media sentiment or news reports. This evolution has paved the way for the development of proprietary algorithms that adapt to and learn from market behavior, continuously updating trading strategies based on new insights.

A notable application includes using natural language processing (NLP) for sentiment analysis, wherein AI models quantify investor sentiment from diverse channels to forecast market movements. Additionally, reinforcement learning techniques are leveraged to refine trading strategies, driven by an ongoing evaluation of historical performance, which contributes to more flexible and responsive trading models.

In examining these significant strategies, it becomes clear that the realm of quantitative finance represents a dynamic interplay between rigorous mathematical analysis and an insightful understanding of market behavioral nuances. As these quantitative techniques continue to evolve, investors must remain attuned to emerging technologies and methodological advancements, constantly refining their strategies to navigate the complex and interconnected world of global financial markets.

Insights Gained from High-Profile Failures
in Quantitative Finance

In the fast-paced realm of quantitative finance, the path to success is often fraught with pitfalls. Even the most well-crafted strategies can falter, reminding us that failures serve not merely as setbacks, but as vital lessons that carry profound implications. This exploration examines prominent failures in quantitative strategies, shedding light on the delicate interplay between mathematical calculation, market behavior, and human oversight.

Long-Term Capital Management (LTCM): A Cautionary Tale

Long-Term Capital Management (LTCM) epitomizes the precarious nature of even the most sophisticated financial strategies. Founded in 1994 by John Meriwether, alongside a cadre of Nobel laureates such as Robert Merton and Myron Scholes, LTCM emerged with a promise to leverage advanced mathematical models to exploit pricing inefficiencies in bond markets. In its nascent years, the firm delivered extraordinary returns, validating the power of quantitative finance.

However, this success bred a perilous overconfidence. In 1998, when the Russian financial crisis erupted, LTCM found itself ensnared in a web of unprecedented market turmoil—one that its models were ill-equipped to handle. The catastrophic losses that ensued underscored a critical lesson: even statistically sound models are vulnerable to "black swan" events that lie outside historical norms. This serves as a stark reminder of the importance of designing models that are both robust and adaptable, and of maintaining an awareness of potential systemic risks and market anomalies that could disrupt even the most well-founded strategies.

Amaranth Advisors: The Dangers of Concentration

The story of Amaranth Advisors acts as another poignant reminder of the dangers posed by concentrated risk. At its zenith, this multi-strategy hedge fund managed more than)9 billion, yet it fell victim to a singular focus on its energy trading operations, led by Brian Hunter. While initial gains from natural gas futures were impressive, Amaranth's extensive positions became increasingly susceptible to erratic weather and sudden regulatory shifts. In September 2006, these vulnerabilities culminated in a jaw-dropping loss of 6 billion within just a few days.

This debacle emphasizes the critical nature of risk management and diversification. Amaranth's downfall can be traced back to insufficient oversight and a lack of positional limits, which allowed the misfortunes of one trading desk to jeopardize the entire fund. For quantitative strategists, the lessons are clear: enforce strict risk management practices, diversify across uncorrelated asset classes, and remain acutely aware of the myriad risk factors influencing different sectors.

The "Quant Quake" of August 2007: A Ripple Effect

The "Quant Quake" of August 2007 stands as a striking example of correlated failures among various hedge funds. During a tumultuous two-week span, numerous quantitative funds faced simultaneous declines, primarily due to rapid market liquidity shifts and a sudden unwinding of positions. This collective crisis unveiled the hidden connections and vulnerabilities among strategies that were assumed to be independent; many funds unwittingly executed similar trades based on analogous models.

The implications of this event are significant. It highlights the urgent necessity for a nuanced understanding of market liquidity dynamics, particularly how quantitative models perform under duress. As many funds scrambled for arbitrage opportunities, liquidity evaporated, triggering a cascading effect across strategies. This situation calls for a heightened awareness of the systemic relationships that exist within the financial ecosystem, underlining the need for greater transparency and cooperation among market participants to mitigate the risks of widespread failure.

Embracing Lessons from Failure

The narratives surrounding high-profile failures in quantitative finance impart essential lessons that extend beyond technical refinements. They highlight the importance of humility, resilience, and an ongoing commitment to learning within a landscape defined by complexity.

Failures serve as illumination points for blind spots that even the most advanced models may overlook. They compel practitioners to remain vigilant, continually challenging established assumptions and rigorously stress-testing strategies across diverse scenarios. Moreover, fostering a culture that encourages open discourse about failure can drive innovation and strengthen the financial fabric, enhancing the overall resilience of the industry.

Ultimately, by drawing lessons from these episodes, we transform past misfortunes into invaluable stepping stones for future endeavors. In doing so, the pursuit of resilient quantitative strategies is not just a goal, but a journey of growth and adaptation that holds the potential to redefine success in the ever-evolving financial landscape.

Practical Applications of Various Models in Quantitative Finance

Regression Models in Predictive Analytics

Regression models are fundamental tools in quantitative finance, particularly in predictive analytics, where they are employed to forecast market movements and pinpoint lucrative trading opportunities. Among these models, linear regression stands out for its ability to elucidate relationships between critical variables—such as stock prices, economic indicators, and financial ratios.

Imagine a financial analyst tasked with forecasting a company's stock price. This approach enables the analyst to derive actionable insights that inform trading strategies.

Here's a practical implementation of a predictive model using Python:

```python
import pandas as pd
from sklearn.model_selection import train_test_split
from sklearn.linear_model import LinearRegression

\#\# Load dataset
data = pd.read_csv('financial_data.csv')
X = data[['revenue_growth', 'interest_rate', 'industry_trend']]
y = data['stock_price']

\#\# Split data into training and testing sets
X_train, X_test, y_train, y_test = train_test_split(X, y, test_size=0.3, random_state=42)

\#\# Initiate and train the regression model
model = LinearRegression()
model.fit(X_train, y_train)

\#\# Predict stock prices
predictions = model.predict(X_test)
```

This predictive model can be enhanced through the incorporation of additional data and advanced techniques, such as regularization, to boost accuracy and minimize the risk of overfitting.

Factor Models for Risk Adjustments

Factor models provide a sophisticated framework for identifying and adjusting for the risks inherent in various financial positions. Notable examples include the Capital Asset Pricing Model (CAPM) and the Fama-French three-factor model, both of which aim to explain the returns of securities based on common risk factors. Portfolio managers utilize these models to assess the expected return of a security in relation to its risk profile, thereby guiding informed asset allocation decisions and effective hedging strategies.

Consider the application of the Fama-French three-factor model. This involves regressing portfolio returns against market risk, size, and value factors, allowing managers to refine their investment strategies based on empirical insights:

```r
```r ## R code for Fama-French three-factor model
library(tseries)

\#\# Load market data and Fama-French factors
portfolio_returns                                      <- as.numeric(read.csv('portfolio_returns.csv'))
market_data <- as.numeric(read.csv('market_returns.csv'))
SMB <- as.numeric(read.csv('SMB.csv'))
HML <- as.numeric(read.csv('HML.csv'))

\#\# Fama-French model estimation
model <- lm(portfolio_returns ~ market_data + SMB + HML)
summary(model)
```
```

By interpreting these coefficients, portfolio managers can better navigate potential premium returns while concurrently managing unnecessary risk exposures.

Monte Carlo Simulations for Derivative Pricing

Monte Carlo simulations present a compelling application of quantitative modeling combined with computational techniques, particularly in the realm of derivative pricing. This method allows for the assessment of intricate financial instruments by simulating numerous potential price paths, thereby calculating the expected payoff of derivatives.

For instance, when pricing a European call option, a Monte Carlo simulation would generate a multitude of random price paths for the underlying asset, facilitating an accurate computation of the option's payoff:

```python
``` python import numpy as np

\#\# Parameters
S0 = 100  \# Initial stock price
K = 105   \# Strike price
T = 1    \# Time to maturity
r = 0.05  \# Risk-free interest rate
sigma = 0.2  \# Volatility
simulations = 10000

\#\# Monte Carlo simulation
np.random.seed(42)
Z = np.random.standard_normal(simulations)
ST = S0 * np.exp((r - 0.5 * sigma**2) * T + sigma * np.sqrt(T) * Z)
payoff = np.maximum(ST - K, 0)
call_price = np.exp(-r * T) * np.mean(payoff)
```
```

Monte Carlo methods are invaluable for their flexibility, particularly when analytical solutions are unattainable. They empower traders with the necessary tools to price and hedge derivatives effectively in complex market environments.

Optimization Models in Portfolio Construction

Portfolio optimization models, such as the Markowitz efficient . frontier, provide investors with a systematic approach to constructing optimal portfolios that balance risk and return. Practical implementation of these models often involves utilizing quadratic programming to determine the optimal asset weights that maximize expected returns for a defined risk level or minimize risk for a target return.

The following Python example illustrates how to implement

these optimization techniques:

```python
``` python from scipy.optimize import minimize

\#\# Assuming expected returns and covariance matrix are already computed
expected_returns = np.array([0.04, 0.06, 0.08])
cov_matrix = np.array([[0.001, 0.0008, 0.0009],
[0.0008, 0.0025, 0.0013],
[0.0009, 0.0013, 0.004]])

def portfolio_volatility(weights):
return     np.sqrt(np.dot(weights.T,     np.dot(cov_matrix, weights)))

\#\# Constraints: sum of weights = 1 and weights >= 0
constraints = 'type': 'eq', 'fun': lambda x: np.sum(x) - 1
bounds = tuple((0, 1) for _ in range(len(expected_returns)))

\#\# Initial guess
initial_weights = np.array([1/3, 1/3, 1/3])

\#\# Optimization
optimized = minimize(portfolio_volatility, initial_weights,
method='SLSQP', bounds=bounds, constraints=constraints)
optimal_weights = optimized.x
` ` `
```

Through these optimization techniques, investors can adeptly navigate complex trade-offs, enhance portfolio performance, and respond effectively to the ever-evolving landscape of financial markets. The continuous adaptation and integration of these models not only foster innovation in quantitative finance but also serve as a foundation for future advancements, ensuring that professionals remain adept in a rapidly changing environment.

Insights from Industry Practitioners

The world of quantitative finance is not solely defined by
```

sophisticated models and complex algorithms; it's equally shaped by the brilliant minds who wield them. Engaging with industry practitioners provides a profound understanding of the real-world challenges and innovative strategies that set this field apart. These discussions bridge the gap between theoretical knowledge and practical application, showcasing the creativity and critical thinking required to thrive in a fast-paced, ever-changing market landscape.

Bridging Theory and Practice

In the vibrant atmosphere of a bustling financial district office, we had the privilege of speaking with Emily Zhang, a senior quantitative analyst at a prominent hedge fund renowned for her adept use of machine learning models. Emily shared her perspective on the multifaceted challenges she encounters: "One of the greatest hurdles we face is transforming established theoretical models into something that resonates with the market's unique characteristics. Each day, we must evaluate the resilience of our strategies—founded on rigorous academic research—when they are put to the test in the unpredictable realm of live trading."

Emily's insights underscored the imperative of continuous learning and adaptability. She recounted a recent initiative where her team incorporated unsupervised learning algorithms into their existing framework, allowing them to identify latent structures within high-dimensional datasets. This innovation provided them with the ability to detect emerging trends and execute timely trades. Such advancements illustrate the delicate balance between harnessing foundational knowledge and daring to explore uncharted territories.

Navigating Ethical Considerations

Our conversation also turned to ethical considerations, shaped by the insights of Rajan Patel, a seasoned risk manager at a proprietary trading firm. "In our relentless pursuit of alpha,"

Rajan explained, "it's easy to overlook the broader implications of our strategies. We must remain acutely aware of the ethical ramifications of our models, particularly concerning market manipulation and data privacy."

He shared a compelling story about an exploratory strategy that, unbeknownst to the team, was inadvertently increasing market volatility. This scenario prompted the firm to promptly reassess their approach. Rajan stressed the importance of embedding ethical reviews as a fundamental aspect of developing and implementing quantitative strategies, emphasizing that this entails not just regulatory compliance, but also a proactive commitment to understanding the societal impact of trading activities.

Leveraging Cross-Disciplinary Expertise

Our exploration continued with Dr. Helen Roberts, who transitioned from academia to finance and now leads a dynamic team of quantitative analysts at a multinational bank. Drawing from her background in computational physics, Helen offered a fresh perspective on financial modeling. "There's immense value in cross-disciplinary knowledge," she asserted. "It enables us to infuse diverse analytical techniques into our work, allowing for innovation that transcends conventional finance paradigms."

For instance, Helen described how her team adapted Monte Carlo methods—originally designed for particle physics simulations—to effectively price complex derivatives with multiple interacting variables. This melding of expertise exemplifies the growing trend of cross-disciplinary collaboration, which not only enhances the robustness of financial solutions but also fosters creative problem-solving.

Case Study: Transformative Trading Technologies

To further illustrate the significance of insights from practitioners, we examined Greenhill Capital's recent strategic overhaul. Engaging seasoned traders alongside computer scientists, the firm set out to create a proprietary algorithmic trading platform that marries rapid execution with adaptive learning capabilities. This initiative stemmed from a keen recognition that speed and adaptability are vital for sustaining a competitive edge.

Interviews with the core team revealed how they implemented real-time feedback loops, allowing the system to learn from past trades and fine-tune execution strategies on the fly. This method not only enhanced trading efficiency but also significantly reduced transaction costs, underscoring the tangible advantages of integrating practitioners' expertise with cutting-edge technology.

These firsthand narratives illuminate the indispensable role of industry practitioners in translating theoretical models into impactful, real-world applications. Their experiences reflect the nuanced dynamics of the field, highlighting the necessity for continuous adaptation and a heightened ethical consciousness.

Incorporating such a diverse array of perspectives not only deepens our insights but also fosters the development of groundbreaking solutions, ensuring that the field intelligently and responsibly evolves. This dynamic interplay between theoretical rigor and practical expertise is what propels the continuous transformation and advancement of quantitative finance.

The Impact of Technology on Strategy
Implementation in Quantitative Finance

In the fast-paced world of quantitative finance, the intersection of innovative technology and strategic insight serves as the cornerstone of successful trading operations. As technological advancements unfold at an exponential rate, their influence on the execution of trading strategies becomes increasingly evident, reshaping the industry landscape and compelling professionals to continuously adapt in order to maintain a competitive edge. Technology now plays a dual role: it not only enhances speed and precision but also delivers insights that were once thought to be unattainable, significantly elevating the efficacy and execution of strategic models.

Transforming Algorithm Execution

The core of strategy implementation hinges on the execution mechanism, a process that has undergone a radical transformation due to technological developments. What was once a tedious, manual endeavor has now evolved into a streamlined, algorithm-driven framework that allows for swift, automated trading. High-frequency trading platforms exemplify this revolution, employing intricate algorithms that conduct transactions in the blink of an eye—often in nanoseconds. These systems thrive on the analysis of vast data sets in real-time, spotting arbitrage opportunities and executing trades with remarkable efficiency.

Consider the innovative practice of co-location, where trading firms strategically position their servers close to exchange data centers. This proximity reduces latency, granting firms a vital advantage in high-speed trading environments. Algorithms can react to market fluctuations in an instant, capturing fleeting price discrepancies that competitors may miss entirely. This not only enhances the timing of trades but also significantly boosts profitability, underscoring the profound impact of technology on strategic execution.

Harnessing Big Data and Machine Learning

The fusion of big data analytics and machine learning has elevated the sophistication of strategy implementation to new heights. The capacity to process and analyze extensive data sets in real-time has unlocked avenues for innovative strategy development and adjustment. Machine learning algorithms excel at identifying complex patterns, offering traders predictive insights that refine decision-making.

Imagine a hedge fund employing a machine learning-based strategy to gauge social media sentiment. Rapidly analyzing tweets and posts, the model can forecast market movements with astounding accuracy, providing traders the foresight to position their portfolios advantageously ahead of market shifts. This integration of natural language processing and sentiment analysis illustrates the transformative potential of machine learning in guiding strategic decisions.

Strengthening Risk Management through Automation

Technology also plays a crucial role in enhancing risk management architectures within trading firms. Automated risk assessment tools are now essential in modern finance, delivering timely alerts and simulations that empower traders to navigate potential hazards. Utilizing advanced technologies like Monte Carlo simulations and value-at-risk (VaR) calculations, firms can dynamically assess and mitigate risks across a range of market conditions.

For example, a multi-strategy hedge fund might employ a sophisticated scenario generator that simulates thousands of potential outcomes based on current market data and historical trends. This advanced tool allows portfolio managers to proactively recalibrate their strategies, ensuring resilience even in turbulent market environments.

Navigating Implementation Challenges

While the advantages of integrating technology into strategy implementation are compelling, the process is not without its challenges. A significant hurdle remains the interoperability of legacy systems with modern technological solutions. As companies strive to leverage new tools, they often face integration roadblocks that can delay progress.

To overcome these challenges, many organizations are transitioning to modular, cloud-based infrastructures that facilitate seamless updates and technology integration. These scalable systems provide the agility required to keep pace with continuous technological advancements, minimizing disruptions and optimizing performance.

One prominent investment bank has successfully navigated this shift by moving from traditional onsite servers to a cloud-based trading platform. This transition not only enhanced operational efficiency and reduced costs but also unlocked vast computational resources, enabling complex simulations and real-time data processing that were previously inconceivable.

The influence of technology on strategy implementation within quantitative finance is both transformative and multifaceted. It empowers traders with accelerated execution capabilities, sophisticated data analytics, and enhanced risk management while posing challenges that necessitate strategic foresight and adaptation. As the technological landscape continues to advance, firms that embrace these changes will secure a competitive advantage, crafting strategies that not only satisfy but surpass the demands of today's dynamic marketplace.

In this intricate relationship between technology and strategy, the ultimate determinant of success lies in the foresight and adaptability of industry practitioners.

Cross-Disciplinary Synergies: Merging AI and Finance for a Transformative Future

In the vibrant world of quantitative finance, the fusion of cross-disciplinary strategies—especially those intertwining artificial intelligence (AI) with financial practices—has emerged as a game-changer. This innovative convergence not only amplifies the analytical prowess of financial models but also ignites fresh pathways that could fundamentally alter market dynamics. The rich interplay between AI and finance opens up a landscape of opportunities, each requiring a sophisticated grasp of these two interrelated domains.

The Power of AI in Financial Modeling

At the heart of financial modeling, AI's influence is strikingly significant, equipping professionals with tools capable of processing and learning from immense datasets that often overwhelm traditional methodologies. Machine learning, a dynamic subset of AI, empowers financial models to evolve and adapt as new information arises, thereby enhancing predictive accuracy and refining investment strategies.

Take, for example, the fascinating realm of reinforcement learning—a type of AI wherein algorithms glean optimal strategies through iterative trial and error. When applied to trading, these algorithms can simulate a multitude of scenarios, adjusting positions based on hypothetical market conditions. A prominent quantitative hedge fund exemplifies this with its use of reinforcement learning to automate portfolio management.

Unraveling Market Sentiment with AI

Another groundbreaking application of AI in finance resides in sentiment analysis, where natural language processing (NLP) algorithms dissect and interpret vast streams of textual data —spanning news articles to social media—enabling a deeper understanding of market sentiment. This proficiency provides traders with actionable insights that were once elusive.

Consider a hedge fund that employs a specialized NLP model, finely tuned to detect subtle linguistic cues reflecting market apprehension or optimism. In effect, it transforms qualitative insights into quantifiable strategies that drive decision-making.

Strengthening Fraud Detection and Compliance

The amalgamation of AI and finance also plays a crucial role in enhancing compliance and fraud detection—areas where the synergy of technology and finance enhances operational integrity. Advanced machine learning techniques can pinpoint unusual patterns that signal potential fraudulent activity, serving as a safeguard for both assets and reputational trust.

Imagine a financial institution leveraging AI-driven anomaly detection to monitor transactions continuously for irregularities. This level of automated vigilance accelerates detection and significantly reduces the risk of human error, thus ensuring robust compliance amidst ever-stricter regulatory frameworks.

Personalized Financial Services Powered by AI

The advent of AI into personalized financial services represents yet another frontier with transformative potential.

Take robo-advisors as a prime example; powered by sophisticated machine learning algorithms, these platforms provide customized investment advice derived from user-specific parameters, including risk tolerance and financial goals.

Collaboration: The Heart of Innovation in Cross-Disciplinary Strategies

The successful adoption of cross-disciplinary strategies in finance hinges on the cultivation of a collaborative environment where expertise in AI and finance can thrive.

For instance, a forward-thinking financial firm might host regular hackathons, where diverse talents convene to brainstorm and prototype AI solutions aimed at addressing specific market challenges. This culture of collaboration fosters continuous innovation, resulting in strategies that are not only cutting-edge but also highly pragmatic.

The intersection of AI and finance has heralded a new era in strategy formulation within quantitative finance. From refining financial modeling and enhancing compliance to personalizing client services, AI significantly broadens the toolkit available to finance professionals. As these cross-disciplinary strategies continue to advance, there is an increasing need for a profound collaborative understanding that intertwines both fields. Embracing this integration positions organizations to meet the present challenges of the market while navigating future opportunities with strategic foresight and agility.

Evolving Challenges in Quantitative Finance

The landscape of quantitative finance has undergone a significant transformation; what was once dominated by straightforward financial models and linear assumptions is now characterized by an intricate web of challenges. As the field evolves, finance professionals must skillfully navigate emerging hurdles that range from the frenetic pace of technological advancements to the pressing need for ethical considerations. Each challenge not only reflects a shift in paradigms but also emphasizes the necessity for rapid adaptation, strategic foresight, and unwavering ethical integrity.

Navigating Market Complexity with Advanced Models

One of the most pressing challenges in quantitative finance today is the escalating complexity of the market. Traditional financial models, which once sufficed in more straightforward environments, now struggle amid the high volatility resulting from interconnected global economies and sophisticated derivative instruments. Consider the complexities involved in accurately pricing options when geopolitical tensions or unexpected monetary policy shifts can trigger significant market movements almost instantaneously.

To address these challenges, finance professionals are increasingly turning to advanced stochastic models based on stochastic differential equations. These models allow for the incorporation of a multitude of variables that influence asset prices. However, their efficacy comes at a cost—they demand not only substantial computational resources but also a high level of expertise. This necessity compels finance professionals to continuously refine their skills and adapt to a rapidly changing analytical landscape.

The Data Deluge Dilemma

The phenomenon known as the 'data deluge' presents both remarkable opportunities and formidable challenges for quantitative finance. On one hand, the wealth of data available—ranging from atmospheric metrics that impact agricultural commodity pricing to social media sentiment analyses—opens the door to unparalleled alpha generation opportunities. On the other hand, sifting through this vast array to extract coherent insights is no small feat.

For example, a hedge fund may find itself overwhelmed with high-frequency trading data combined with unconventional datasets. The real challenge lies in designing scalable data architectures that can efficiently filter the noise while capturing valuable signals. This intricate balancing act requires a significant investment in both advanced technology and specialized skills, underscoring the necessity of a robust data strategy.

Balancing Automation and Human Oversight

The advent of algorithmic trading has revolutionized trade execution, allowing transactions to be conducted at breathtaking speeds. Yet, this innovation brings with it the critical challenge of ensuring effective human oversight. As algorithms gain increasing autonomy in making trading decisions, the risk of erratic market movements—such as those exemplified by the infamous 2010 flash crash—raises serious concerns about market stability.

Maintaining a delicate balance between the advantages of automation and the imperative for human judgment necessitates rigorous protocol, including detailed algorithm audits and well-structured contingency plans. Crafting these systems requires not only technological sophistication but also a commitment to prudent risk management, ensuring that human expertise remains a cornerstone of the decision-making framework.

Ethical Concerns and Regulatory Compliance

In the rush to capitalize on innovative quantitative models, the specter of ethical concerns looms large. Questions surrounding the fairness of algorithm-driven market impacts, potential biases embedded in AI models, and the ethical ramifications of utilizing specific datasets are more pertinent than ever. As regulations continue to evolve in response to these concerns, finance professionals must adopt an agile approach to ensure compliance.

For instance, consider the repercussions of biases in AI-driven credit scoring systems, where unconscious discrimination can have far-reaching ethical and legal consequences. To mitigate these risks, it is essential for finance professionals to embrace transparency in their modeling practices and continually assess and rectify biases. This not only aligns with regulatory standards but also meets societal expectations for fairness and accountability.

The Cost of Technological Advancements

While technological breakthroughs offer significant advantages, they also introduce challenges related to cost and resource allocation. Investments in high-tech infrastructure for high-frequency trading, the integration of artificial intelligence, and robust data processing capabilities necessitate substantial capital outlays. This can pose significant barriers for smaller firms striving to compete against established industry leaders.

For instance, the disparity in trading efficiency between firms that invest in cutting-edge photon-based data transfer systems—gaining microseconds in trade execution—and those that cannot afford such innovations exemplifies this issue. Competing on a technological basis often drives firms toward strategic collaborations and partnerships, allowing them to pool resources and enhance their competitive edge.

As we delve deeper into the complexities of quantitative finance, it becomes evident that each challenge serves as a clarion call for innovation and adaptability. Finance professionals must leverage interdisciplinary expertise, invest in state-of-the-art technology, and cultivate a culture of ethical behavior to successfully navigate this evolving landscape. Ultimately, the path forward requires not just simplistic solutions, but the construction of a resilient framework capable of withstanding the dynamic nature of market developments—while judiciously employing technology with a strong ethical foundation.

Practical Considerations in Strategy Deployment

In the complex world of quantitative finance, the deployment of trading strategies is where theoretical insights confront the realities of the market. While meticulously designed models and algorithms form the foundation of these strategies, transitioning from academic or simulated environments into live markets presents a myriad of practical challenges. A successful strategy implementation necessitates a thoughtful combination of technical expertise, strategic foresight, and the ability to adapt to the constantly shifting landscape of financial markets.

Understanding Market Conditions and Adapting Strategies

The inherently dynamic nature of financial markets means that deploying a trading strategy is not a one-off task. Professionals must engage in continuous monitoring and assessment of market conditions to ensure their strategies remain robust and effective. Take, for instance, a momentum-based trading strategy that flourishes in trending markets; if the market shifts into a range-bound phase, this approach may struggle, calling for timely adjustments or even a complete re deployment.

For example, a quantitative trader utilizing a momentum strategy may observe that the current volatility index (VIX) is at historically low levels, suggesting a period of market complacency. In this environment, momentum signals may become unreliable, prompting the trader to pivot to a mean reversion strategy instead. This scenario highlights the necessity of having a repertoire of adaptable strategies and the agility to respond promptly to real-time market signals.

Infrastructure and Technology Considerations

The technological infrastructure underpinning a trading operation is crucial to successful strategy deployment. Whether dealing with high-frequency trading that demands ultra-low latency networks or sophisticated environments for backtesting, having the right technological framework in place is essential. Choosing between developing in-house solutions or collaborating with external providers can dramatically impact the efficiency and cost-effectiveness of strategy execution.

For instance, implementing high-frequency trading algorithms necessitates an infrastructure capable of processing vast amounts of data within milliseconds. Decisions about hosting servers near major exchange data centers to minimize latency must be carefully considered against their associated costs. This decision-making process underscores the importance of aligning infrastructure investments with the operational needs of specific trading strategies.

Risk Management and Compliance

A comprehensive risk management framework is vital for the successful deployment of trading strategies. Professionals need to anticipate potential risks associated with each strategy and establish controls to mitigate them. Employing risk metrics such as Value-at-Risk (VaR) and Conditional Value-at-Risk (CVaR) is essential for gauging potential losses during deployment, enabling teams to prepare for sudden adverse market events.

Compliance also plays a critical role, particularly given the ever-evolving regulatory landscape that governs financial markets. Consider an algorithm designed to capitalize on small price discrepancies in exotic options markets; a thorough legal assessment is necessary to ensure compliance with regulatory requirements, avoiding potentially significant penalties or sanctions.

Performance Monitoring and Real-Time Analytics

Initiating a strategy in the market is merely the first step; ongoing performance monitoring is crucial. Real-time analytics empower practitioners to evaluate the current effectiveness of strategies, make informed adjustments, and minimize lag time in decision-making. Utilizing dashboards to track key performance indicators such as the Sharpe ratio, maximum drawdown, and alpha generation can provide immediate feedback on the status of deployed strategies.

For instance, a portfolio manager might observe an unexpected increase in drawdown for one of their strategies during a routine performance analysis. A thorough investigation into real-time data could reveal the root cause— perhaps a glitch in a data feed or a significant macroeconomic event—prompting swift corrective measures. This scenario illustrates the pivotal role of timely information in sustaining the health of trading strategies.

Leveraging Historical Insights and Feedback Loops

The deployment phase can be significantly enhanced by leveraging historical performance insights and establishing robust feedback loops. Analyzing previous strategy iterations can illuminate patterns of success and areas for improvement, creating a continuous improvement ethos. Feedback loops, where insights gleaned from live deployments inform the development cycle, play a crucial role in refining and optimizing future strategy iterations.

Imagine a machine learning-driven strategy that had previously suffered due to fluctuations in model training quality caused by changing market conditions. Incorporating real-world performance feedback into the retraining process for each deployment cycle allows for more accurate model adaptation—demonstrating the iterative nature of learning-based strategies and their responsiveness to real market dynamics.

Deploying quantitative strategies in live markets entails much more than simply executing a trade; it requires a comprehensive approach that integrates market awareness, technological proficiency, risk management, and continuous performance evaluation. This discussion not only emphasizes the importance of pragmatism and adaptability but also highlights the essential steps needed to transform theoretical models into actionable, effective market solutions.

The Future of Alpha Generation in Quantitative Investing

The landscape of alpha generation in quantitative investing is entering a new era, one shaped by rapid technological advancements, shifting market dynamics, and an unparalleled availability of data. As we embark on this journey through an evolving financial ecosystem, the challenge of capturing excess returns beyond market benchmarks—often referred to as "alpha"—is becoming intricately linked with breakthrough innovations in machine learning, big data analytics, and advanced risk management methodologies. This transformation is not only redefining the strategies employed in investment but also reshaping the foundational principles of quantitative finance.

Leveraging Artificial Intelligence and Machine Learning

Artificial intelligence (AI) and machine learning (ML) are at the forefront of revolutionizing alpha generation methods. These technologies empower the development of predictive models that can adapt and refine themselves as they process vast amounts of market data. Algorithms capable of self-learning can detect intricate patterns and correlations that traditional analytical approaches might overlook, unveiling lucrative opportunities for generating alpha.

Imagine a scenario where an AI-driven strategy employs deep learning models to analyze stock price movements by synthesizing complex variables, including sentiment derived from financial news, trading volumes, and historical pricing trends. This model, continually enhanced by real-time data, can potentially preserve its competitive edge even in fluctuating market conditions, enabling sustained alpha generation over time.

Embracing Alternative Data Sources

The integration of alternative data—encompassing everything from satellite imagery to social media insights—is fundamentally altering how quantitative analysts uncover alpha. The challenge, however, lies in skillfully converting these varied data streams into actionable intelligence.

Consider hedge funds utilizing weather sensor data to predict agricultural commodity price movements or employing geolocation analytics to monitor foot traffic at retail locations. These examples exemplify how alternative data can be effectively leveraged to identify neglected investment opportunities. In the coming years, the ability to adeptly harness this diverse array of data will be a crucial determinant of alpha generation success.

Exploring Decentralized Finance (DeFi) Innovations

The emergence of decentralized finance (DeFi) is opening up innovative pathways for alpha generation, fundamentally reinventing traditional financial concepts through blockchain technology. Within this burgeoning domain, opportunities abound in areas such as tokenization, automated market-making, and smart contracts—novel frameworks that enable quantitative strategies to exploit arbitrage and yield farming within digital asset markets.

Picture a trading strategy that utilizes smart contracts to execute transactions automatically based on predefined conditions linked to liquidity pools in decentralized exchanges.

Addressing Complexity with Enhanced Risk Management

As quantitative strategies become more sophisticated, the complexities associated with risk management grow correspondingly. Therefore, robust risk management frameworks are essential in effectively addressing the multifaceted risks that accompany alpha generation strategies. Cutting-edge risk management systems that utilize AI-driven scenario analysis and stress testing capabilities can significantly enhance the ability to foresee and manage adverse market events.

A quant strategy that integrates these advanced risk management techniques would not only monitor traditional indicators like Value-at-Risk (VaR) but would also dynamically adjust risk exposure based on predictive analytics derived from AI models. This ensures not only consistent alpha generation but also provides a safeguard against volatile market conditions.

Navigating Ethical Considerations and Regulatory Evolution

In tandem with these technological advancements, ethical and regulatory considerations are emerging as crucial factors influencing the future of alpha generation. With heightened attention on data privacy, algorithmic accountability, and ethical investing practices, quantitative analysts must adeptly navigate a complex regulatory environment to maintain compliance and uphold responsible investment strategies.

For instance, potential regulations might call for increased transparency in algorithmic decision-making processes, compelling quants to craft strategies that are not only high-performing but also ethically conscientious and in alignment with existing legal frameworks. This challenge presents a delicate balancing act: pursuing alpha while ensuring adherence to ethical guidelines and regulatory standards.

The future of alpha generation in quantitative investing will hinge on the seamless integration of advanced technologies, innovative data approaches, and resilient risk management frameworks. As the financial landscape continues to evolve, quants must cultivate a blend of analytical skill and ethical foresight to formulate transformative investment strategies that surpass traditional methodologies.

APPENDIX A: TUTORIALS

Comprehensive Project: Data Acquisition and Management

Objective:

To provide students with hands-on experience in acquiring, cleaning, preprocessing, and managing financial data. The project will culminate in creating a clean and comprehensive dataset suitable for quantitative analysis.

Project Overview:

1. Introduction to Data Types and Sources
2. Data Collection and Acquisition
3. Data Cleaning and Preprocessing
4. Handling Missing Data and Outliers
5. Data Storage and Retrieval Frameworks
6. Time Series vs. Cross-Sectional Data Analysis

Step-by-Step Instructions:

Step 1: Introduction to Data Types and Sources

Objective: Understand different types of data in quantitative finance and familiarize with common data sources and platforms.

1. Research and Report:
2. Write a brief report (1-2 pages) on the types of data used in quantitative finance (historical, real-time, alternative data).

3. Identify at least three data sources/platforms (e.g., Bloomberg, Reuters, Quandl) and describe the type of data they provide.

Deliverable: A written report on data types and sources.

Step 2: Data Collection and Acquisition

Objective: Acquire a dataset from a reliable financial data source.

1. Choose a Dataset:
2. Select a financial dataset from one of the identified sources (e.g., historical stock prices from Yahoo Finance, economic indicators from FRED).
3. Download Data:
4. Download the dataset in CSV format. Ensure it covers a sufficient time period (e.g., 5 years of daily stock prices).
5. Document Data Source:
6. Create a document detailing the source of the data, the variables included, and the time period covered.

Deliverable: A CSV file of the dataset and a document describing the dataset.

Step 3: Data Cleaning and Preprocessing

Objective: Clean and preprocess the acquired data to make it suitable for analysis.

1. Import Data:
2. Write a script in Python or R to import the CSV file.
3. Inspect Data:
4. Inspect the data for any inconsistencies or errors (e.g., incorrect data types, duplicated rows).
5. Clean Data:

6. Perform data cleaning tasks such as:
7. Converting data types (e.g., dates to datetime format).
8. Removing duplicate rows.
9. Renaming columns for clarity.

Deliverable: A cleaned dataset and the code used for cleaning.

Step 4: Handling Missing Data and Outliers

Objective: Address missing values and outliers in the dataset.

1. Identify Missing Values:
2. Identify any missing values in the dataset and summarize the extent of missing data.

3. Handle Missing Values:

4. Choose an appropriate method to handle missing values (e.g., imputation, removal).

5. Detect Outliers:

6. Use statistical methods to detect outliers in the dataset (e.g., Z-score, IQR method).

7. Treat Outliers:

8. Decide on a method to treat outliers (e.g., capping, removal).

Deliverable: A dataset with handled missing values and outliers, and the code used for these tasks.

Step 5: Data Storage and Retrieval Frameworks

Objective: Implement a framework for storing and retrieving the cleaned data.

1. Choose a Storage Solution:
2. Select a suitable data storage solution (e.g., SQL database, NoSQL database, cloud storage).

3. Store Data:

4. Write a script to store the cleaned dataset in the chosen storage solution.

5. Retrieve Data:

6. Write a script to retrieve data from the storage solution for future use.

Deliverable: Scripts for storing and retrieving data, and confirmation of data being stored correctly.

Step 6: Time Series vs. Cross-Sectional Data Analysis

Objective: Understand the differences between time series and cross-sectional data analysis.

1. Time Series Analysis:
2. Perform a basic time series analysis on the dataset (e.g., plotting time series data, calculating moving averages).

3. Cross-Sectional Analysis:
4. Perform a basic cross-sectional analysis on the dataset (e.g., comparing the performance of different stocks at a specific point in time).

5. Write a Report:

6. Write a brief report (1-2 pages) summarizing the differences between time series and cross-sectional data analysis and presenting your findings from the analyses performed.

Deliverable: A written report and accompanying analysis scripts.

Final Submission:

Students should compile all deliverables into a single project folder, including:

- Reports and documentation (in PDF format).
- Cleaned dataset (in CSV format).

- All scripts used for data cleaning, handling missing values and outliers, storing and retrieving data, and performing analyses.

Evaluation Criteria:

- Completeness: All steps are completed, and all deliverables are submitted.
- Accuracy: Data cleaning, handling of missing values and outliers, and analyses are performed correctly.
- Documentation: Clear and concise documentation is provided for each step.
- Code Quality: Code is well-organized, readable, and properly commented.
- Analysis and Insight: Demonstrates a clear understanding of the differences between time series and cross-sectional data analysis with insightful findings.

This project will equip students with practical skills in data acquisition and management, essential for any aspiring quantitative finance professional.

Comprehensive Project: Statistical Foundations for Quantitative Models

Objective:

To provide students with a thorough understanding and practical experience in the statistical foundations essential for building quantitative models. The project will culminate in a comprehensive report showcasing the analysis and insights derived from the selected financial dataset.

Project Overview:

1. Basic Statistical Concepts
2. Probability Distributions
3. Hypothesis Testing and Confidence Intervals
4. Regression Analysis
5. Time Series Analysis

6. Advanced Statistical Techniques (ARIMA, GARCH)
7. Exploratory Data Analysis (EDA)
8. Non-Parametric Methods
9. Multivariate Analysis
10. Simulation Methods

Step-by-Step Instructions:

Step 1: Basic Statistical Concepts

Objective: Understand and apply basic statistical concepts such as mean, variance, and correlation to a financial dataset.

1. Select Dataset:
2. Choose a financial dataset (e.g., daily stock prices, interest rates) from a reliable source.
3. Calculate Basic Statistics:
4. Calculate the mean, variance, and standard deviation for the selected variables in the dataset.
5. Compute the correlation matrix to understand the relationships between different variables.

Deliverable: A Jupyter notebook or R script with calculations and interpretations of the basic statistics.

Step 2: Probability Distributions

Objective: Explore and apply probability distributions to model financial data.

1. Visualize Distributions:
2. Plot histograms and probability density functions (PDFs) for key variables in the dataset.
3. Fit Distributions:
4. Fit common probability distributions (e.g., normal, log-normal, t-distribution) to the data.
5. Use goodness-of-fit tests (e.g., KS test) to evaluate the fit.

Deliverable: A Jupyter notebook or R script with

distribution fitting and evaluation, including visualizations and interpretations.

Step 3: Hypothesis Testing and Confidence Intervals

Objective: Conduct hypothesis testing and calculate confidence intervals for financial data.

1. Formulate Hypotheses:
2. Formulate null and alternative hypotheses for a selected financial metric (e.g., mean return).

3. Perform Tests:

4. Perform hypothesis tests (e.g., t-test, chi-square test) and interpret the results.
5. Calculate and interpret confidence intervals for key statistics.

Deliverable: A Jupyter notebook or R script with hypothesis testing procedures and results, including explanations.

Step 4: Regression Analysis

Objective: Perform regression analysis to identify relationships between financial variables.

1. Linear Regression:
2. Conduct a linear regression analysis to model the relationship between a dependent variable (e.g., stock returns) and one or more independent variables (e.g., market index).

3. Evaluate Model:

4. Assess the model's goodness-of-fit (e.g., R-squared, adjusted R-squared).
5. Check for assumptions (e.g., linearity, homoscedasticity) and potential issues (e.g., multicollinearity).

Deliverable: A Jupyter notebook or R script with regression analysis, model evaluation, and interpretations.

Step 5: Time Series Analysis

Objective: Analyze and model financial time series data.

1. Plot Time Series:
2. Plot the time series data to visualize trends, seasonality, and any anomalies.
3. Stationarity Tests:
4. Perform stationarity tests (e.g., ADF test) to determine if the time series is stationary.
5. Basic Models:
6. Apply basic time series models (e.g., moving averages, exponential smoothing).

Deliverable: A Jupyter notebook or R script with time series plots, stationarity test results, and basic time series models.

Step 6: Advanced Statistical Techniques (ARIMA, GARCH)

Objective: Apply advanced time series models to financial data.

1. ARIMA Modeling:
2. Identify and fit an ARIMA model to the time series data.
3. Evaluate the model using diagnostics (e.g., ACF, PACF plots) and forecast future values.
4. GARCH Modeling:
5. Fit a GARCH model to the financial time series to model volatility.
6. Assess the model's performance using appropriate metrics.

Deliverable: A Jupyter notebook or R script with ARIMA and GARCH modeling, including diagnostics and forecasts.

Step 7: Exploratory Data Analysis (EDA)

Objective: Perform exploratory data analysis to uncover

patterns and insights in the dataset.

1. Visual Analysis:
2. Create visualizations (e.g., scatter plots, heatmaps) to explore relationships and patterns in the data.
3. Summary Statistics:
4. Calculate and interpret summary statistics to gain insights into the dataset's characteristics.

Deliverable: A Jupyter notebook or R script with EDA visualizations and summary statistics.

Step 8: Non-Parametric Methods

Objective: Apply non-parametric methods to financial data.

1. Rank-Based Tests:
2. Conduct non-parametric tests (e.g., Wilcoxon signed-rank test) to compare distributions.
3. Kernel Density Estimation:
4. Use kernel density estimation (KDE) to estimate the probability density function of a variable.

Deliverable: A Jupyter notebook or R script with non-parametric tests and KDE, including interpretations.

Step 9: Multivariate Analysis

Objective: Perform multivariate analysis to understand the interactions between multiple financial variables.

1. Principal Component Analysis (PCA):
2. Apply PCA to reduce dimensionality and identify key components.
3. Cluster Analysis:
4. Perform cluster analysis (e.g., k-means) to group similar observations.

Deliverable: A Jupyter notebook or R script with PCA and

cluster analysis, including visualizations and interpretations.

Step 10: Simulation Methods

Objective: Use simulation methods to model and analyze financial data.

1. Monte Carlo Simulation:
2. Implement Monte Carlo simulation to model the uncertainty in financial forecasts.
3. Scenario Analysis:
4. Conduct scenario analysis to evaluate the impact of different market conditions.

Deliverable: A Jupyter notebook or R script with Monte Carlo simulations and scenario analysis, including results and interpretations.

Final Submission:

Students should compile all deliverables into a single project folder, including:

- Reports and documentation (in PDF format).
- Cleaned dataset (in CSV format).
- All scripts used for statistical analysis and modeling.

Evaluation Criteria:

- Completeness: All steps are completed, and all deliverables are submitted.
- Accuracy: Statistical analyses and modeling are performed correctly.
- Documentation: Clear and concise documentation is provided for each step.
- Code Quality: Code is well-organized, readable, and properly commented.
- Analysis and Insight: Demonstrates a clear understanding of statistical methods with insightful findings.

This project will equip students with practical skills in statistical analysis, essential for building robust quantitative models in finance.

Comprehensive Project: Building Alpha Models

Objective:

To provide students with a thorough understanding and practical experience in building alpha models. The project will culminate in a comprehensive report showcasing the development of an alpha model, its backtesting results, and insights derived from the analysis.

Project Overview:

1. Understanding Alpha
2. Factor Models in Finance
3. Risk-Adjusted Return Metrics
4. Valuation Metrics
5. Designing a Systematic Trading Strategy
6. Backtesting Frameworks
7. Common Pitfalls in Strategy Development
8. Case Studies of Successful Alpha Models
9. Portfolio Construction for Alpha Generation
10. Continuous Improvement of Models

Step-by-Step Instructions:

Step 1: Understanding Alpha

Objective: Understand the concept of alpha and its significance in investment strategies.

1. Research Alpha:
2. Read academic papers and industry reports on alpha.
3. Summarize the key points about what alpha represents and its importance.
4. Identify Alpha Opportunities:
5. List potential sources of alpha (e.g., market

inefficiencies, behavioral biases).

Deliverable: A brief report summarizing the concept of alpha, its significance, and identified sources of alpha.

Step 2: Factor Models in Finance

Objective: Apply factor models to identify sources of alpha.

1. Select Dataset:
2. Choose a financial dataset (e.g., stock returns, economic indicators).
3. Apply Factor Models:
4. Use factor models (e.g., Fama-French three-factor model) to analyze the dataset.
5. Identify which factors are significant in explaining returns.

Deliverable: A Jupyter notebook or R script with the factor model analysis, including visualizations and interpretations.

Step 3: Risk-Adjusted Return Metrics

Objective: Evaluate the performance of investment strategies using risk-adjusted return metrics.

1. Calculate Metrics:
2. Compute risk-adjusted return metrics (e.g., Sharpe ratio, Sortino ratio) for the dataset.
3. Interpret Results:
4. Interpret the calculated metrics to understand the risk-return profile of the investment.

Deliverable: A Jupyter notebook or R script with the calculation of risk-adjusted return metrics and their interpretations.

Step 4: Valuation Metrics

Objective: Use valuation metrics to assess the attractiveness of securities.

1. Select Valuation Metrics:
2. Choose relevant valuation metrics (e.g., P/E ratio, P/B ratio).
3. Analyze Securities:
4. Apply the selected valuation metrics to the dataset to identify undervalued or overvalued securities.

Deliverable: A Jupyter notebook or R script with valuation metric analysis and interpretation.

Step 5: Designing a Systematic Trading Strategy

Objective: Design a systematic trading strategy based on identified alpha opportunities.

1. Define Strategy Rules:
2. Clearly define the rules and logic of the trading strategy.
3. Implement Strategy:
4. Code the systematic trading strategy using a programming language (e.g., Python, R).

Deliverable: A Jupyter notebook or R script with the implementation of the trading strategy.

Step 6: Backtesting Frameworks

Objective: Backtest the trading strategy to evaluate its performance.

1. Set Up Backtesting Framework:
2. Use a backtesting framework (e.g., Backtrader, QuantConnect) to test the strategy.
3. Run Backtests:
4. Run the backtests on historical data and analyze the results.

Deliverable: A Jupyter notebook or R script with backtesting results, including performance metrics and visualizations.

Step 7: Common Pitfalls in Strategy Development

Objective: Identify and avoid common pitfalls in strategy development.

1. Research Pitfalls:
2. Read about common pitfalls (e.g., overfitting, data snooping) in strategy development.
3. Apply Best Practices:
4. Apply best practices to avoid these pitfalls in your strategy.

Deliverable: A brief report summarizing the common pitfalls and how they were addressed in the strategy development.

Step 8: Case Studies of Successful Alpha Models

Objective: Learn from case studies of successful alpha models.

1. Select Case Studies:
2. Choose case studies of successful alpha models from academic literature or industry reports.
3. Analyze Case Studies:
4. Analyze the selected case studies to identify key success factors and lessons learned.

Deliverable: A brief report summarizing the analysis of the case studies and key takeaways.

Step 9: Portfolio Construction for Alpha Generation

Objective: Construct a portfolio that maximizes alpha generation.

1. Select Securities:
2. Select a set of securities based on the alpha identified from the factor models and valuation metrics.
3. Construct Portfolio:

4. Use portfolio optimization techniques to construct a portfolio that aims to maximize alpha generation.

Deliverable: A Jupyter notebook or R script with the portfolio construction process and results.

Step 10: Continuous Improvement of Models

Objective: Continuously improve the alpha models using feedback and new data.

1. Implement Feedback Loop:
2. Set up a feedback loop to continuously monitor and improve the model.

3. Incorporate New Data:

4. Periodically incorporate new data and reassess the model's performance.

Deliverable: A brief report describing the continuous improvement process and any updates made to the model.

Final Submission:

Students should compile all deliverables into a single project folder, including:

- Reports and documentation (in PDF format).
- Cleaned dataset (in CSV format).
- All scripts used for analysis, modeling, and backtesting.

Evaluation Criteria:

- Completeness: All steps are completed, and all deliverables are submitted.
- Accuracy: Analyses and modeling are performed correctly.
- Documentation: Clear and concise documentation is provided for each step.
- Code Quality: Code is well-organized, readable, and properly commented.

- Analysis and Insight: Demonstrates a clear understanding of alpha models with insightful findings.

This project will equip students with practical skills in developing and backtesting alpha models, essential for successful quantitative finance strategies.

Comprehensive Project: Advanced Machine Learning Techniques

Objective:

To provide students with a deep understanding and hands-on experience with advanced machine learning techniques applied to financial data. The project will culminate in a comprehensive report showcasing the development, validation, and performance of machine learning models applied to a financial dataset.

Project Overview:

1. Overview of Machine Learning in Finance
2. Supervised vs. Unsupervised Learning
3. Popular Algorithms (Decision Trees, Neural Networks, SVM)
4. Feature Selection and Engineering
5. Model Validation and Testing
6. Ensemble Methods for Enhanced Performance
7. Overfitting and Regularization Techniques
8. Using Natural Language Processing (NLP) for Sentiment Analysis
9. Reinforcement Learning Applications in Trading
10. Ethical Implications of Machine Learning in Finance

Step-by-Step Instructions:

Step 1: Overview of Machine Learning in Finance

Objective: Understand the role and applications of machine learning in finance.

1. Research Applications:
2. Read academic papers and industry reports on machine learning applications in finance.
3. Summarize the key points about how machine learning is used in financial markets.
4. Identify Use Cases:
5. List potential use cases of machine learning in finance (e.g., fraud detection, algorithmic trading).

Deliverable: A brief report summarizing the applications and use cases of machine learning in finance.

Step 2: Supervised vs. Unsupervised Learning

Objective: Understand the difference between supervised and unsupervised learning and their applications.

1. Select Dataset:
2. Choose a financial dataset (e.g., stock prices, transaction data).
3. Apply Supervised Learning:
4. Use a supervised learning algorithm (e.g., linear regression, classification) to predict an outcome.
5. Evaluate the model's performance using appropriate metrics.
6. Apply Unsupervised Learning:
7. Use an unsupervised learning algorithm (e.g., clustering, PCA) to uncover patterns.

Deliverable: A Jupyter notebook or R script with both supervised and unsupervised learning models, including visualizations and interpretations.

Step 3: Popular Algorithms (Decision Trees, Neural Networks, SVM)

Objective: Implement and compare the performance of

popular machine learning algorithms.

1. Implement Algorithms:
2. Decision Trees
3. Neural Networks
4. Support Vector Machines (SVM)
5. Compare Performance:
6. Evaluate and compare the performance of these algorithms on the chosen dataset.

Deliverable: A Jupyter notebook or R script with the implementation of the algorithms, performance comparisons, and visualizations.

Step 4: Feature Selection and Engineering

Objective: Enhance model performance through feature selection and engineering.

1. Feature Selection:
2. Use techniques like correlation analysis, mutual information, and recursive feature elimination.
3. Feature Engineering:
4. Create new features based on domain knowledge and data transformations.

Deliverable: A Jupyter notebook or R script with feature selection and engineering processes, including the rationale for chosen features.

Step 5: Model Validation and Testing

Objective: Validate and test the machine learning models to ensure robustness.

1. Validation Techniques:
2. Use cross-validation, train-test split, and other techniques to validate models.
3. Performance Metrics:

4. Evaluate models using metrics like accuracy, precision, recall, F1-score, and ROC-AUC.

Deliverable: A Jupyter notebook or R script with model validation, testing processes, and performance metrics.

Step 6: Ensemble Methods for Enhanced Performance

Objective: Improve model performance using ensemble methods.

1. Implement Ensemble Methods:
2. Bagging (e.g., Random Forest)
3. Boosting (e.g., XGBoost, AdaBoost)
4. Stacking

5. Evaluate Performance:

6. Compare the performance of ensemble methods with individual models.

Deliverable: A Jupyter notebook or R script with the implementation of ensemble methods, performance comparisons, and visualizations.

Step 7: Overfitting and Regularization Techniques

Objective: Address overfitting using regularization techniques.

1. Identify Overfitting:
2. Detect overfitting through training and validation performance discrepancies.

3. Apply Regularization:

4. Use techniques like Lasso, Ridge, and Elastic Net regularization.

Deliverable: A Jupyter notebook or R script with regularization techniques applied and their impact on model performance.

Step 8: Using Natural Language Processing (NLP) for Sentiment Analysis

Objective: Apply NLP techniques to perform sentiment analysis on financial news or social media data.

1. Collect Text Data:
2. Gather financial news or social media data relevant to the chosen financial dataset.
3. Perform Sentiment Analysis:
4. Use NLP libraries (e.g., NLTK, spaCy) to preprocess text and perform sentiment analysis.

Deliverable: A Jupyter notebook or R script with the NLP process, sentiment analysis results, and their application to the financial dataset.

Step 9: Reinforcement Learning Applications in Trading

Objective: Explore the application of reinforcement learning in trading strategies.

1. Implement Reinforcement Learning:
2. Use libraries like OpenAI Gym to develop and train a reinforcement learning trading agent.
3. Evaluate Performance:
4. Assess the agent's performance in a simulated trading environment.

Deliverable: A Jupyter notebook or R script with the reinforcement learning model, training process, and performance evaluation.

Step 10: Ethical Implications of Machine Learning in Finance

Objective: Understand and address the ethical implications of machine learning in finance.

1. Research Ethical Issues:
2. Read about ethical concerns (e.g., bias, transparency, accountability) in machine learning applications.
3. Propose Solutions:

4. Suggest methods to mitigate ethical issues in financial machine learning models.

Deliverable: A brief report summarizing the ethical implications and proposed solutions to mitigate them.

Final Submission:

Students should compile all deliverables into a single project folder, including:

- Reports and documentation (in PDF format).
- Cleaned dataset (in CSV format).
- All scripts used for analysis, modeling, and validation.

Evaluation Criteria:

- Completeness: All steps are completed, and all deliverables are submitted.
- Accuracy: Analyses and modeling are performed correctly.
- Documentation: Clear and concise documentation is provided for each step.
- Code Quality: Code is well-organized, readable, and properly commented.
- Analysis and Insight: Demonstrates a clear understanding of machine learning techniques with insightful findings.

This project will equip students with practical skills in applying advanced machine learning techniques to financial data, essential for successful quantitative finance strategies.

Comprehensive Project: Risk Management in Quantitative Strategies

Objective:

To provide students with a thorough understanding and practical experience in risk management within quantitative finance. The project will culminate in a comprehensive report showcasing the development and application of risk management strategies based on a financial dataset.

Project Overview:

1. Importance of Risk Management
2. Types of Financial Risk (Market, Credit, Operational)
3. Measuring Risk (VaR, CVaR, Stress Testing)
4. Risk-Reward Trade-offs in Alpha Generation
5. Diversification Strategies
6. Dynamic Risk Management Techniques
7. Implementing Risk Limits in Trading Systems
8. Crisis Management and Contingency Planning
9. Case Studies of Risk Management Failures
10. Future Trends in Risk Management Strategies

Step-by-Step Instructions:

Step 1: Importance of Risk Management

Objective: Understand the fundamental importance of risk management in quantitative finance.

1. Research Key Concepts:
2. Read academic papers and industry reports on risk management in finance.
3. Summarize the key points about why risk management is critical in quantitative finance.
4. Identify Real-World Examples:
5. List real-world examples where effective risk management prevented significant losses.

Deliverable: A brief report summarizing the importance of risk management in quantitative finance and real-world examples.

Step 2: Types of Financial Risk (Market, Credit, Operational)

Objective: Understand and differentiate between market, credit, and operational risks.

1. Define Each Risk Type:

2. Provide clear definitions and examples of market risk, credit risk, and operational risk.

3. Identify Risk Factors:

4. Identify and list factors contributing to each type of risk in a chosen financial dataset.

Deliverable: A document detailing the types of financial risk, their definitions, and contributing factors.

Step 3: Measuring Risk (VaR, CVaR, Stress Testing)

Objective: Measure financial risk using VaR (Value at Risk), CVaR (Conditional Value at Risk), and stress testing techniques.

1. Implement VaR:
2. Calculate VaR using historical and parametric methods.

3. Implement CVaR:

4. Calculate CVaR to understand potential losses beyond VaR.

5. Conduct Stress Testing:

6. Perform stress testing to evaluate the impact of extreme market conditions.

Deliverable: A Jupyter notebook or R script with the implementation of VaR, CVaR, and stress testing, including visualizations and interpretations.

Step 4: Risk-Reward Trade-offs in Alpha Generation

Objective: Analyze the trade-offs between risk and reward in alpha generation strategies.

1. Calculate Risk-Adjusted Returns:
2. Use metrics like Sharpe Ratio, Sortino Ratio, and Information Ratio.

3. Evaluate Trade-offs:

4. Analyze the trade-offs between risk and reward for different alpha generation strategies.

Deliverable: A Jupyter notebook or R script with calculations of risk-adjusted returns and an analysis of risk-reward trade-offs.

Step 5: Diversification Strategies

Objective: Understand and apply diversification strategies to manage risk.

1. Construct Diversified Portfolios:
2. Create portfolios using different asset classes and sectors to diversify risk.
3. Evaluate Diversification Benefits:
4. Measure the impact of diversification on portfolio risk and return.

Deliverable: A Jupyter notebook or R script with diversified portfolio construction and an evaluation of diversification benefits.

Step 6: Dynamic Risk Management Techniques

Objective: Apply dynamic risk management techniques to adapt to changing market conditions.

1. Implement Dynamic Hedging:
2. Use techniques like delta hedging and volatility targeting.
3. Adjust Portfolios Dynamically:
4. Rebalance portfolios based on changing market conditions and risk profiles.

Deliverable: A Jupyter notebook or R script with dynamic risk management techniques applied and their impact on portfolio risk and return.

Step 7: Implementing Risk Limits in Trading Systems

Objective: Implement risk limits to control exposure in trading systems.

1. Define Risk Limits:
2. Set limits for various risk factors (e.g., position size, leverage, drawdown).
3. Monitor and Enforce Limits:
4. Develop a system to continuously monitor and enforce risk limits.

Deliverable: A Jupyter notebook or R script with the implementation of risk limits and monitoring system.

Step 8: Crisis Management and Contingency Planning

Objective: Develop crisis management and contingency plans for extreme market events.

1. Identify Potential Crises:
2. List potential crises and their triggers (e.g., market crashes, liquidity crunches).
3. Develop Contingency Plans:
4. Create detailed plans to manage and mitigate the impact of identified crises.

Deliverable: A document outlining potential crises and detailed contingency plans.

Step 9: Case Studies of Risk Management Failures

Objective: Learn from historical cases of risk management failures.

1. Research Notable Failures:
2. Study cases like the 2008 financial crisis, LTCM collapse, and others.
3. Analyze Causes and Lessons:
4. Analyze the causes of these failures and the lessons learned.

Deliverable: A report summarizing case studies of risk management failures, their causes, and lessons learned.

Step 10: Future Trends in Risk Management Strategies

Objective: Explore future trends and innovations in risk management strategies.

1. Research Emerging Trends:
2. Read about new techniques and technologies in risk management (e.g., AI, blockchain).
3. Identify Potential Impacts:
4. Discuss how these trends could impact future risk management practices.

Deliverable: A report discussing future trends in risk management strategies and their potential impacts.

Final Submission:

Students should compile all deliverables into a single project folder, including:

- Reports and documentation (in PDF format).
- Cleaned dataset (in CSV format).
- All scripts used for analysis, modeling, and validation.

Evaluation Criteria:

- Completeness: All steps are completed, and all deliverables are submitted.
- Accuracy: Analyses and modeling are performed correctly.
- Documentation: Clear and concise documentation is provided for each step.
- Code Quality: Code is well-organized, readable, and properly commented.
- Analysis and Insight: Demonstrates a clear understanding of risk management techniques with

insightful findings.

This project will equip students with practical skills in applying risk management techniques to quantitative finance, essential for developing robust and resilient financial strategies.

Comprehensive Project: Algorithmic Trading and Execution Strategies

Objective:

To provide students with a thorough understanding and hands-on experience in algorithmic trading and execution strategies. The project will culminate in a comprehensive report and presentation showcasing their developed trading algorithms and execution strategies.

Project Overview:

1. Overview of Algorithmic Trading
2. Types of Trading Algorithms (Market Making, Arbitrage)
3. Execution Strategies (VWAP, TWAP)
4. Importance of Latency and Technology in Execution
5. Performance Metrics for Trading Algorithms
6. The Role of Market Microstructure
7. Regulatory Implications of Algorithmic Trading
8. Backtesting Execution Strategies
9. Cross-Asset and Multi-Market Trading Considerations
10. Future Developments in Trading Technology

Step-by-Step Instructions:

Step 1: Overview of Algorithmic Trading

Objective: Understand the basic concepts and significance of algorithmic trading.

1. Research Key Concepts:
2. Read academic papers, industry reports, and

QUANTITATIVE STRATEGIES: ADVANCED MODELS FOR ALPHA GENERAT...

textbooks on algorithmic trading.

3. Summarize key points about the history, evolution, and current state of algorithmic trading.

4. Identify Real-World Examples:

5. List real-world examples of successful algorithmic trading strategies and firms.

Deliverable: A brief report summarizing the overview of algorithmic trading and real-world examples.

Step 2: Types of Trading Algorithms
(Market Making, Arbitrage)

Objective: Understand and implement different types of trading algorithms.

1. Define Each Algorithm Type:

2. Provide clear definitions and examples of market-making and arbitrage algorithms.

3. Implement Market Making Algorithm:

4. Develop a simple market-making algorithm using historical price data.

5. Implement Arbitrage Algorithm:

6. Develop a basic arbitrage algorithm focusing on price discrepancies between markets.

Deliverable: A Jupyter notebook or R script with the implementation of market-making and arbitrage algorithms, including visualizations and explanations.

Step 3: Execution Strategies (VWAP, TWAP)

Objective: Implement and evaluate various execution strategies.

1. Define VWAP and TWAP:

2. Provide clear definitions and the mathematical formulations for VWAP (Volume Weighted Average

Price) and TWAP (Time Weighted Average Price).

3. Implement VWAP Execution Strategy:
4. Develop a VWAP strategy using historical trade data.
5. Implement TWAP Execution Strategy:
6. Develop a TWAP strategy using historical trade data.

Deliverable: A Jupyter notebook or R script with the implementation of VWAP and TWAP strategies, including visualizations and performance analysis.

Step 4: Importance of Latency and Technology in Execution

Objective: Understand the impact of latency and technology on trading execution.

1. Research the Impact of Latency:
2. Read articles and papers on the importance of low latency in high-frequency trading.
3. Evaluate Technology Solutions:
4. List and evaluate different technology solutions used to reduce latency (e.g., co-location, FPGA).

Deliverable: A report discussing the importance of latency and the role of technology in trading execution.

Step 5: Performance Metrics for Trading Algorithms

Objective: Measure and evaluate the performance of trading algorithms.

1. Identify Key Metrics:
2. Define metrics such as Sharpe Ratio, Sortino Ratio, Information Ratio, and execution cost.
3. Evaluate Algorithms:
4. Apply these metrics to evaluate the performance of the previously implemented trading algorithms.

Deliverable: A Jupyter notebook or R script with the

performance evaluation of trading algorithms using key metrics.

Step 6: The Role of Market Microstructure

Objective: Understand the role of market microstructure in algorithmic trading.

1. Research Market Microstructure:
2. Study the components of market microstructure, including order types, order books, and matching engines.
3. Analyze Order Book Data:
4. Use order book data to analyze and visualize market microstructure.

Deliverable: A report and visualizations analyzing the market microstructure based on order book data.

Step 7: Regulatory Implications of Algorithmic Trading

Objective: Understand the regulatory landscape affecting algorithmic trading.

1. Research Regulations:
2. Study regulations and guidelines from financial authorities (e.g., SEC, CFTC) regarding algorithmic trading.
3. Analyze Compliance Requirements:
4. Identify key compliance requirements for algorithmic trading systems.

Deliverable: A report summarizing the regulatory implications and compliance requirements for algorithmic trading.

Step 8: Backtesting Execution Strategies

Objective: Backtest the developed execution strategies using historical data.

1. Set Up Backtesting Environment:

2. Use Python libraries like Backtrader or R packages for backtesting.

3. Perform Backtesting:

4. Backtest the VWAP and TWAP strategies on historical data, adjusting parameters to optimize performance.

Deliverable: A Jupyter notebook or R script with backtesting results, including performance metrics and visualizations.

Step 9: Cross-Asset and Multi-Market Trading Considerations

Objective: Consider the challenges and strategies for cross-asset and multi-market trading.

1. Identify Challenges:
2. List challenges in cross-asset and multi-market trading, such as liquidity, correlation, and execution.

3. Develop Strategies:

4. Propose strategies to overcome these challenges, including portfolio diversification and multi-market execution techniques.

Deliverable: A report discussing the challenges and proposed strategies for cross-asset and multi-market trading.

Step 10: Future Developments in Trading Technology

Objective: Explore future trends and innovations in trading technology.

1. Research Emerging Technologies:
2. Read about new technologies and innovations in trading, such as AI, machine learning, and blockchain.

3. Identify Potential Impacts:

4. Discuss how these technologies could impact future trading strategies and market dynamics.

Deliverable: A report discussing future developments in

trading technology and their potential impacts.

Final Submission:

Students should compile all deliverables into a single project folder, including:

- Reports and documentation (in PDF format).
- Cleaned dataset (in CSV format).
- All scripts used for analysis, modeling, and validation.

Evaluation Criteria:

- Completeness: All steps are completed, and all deliverables are submitted.
- Accuracy: Analyses and modeling are performed correctly.
- Documentation: Clear and concise documentation is provided for each step.
- Code Quality: Code is well-organized, readable, and properly commented.
- Analysis and Insight: Demonstrates a clear understanding of algorithmic trading techniques with insightful findings.

This project will equip students with practical skills in applying algorithmic trading techniques, essential for developing robust and efficient trading strategies in quantitative finance.

Comprehensive Project: Behavioral Finance and Market Inefficiencies

Objective:

To provide students with a deep understanding of behavioral finance concepts and their impact on market inefficiencies. The project will culminate in a comprehensive report and presentation showcasing their findings and insights.

Project Overview:

1. Introduction to Behavioral Finance Concepts
2. Common Cognitive Biases Affecting Traders
3. The Influence of Sentiment on Market Movements
4. Identifying Market Inefficiencies
5. Quantitative Approaches to Behavioral Finance
6. Case Studies of Behavioral Anomalies
7. Integrating Behavioral Insights into Quantitative Models
8. Risk Management in the Context of Behavioral Finance
9. Predictive Power of Sentiment Indicators
10. The Role of Behavioral Finance in Alpha Generation

Step-by-Step Instructions:

Step 1: Introduction to Behavioral Finance Concepts

Objective: Understand the foundational concepts of behavioral finance.

1. Research Key Concepts:
2. Read academic papers, books, and articles on behavioral finance.
3. Summarize key concepts such as prospect theory, loss aversion, and mental accounting.
4. Create a Conceptual Framework:
5. Develop a visual framework or mind map illustrating the core principles of behavioral finance.

Deliverable: A brief report summarizing the key concepts of behavioral finance and a conceptual framework.

Step 2: Common Cognitive Biases Affecting Traders

Objective: Identify and understand common cognitive biases that affect traders.

1. Research Cognitive Biases:
2. List and define common cognitive biases such as

overconfidence, herd behavior, and anchoring.

3. Analyze Real-World Examples:

4. Provide examples of how these biases have affected trading decisions in real-world scenarios.

Deliverable: A report detailing common cognitive biases and real-world examples of their impact on trading.

Step 3: The Influence of Sentiment on Market Movements

Objective: Analyze the impact of market sentiment on price movements and trading decisions.

1. Collect Sentiment Data:
2. Gather sentiment data from social media, news, and financial reports.

3. Perform Sentiment Analysis:

4. Use natural language processing (NLP) techniques to analyze sentiment data and correlate it with market movements.

Deliverable: A Jupyter notebook or R script with sentiment analysis results, including visualizations and correlations with market movements.

Step 4: Identifying Market Inefficiencies

Objective: Identify and analyze market inefficiencies caused by behavioral factors.

1. Define Market Inefficiencies:
2. Provide clear definitions and examples of market inefficiencies.

3. Analyze Historical Data:

4. Use historical market data to identify patterns and anomalies indicative of inefficiencies.

Deliverable: A report and visualizations identifying market inefficiencies based on historical data analysis.

Step 5: Quantitative Approaches to Behavioral Finance

Objective: Apply quantitative methods to analyze and model behavioral finance phenomena.

1. Develop Quantitative Models:
2. Create models that incorporate behavioral finance concepts (e.g., sentiment-based trading strategies).
3. Evaluate Model Performance:
4. Backtest and evaluate the performance of these models using historical data.

Deliverable: A Jupyter notebook or R script with the development and evaluation of quantitative models, including performance analysis.

Step 6: Case Studies of Behavioral Anomalies

Objective: Study and analyze notable cases of behavioral anomalies in financial markets.

1. Select Case Studies:
2. Choose case studies of well-known behavioral anomalies (e.g., dot-com bubble, 2008 financial crisis).
3. Conduct In-Depth Analysis:
4. Analyze the selected cases to understand the role of behavioral factors.

Deliverable: A report with in-depth analyses of selected case studies, highlighting the behavioral factors involved.

Step 7: Integrating Behavioral Insights
into Quantitative Models

Objective: Integrate behavioral finance insights into existing quantitative models.

1. Modify Existing Models:
2. Adjust existing trading models to incorporate

behavioral insights (e.g., sentiment indicators).

3. Test and Validate:

4. Backtest and validate the modified models to assess improvements in performance.

Deliverable: A Jupyter notebook or R script showing the integration of behavioral insights into quantitative models, including backtesting results.

Step 8: Risk Management in the Context of Behavioral Finance

Objective: Develop risk management strategies that account for behavioral factors.

1. Identify Behavioral Risks:
2. List potential risks that arise from behavioral biases.

3. Develop Mitigation Strategies:

4. Propose risk management strategies to mitigate these behavioral risks.

Deliverable: A report detailing behavioral risks and proposed risk management strategies.

Step 9: Predictive Power of Sentiment Indicators

Objective: Assess the predictive power of sentiment indicators in trading strategies.

1. Develop Sentiment-Based Indicators:
2. Create sentiment indicators based on NLP analysis of news and social media.

3. Evaluate Predictive Performance:

4. Backtest trading strategies using these indicators to evaluate their predictive power.

Deliverable: A Jupyter notebook or R script with the development and evaluation of sentiment indicators, including backtesting results.

Step 10: The Role of Behavioral Finance in Alpha Generation

Objective: Explore the role of behavioral finance in generating alpha.

1. Analyze Successful Strategies:
2. Study successful trading strategies that leverage behavioral finance concepts.
3. Develop a Comprehensive Strategy:
4. Propose a comprehensive trading strategy that incorporates behavioral finance insights.

Deliverable: A report and presentation detailing the role of behavioral finance in alpha generation and a proposed comprehensive trading strategy.

Final Submission:

Students should compile all deliverables into a single project folder, including:

- Reports and documentation (in PDF format).
- Cleaned dataset (in CSV format).
- All scripts used for analysis, modeling, and validation.

Evaluation Criteria:

- Completeness: All steps are completed, and all deliverables are submitted.
- Accuracy: Analyses and modeling are performed correctly.
- Documentation: Clear and concise documentation is provided for each step.
- Code Quality: Code is well-organized, readable, and properly commented.
- Analysis and Insight: Demonstrates a clear understanding of behavioral finance concepts with insightful findings.

This project will equip students with practical skills and deep insights into how behavioral finance impacts market inefficiencies, essential for developing robust and effective trading strategies in quantitative finance.

Comprehensive Project: Portfolio Construction and Optimization

Objective:

To provide students with a thorough understanding of portfolio construction and optimization techniques. The project will culminate in a comprehensive report and presentation showcasing their findings and insights.

Project Overview:

1. Principles of Portfolio Theory
2. The Efficient Frontier and Risk-Return Trade-Off
3. Asset Allocation Strategies
4. Techniques for Portfolio Optimization (Markowitz, Black-Litterman)
5. Incorporating Alternative Assets in Portfolios
6. Dynamic Portfolio Adjustment Methodologies
7. Performance Evaluation and Attribution Analysis
8. The Role of Constraints in Portfolio Construction
9. Developing a Multi-Strategy Portfolio
10. Future Trends in Portfolio Management

Step-by-Step Instructions:

Step 1: Principles of Portfolio Theory

Objective: Understand the foundational principles of portfolio theory.

1. Research Key Concepts:
2. Study the basics of portfolio theory, including diversification, risk, return, and the relationship between them.
3. Read academic papers and textbooks on modern

portfolio theory (MPT).

4. Summarize Key Concepts:

5. Write a summary explaining the core principles of portfolio theory, including the benefits of diversification.

Deliverable: A brief report summarizing the key principles of portfolio theory.

Step 2: The Efficient Frontier and Risk-Return Trade-Off

Objective: Analyze and visualize the efficient frontier and understand the risk-return trade-off.

1. Collect Data:
2. Gather historical price data for a selection of stocks or assets.

3. Calculate Metrics:

4. Compute expected returns, standard deviations, and the covariance matrix for the selected assets.

5. Construct the Efficient Frontier:

6. Use Python or R to construct and visualize the efficient frontier.

Deliverable: A Jupyter notebook or R script with calculations and visualizations of the efficient frontier, along with a report explaining the findings.

Step 3: Asset Allocation Strategies

Objective: Explore different asset allocation strategies and their implications.

1. Research Asset Allocation Models:
2. Study various asset allocation strategies such as strategic, tactical, and dynamic asset allocation.

3. Apply Asset Allocation Models:

4. Implement different asset allocation strategies using historical data.

Deliverable: A report detailing the different asset allocation strategies and their application results, including visualizations.

Step 4: Techniques for Portfolio Optimization (Markowitz, Black-Litterman)

Objective: Optimize portfolios using different methodologies.

1. Markowitz Optimization:
2. Implement the Markowitz mean-variance optimization model.
3. Black-Litterman Model:
4. Study and implement the Black-Litterman model for portfolio optimization.

Deliverable: A Jupyter notebook or R script implementing both optimization techniques, along with a report comparing their performance.

Step 5: Incorporating Alternative Assets in Portfolios

Objective: Understand the role of alternative assets in portfolio construction.

1. Research Alternative Assets:
2. Study different types of alternative assets (e.g., real estate, commodities, hedge funds).
3. Analyze Impact:
4. Analyze the impact of including alternative assets in a portfolio on risk and return.

Deliverable: A report detailing the analysis of alternative assets' impact on portfolio performance, including visualizations.

Step 6: Dynamic Portfolio Adjustment Methodologies

Objective: Explore methodologies for dynamically adjusting portfolio allocations.

1. Research Dynamic Adjustment Techniques:
2. Study techniques such as constant proportion portfolio insurance (CPPI) and time-varying asset allocation.
3. Implement Dynamic Adjustments:
4. Apply dynamic adjustment techniques to a sample portfolio.

Deliverable: A Jupyter notebook or R script with the implementation of dynamic adjustment techniques, along with a report explaining the results.

Step 7: Performance Evaluation and Attribution Analysis

Objective: Evaluate and attribute the performance of constructed portfolios.

1. Develop Evaluation Metrics:
2. Define performance metrics such as Sharpe ratio, Sortino ratio, and alpha.
3. Conduct Attribution Analysis:
4. Perform attribution analysis to determine the sources of portfolio returns.

Deliverable: A report detailing the performance evaluation and attribution analysis of the constructed portfolios, including visualizations.

Step 8: The Role of Constraints in Portfolio Construction

Objective: Understand and apply constraints in portfolio construction.

1. Research Constraints:
2. Study different types of constraints (e.g., budget, regulatory, ESG).

3. Apply Constraints:

4. Implement constraints in the portfolio optimization process.

Deliverable: A Jupyter notebook or R script with the implementation of constrained optimization, along with a report explaining the impact of constraints on the portfolio.

Step 9: Developing a Multi-Strategy Portfolio

Objective: Develop a multi-strategy portfolio combining different investment strategies.

1. Research Multi-Strategy Approaches:
2. Study various multi-strategy approaches and their benefits.

3. Construct a Multi-Strategy Portfolio:

4. Develop and implement a multi-strategy portfolio using historical data.

Deliverable: A report detailing the development and performance of the multi-strategy portfolio, including visualizations.

Step 10: Future Trends in Portfolio Management

Objective: Explore future trends and developments in portfolio management.

1. Research Emerging Trends:
2. Study emerging trends such as robo-advisors, AI in portfolio management, and sustainable investing.

3. Analyze Potential Impact:

4. Analyze the potential impact of these trends on portfolio management practices.

Deliverable: A report summarizing the future trends in portfolio management and their potential impact on the industry.

Final Submission:

Students should compile all deliverables into a single project folder, including:

- Reports and documentation (in PDF format).
- Cleaned dataset (in CSV format).
- All scripts used for analysis, modeling, and validation.

Evaluation Criteria:

- Completeness: All steps are completed, and all deliverables are submitted.
- Accuracy: Analyses and modeling are performed correctly.
- Documentation: Clear and concise documentation is provided for each step.
- Code Quality: Code is well-organized, readable, and properly commented.
- Analysis and Insight: Demonstrates a clear understanding of portfolio construction and optimization concepts with insightful findings.

This project will equip students with practical skills and deep insights into portfolio construction and optimization, essential for developing robust and effective investment strategies in quantitative finance.

Comprehensive Project: Case Studies and Real-World Applications

Objective:

To provide students with a practical understanding of quantitative finance through the analysis of real-world case studies. The project will culminate in a detailed report and presentation.

Project Overview:

1. Overview of Successful Quantitative Hedge Funds
2. Analysis of Notable Quantitative Strategies

3. Lessons Learned from High-Profile Failure Cases
4. Practical Applications of Various Models
5. Interviews with Industry Practitioners
6. The Impact of Technology on Strategy Implementation
7. Cross-Disciplinary Strategies (AI, Finance, etc.)
8. Evolving Challenges in Quantitative Finance
9. Practical Considerations in Strategy Deployment
10. Future of Alpha Generation in Quantitative Investing

Step-by-Step Instructions:

Step 1: Overview of Successful Quantitative Hedge Funds

Objective: Understand the characteristics and strategies of successful quantitative hedge funds.

1. Research Successful Hedge Funds:
2. Identify and research at least three successful quantitative hedge funds (e.g., Renaissance Technologies, Two Sigma, D.E. Shaw & Co.).
3. Study their founding history, primary strategies, and key success factors.
4. Summarize Findings:
5. Write a summary highlighting the key strategies and success factors of these hedge funds.

Deliverable: A report summarizing the characteristics and strategies of successful quantitative hedge funds.

Step 2: Analysis of Notable Quantitative Strategies

Objective: Analyze and evaluate notable quantitative strategies.

1. Select Strategies:
2. Choose at least three notable quantitative strategies (e.g., statistical arbitrage, trend-following, high-frequency trading).

3. Perform Analysis:

4. Analyze the mechanics, data requirements, and risk management techniques of each strategy.

5. Evaluate their historical performance and limitations.

Deliverable: A detailed report analyzing the selected quantitative strategies, including visualizations and performance metrics.

Step 3: Lessons Learned from High-Profile Failure Cases

Objective: Understand the reasons behind the failure of high-profile quantitative strategies.

1. Research Failure Cases:

2. Identify and research at least two high-profile failure cases in quantitative finance (e.g., Long-Term Capital Management, Knight Capital).

3. Analyze Causes of Failure:

4. Analyze the key factors that led to the failure of these strategies (e.g., over-leverage, model risk, market anomalies).

Deliverable: A report detailing the lessons learned from high-profile failure cases, including an analysis of the causes and preventive measures.

Step 4: Practical Applications of Various Models

Objective: Apply quantitative models to real-world data and evaluate their performance.

1. Select Models:

2. Choose at least two quantitative models to apply (e.g., Black-Scholes model, CAPM, GARCH).

3. Collect Data:

4. Gather relevant historical data for the application of

the selected models.

5. Apply Models:

6. Implement the models using Python or R and evaluate their performance on the collected data.

Deliverable: A Jupyter notebook or R script with the implementation of the models, along with a report discussing their practical applications and results.

Step 5: Interviews with Industry Practitioners

Objective: Gain insights from industry practitioners on the implementation and challenges of quantitative strategies.

1. Identify Practitioners:
2. Reach out to at least two industry practitioners working in quantitative finance.
3. Conduct Interviews:
4. Prepare a set of questions to ask about their experiences, challenges, and insights.
5. Conduct and document the interviews.

Deliverable: A report summarizing the insights gained from the interviews with industry practitioners.

Step 6: The Impact of Technology on Strategy Implementation

Objective: Explore how technological advancements have influenced quantitative strategy implementation.

1. Research Technological Impact:
2. Study the impact of technologies such as high-frequency trading platforms, machine learning algorithms, and big data analytics on quantitative finance.
3. Analyze Case Studies:
4. Analyze case studies where technology has played a crucial role in strategy implementation and

performance.

Deliverable: A report detailing the impact of technology on quantitative strategy implementation, including case study analyses.

Step 7: Cross-Disciplinary Strategies (AI, Finance, etc.)

Objective: Explore the integration of cross-disciplinary strategies in quantitative finance.

1. Research Cross-Disciplinary Approaches:
2. Study how artificial intelligence, machine learning, and other disciplines are being integrated into quantitative finance.
3. Analyze Applications:
4. Analyze specific applications of cross-disciplinary strategies in quantitative models.

Deliverable: A report discussing cross-disciplinary strategies and their applications in quantitative finance.

Step 8: Evolving Challenges in Quantitative Finance

Objective: Identify and discuss the evolving challenges in the field of quantitative finance.

1. Research Challenges:
2. Study the current and emerging challenges faced by quantitative finance practitioners (e.g., regulatory changes, data privacy issues, model risk).
3. Analyze Impact:
4. Analyze how these challenges impact the development and implementation of quantitative strategies.

Deliverable: A report detailing the evolving challenges in quantitative finance and their potential impact on the industry.

Step 9: Practical Considerations in Strategy Deployment

Objective: Understand the practical considerations for deploying quantitative strategies.

1. Research Deployment Considerations:
2. Study the practical aspects of deploying quantitative strategies, including infrastructure, risk management, and compliance.
3. Develop Deployment Plan:
4. Develop a detailed deployment plan for a selected quantitative strategy.

Deliverable: A report outlining the practical considerations and a deployment plan for a selected quantitative strategy.

Step 10: Future of Alpha Generation in Quantitative Investing

Objective: Explore the future trends and developments in alpha generation.

1. Research Future Trends:
2. Study emerging trends and innovations in alpha generation, such as alternative data sources, advanced machine learning models, and ESG investing.
3. Analyze Potential Impact:
4. Analyze the potential impact of these trends on the future of quantitative investing.

Deliverable: A report summarizing the future trends in alpha generation and their potential impact on quantitative investing.

Final Submission:

Students should compile all deliverables into a single project folder, including:

- Reports and documentation (in PDF format).

- Cleaned dataset (in CSV format).
- All scripts used for analysis, modeling, and validation.
- Interview transcripts (if applicable).

Evaluation Criteria:

- Completeness: All steps are completed, and all deliverables are submitted.
- Accuracy: Analyses and modeling are performed correctly.
- Documentation: Clear and concise documentation is provided for each step.
- Code Quality: Code is well-organized, readable, and properly commented.
- Analysis and Insight: Demonstrates a clear understanding of case studies and real-world applications with insightful findings.

This project will equip students with practical skills and deep insights into real-world applications of quantitative finance, essential for developing robust and effective investment strategies.

APPENDIX B:
GLOSSARY OF TERMS

A

Alpha: A measure of investment performance on a risk-adjusted basis. Alpha represents the value that a portfolio manager adds to or subtracts from a portfolio's return.

Algorithmic Trading: The use of computer algorithms to automate trading decisions, often involving the timing, pricing, or volume of trades, to achieve the best possible outcomes.

Alternative Data: Non-traditional data sources that can provide unique insights into market conditions or company performance, such as satellite imagery, social media sentiment, or transaction data.

ARIMA (AutoRegressive Integrated Moving Average): A statistical analysis model used to forecast future points in a series by using parameters that account for autoregression, differencing, and moving averages.

B

Backtesting: The process of testing a trading strategy on historical data to evaluate its performance before applying it in live trading.

Behavioral Finance: A field of finance that studies how psychological influences and biases affect the financial behaviors of investors and financial practitioners.

Big Data: Extremely large data sets that may be analyzed computationally to reveal patterns, trends, and associations, especially relating to human behavior and interactions.

C

Correlation: A statistical measure that expresses the extent to which two variables are linearly related (ranges from -1 to 1).

Cross-Sectional Data: Data collected from multiple subjects (such as individuals, firms, or countries) at a single point in time.

CVaR (Conditional Value at Risk): A risk assessment measure that quantifies the amount of tail risk in a portfolio. It represents the average loss exceeding the VaR (Value at Risk).

D

Data Preprocessing: The process of transforming raw data into an understandable format before analytics. Steps include cleaning, integration, transformation, and reduction of data.

Diversification: A risk management strategy that mixes a wide variety of investments within a portfolio to reduce exposure to any single asset or risk.

E

EDA (Exploratory Data Analysis): Analyzing data sets to summarize their main characteristics, often using visual methods, before applying formal modeling or hypothesis testing.

Efficient Frontier: A concept in portfolio theory, it reflects portfolios that provide the highest expected return for a defined level of risk or the lowest risk for a given level of expected return.

Ensemble Methods: Machine learning techniques that combine multiple models to improve performance and robustness over individual models.

F

Factor Models: Financial models that explain the returns of an asset or portfolio through various factors, such as economic, fundamental, or statistical factors.

Feature Engineering: The process of using domain knowledge to create new features or variables that can enhance the performance of machine learning models.

Future Trends: Predictions about how current events and potential changes will shape future developments in quantitative strategies and financial markets.

G

GARCH (Generalized Autoregressive Conditional Heteroskedasticity): A statistical model used to estimate the volatility of financial returns, often employed in risk management.

H

Hypothesis Testing: A method in statistics to test an assumption regarding a population parameter. It's used to infer the probability that a given hypothesis is true.

I

Inefficiencies: Deviations from the ideal market conditions where all information is reflected in asset prices, allowing for potential profit opportunities.

L

Latency: The time delay between the input of an electronic signal and the occurrence of the desired response, critical in high-frequency trading environments.

M

Markowitz Model: A portfolio optimization theory stating that an investment portfolio is designed to maximize returns for a given level of risk through diversification.

Monte Carlo Simulation: A computational algorithm that uses repeated random sampling to obtain numerical results, often used to assess risk and uncertainty in financial modeling.

N

Natural Language Processing (NLP): A branch of artificial intelligence that explores the interaction between computers and human language, used for sentiment analysis and extracting insights from text data.

O

Overfitting: A modeling error which occurs when a function is too closely aligned to a limited set of data points, causing poor performance on new data.

P

Portfolio Optimization: The process of choosing the proportions of various assets to be included in a portfolio, so as to make the portfolio better than any other portfolio according to some criterion (usually maximizing expected return for a given amount of risk).

R

Regression Analysis: A statistical method for estimating the relationships among variables, often used in finance to model the relationship between asset prices and other variables.

Reinforcement Learning: A type of machine learning where agents learn to make decisions by performing actions and receiving rewards.

Risk Management: The process of identification, analysis, and acceptance or mitigation of uncertainty in investment decisions.

S

Simulation Methods: Techniques used to model the behavior of a system as it evolves over time. Monte Carlo methods are a common example.

Stress Testing: A simulation technique used on asset and liability portfolios to determine their reactions to different financial situations.

T

Time Series Analysis: Methods for analyzing time-series data to extract meaningful statistics and identify characteristics of the data.

V

VaR (Value at Risk): A measure of the risk of loss for investments based on a specific time frame and confidence interval.

VWAP (Volume-Weighted Average Price): A trading benchmark calculated by dividing the total dollar value of trades by the total trading volume, used by traders to assess the quality of execution.

W

Weight: The proportion of an individual asset in an investment portfolio.

Y

Yield Curve: A graph that plots interest rates of bonds having equal credit quality but differing maturity dates.

Z

Zero-Coupon Bond: A bond that does not pay periodic interest but is sold at a discount from its face value.

This glossary covers key terms and concepts essential for understanding "Quantitative Strategies for Alpha Generation: Advanced Models for Outperforming the Market."

APPENDIX C: ADDITIONAL RESOURCES

To further enhance the reader's understanding of the topics covered in "Quantitative Strategies for Alpha Generation: Advanced Models for Outperforming the Market," the following resources are recommended. These resources encompass a wide range of topics including quantitative finance, data management, statistical modeling, machine learning, risk management, algorithmic trading, behavioral finance, portfolio construction, and case studies of real-world applications.

Books

1. "Quantitative Financial Analytics: The Path to Investment Profits" by Edward E. Qian
2. Focuses on quantitative investment strategies and the practical aspects of implementing these strategies.
3. "Active Portfolio Management: A Quantitative Approach for Producing Superior Returns and Controlling Risk" by Richard C. Grinold and Ronald N. Kahn
4. Provides a comprehensive guide to quantitative investment management, with a focus on active portfolio management.

5. "Advances in Financial Machine Learning" by Marcos López de Prado

6. Offers in-depth insights into machine learning applications in finance, including feature engineering, model validation, and backtesting.

7. "The Econometrics of Financial Markets" by John Y. Campbell, Andrew W. Lo, and A. Craig MacKinlay

8. Explores econometric models and their applications to financial markets, emphasizing empirical techniques.

Research Papers and Articles

1. "Factor Investing in the Corporate Bond Market" by Jozef Donders and Patrick Houweling (Journal of Fixed Income)

2. Discusses the application of factor investing principles in the corporate bond market.

3. "Backtesting Strategies in Finance: Pitfalls and Remedies" by Bailey, Borwein, López de Prado, and Zhu (Journal of Computational Finance)

4. Highlights common pitfalls in backtesting quantitative strategies and offers solutions to avoid these issues.

5. "A Survey of Machine Learning in Finance" by Robert Miller, Dave Cliff, and Marc Deissenberg (International Journal of Computer Applications)

6. Provides a survey of the various machine learning techniques used in finance and their applications.

Online Courses and Tutorials

1. Coursera: "Machine Learning for Trading" by Georgia Tech

2. An online course that covers the application of machine learning techniques to trading strategies,

including supervised and unsupervised learning.

3. edX: "Financial Engineering and Risk Management" by Columbia University

4. Offers insights into financial engineering and risk management, focusing on quantitative finance and the application of tools and techniques.

5. Khan Academy: "Probability and Statistics"

6. A comprehensive set of tutorials on the fundamental concepts of probability and statistics, essential for quantitative finance.

Software and Tools

1. R and Python Programming Languages

2. Key tools for quantitative analysts. Libraries like Quantlib (Python) and quantmod (R) are especially useful for financial modeling and analysis.

3. Bloomberg Terminal

4. A leading source of real-time and historical financial data, essential for data acquisition and management in quantitative finance.

5. Hadoop and Spark

6. Big data technologies critical for handling large-scale financial data and improving computational efficiency.

Industry Reports and Blogs

1. BlackRock Investment Institute Reports

2. Offers research and insights on market trends, investment strategies, and quantitative finance applications.

3. QuantStart Blog

4. A blog dedicated to algorithmic trading and quantitative finance, featuring tutorials, research

articles, and case studies.

5. Financial Analysts Journal

6. Publishes scholarly articles on financial theory and its application, providing valuable insights into various aspects of quantitative finance.

Professional Organizations

1. CFA Institute

2. Provides resources, certifications, and networking opportunities for finance professionals, including those specializing in quantitative finance.

3. International Association for Quantitative Finance (IAQF)

4. Offers educational resources, networking opportunities, and industry events for professionals in quantitative finance.

Conferences and Workshops

1. Quantitative Finance Conference

2. Hosts speakers and experts in the field, providing an opportunity to learn about the latest trends and research in quantitative finance.

3. NeurIPS (Conference on Neural Information Processing Systems)

4. Focuses on machine learning and computational neuroscience, with applications in finance.

These additional resources will provide readers with a deeper understanding of the complex topics covered in the book and the practical skills necessary to apply these concepts in real-world financial contexts.

Epilogue: The Journey Ahead - Mastering the Art and Science of Alpha Generation

As we conclude this extensive exploration into the realm of

quantitative strategies for alpha generation, it's essential to reflect on the knowledge amassed and to contemplate the journey that lies ahead. This book aimed to equip you with a profound understanding of advanced models, data techniques, statistical methodologies, machine learning applications, risk management frameworks, behavioral insights, and portfolio optimization strategies — all pivotal in your quest to outperform the market.

The Integration of Foundations

The Essence of Data

Mastering Statistical Tools

Crafting Alpha Models

Embracing Machine Learning

Navigating Risk

Efficient Execution

Behavioral Insights

Optimizing Portfolios

Real-World Reflections

Looking Forward

As we look to the future of alpha generation, several trends stand out. Advances in artificial intelligence, the increasing use of alternative data, and the integration of behavioral insights will continue to shape our strategies. Regulatory developments and ethical considerations will also play a significant role, ensuring that our pursuit of alpha remains sustainable and responsible.

In conclusion, mastering the art and science of alpha generation requires continuous learning, adaptation, and innovation. Armed with the comprehensive knowledge from this book, you are well-equipped to navigate the complexities of financial markets and achieve your alpha generation goals. The journey ahead is one of perpetual discovery, where curiosity and rigor will be your guiding stars in the quest for market outperformance.

www.ingramcontent.com/pod-product-compliance
Lightning Source LLC
LaVergne TN
LVHW051221050326
832903LV00028B/2190